Progressive Business Plan for a Yoga Studio

Yoga Studio
Business Plan

_____ (date)

Business Name: _____

Plan Time Period: 2018 - 2020

Founding Directors:

Name: _____

Name: _____

Contact Information:

Owner: _____

Address: _____

City/State/Zip: _____

Phone: _____

Cell: _____

Fax: _____

Website: _____

Email: _____

Submitted to: _____

Date: _____

Contact Info: _____

NON-DISCLOSURE AGREEMENT

_____ (Company)., and _____ (Person Name), agrees:

_____ (Company) Corp. may from time to time disclose to _____ (Person Name) certain confidential information or trade secrets generally regarding Business plan and financials of _____ (Company) corp.

_____ (Person Name) agrees that it shall not disclose the information so conveyed, unless in conformity with this agreement. _____ (Person Name) shall limit disclosure to the officers and employees of _____ (Person Name) with a reasonable "need to know" the information, and shall protect the same from disclosure with reasonable diligence.

As to all information which _____ (Company) Corp. claims is confidential, _____ (Company) Corp. shall reduce the same to writing prior to disclosure and shall conspicuously mark the same as "confidential," "not to be disclosed" or with other clear indication of its status. If the information which _____ (Company) Corp. is disclosing is not in written form, for example, a machine or device, _____ (Company) Corp. shall be required prior to or at the same time that the disclosure is made to provide written notice of the secrecy claimed by _____ (Company) Corp.. _____ (Person Name) agrees upon reasonable notice to return the confidential tangible material provided by it by _____ (Company) Corp. upon reasonable request.

The obligation of non-disclosure shall terminate when if any of the following occurs:
(a) The confidential information becomes known to the public without the fault of _____ (Person Name), or;
(b) The information is disclosed publicly by _____ (Company) Corp., or ;
(c) a period of 12 months passes from the disclosure, or;
(d) the information loses its status as confidential through no fault of _____ (Person Name).

In any event, the obligation of non-disclosure shall not apply to information which was known to _____ (Person Name) prior to the execution of this agreement.

Dated: _____

_____
_____ (Company) Corp.
_____(Person Name)

Yoga Studio Business Plan: Table of Contents

Section	Description	Page
1.0	**Executive Summary**	___
1.1.0	Tactical Objectives	___
1.1.1	Strategic Objectives	___
1.2	Mission Statement	___
1.2.1	Core Values Statement	___
1.3	Vision Statement	___
1.4	Keys to Success	___
2.0	**Company Summary**	___
2.1	Company Ownership	___
2.2	Company Licensing and Liability Protection	___
2.3	Start-up To-do Checklist	___
2.4.0	Company Location	___
2.4.1	Company Facilities	___
2.5.0	Start-up Summary	___
2.5.1	Inventory	___
2.5.2	Supply Sourcing	___
2.6	Start-up Requirements	___
2.7	SBA Loan Key Requirements	___
2.7.1	Other Financing Options	___
3.0	**Products and Services**	___
3.1	Service Descriptions	___
3.1.1	Product Descriptions	___
3.2	Alternate Revenue Streams	___
3.3	Production of Products and Services	___
3.4	Competitive Comparison	___
3.5	Sale Literature	___
3.6	Fulfillment	___
3.7	Technology	___
3.8	Future Products and Services	___
4.0	**Market Analysis Summary**	___
4.1.0	Secondary Market Research	___
4.1.1	Primary Market Research	___
4.2	Market Segmentation	___
4.3	Target Market Segment Strategy	___
4.3.1	Market Needs	___
4.4	Buying Patterns	___
4.5	Market Growth	___

Section	Description	Page
4.6	Service Business Analysis	_____
4.7	Barrier to Entry	_____
4.8	Competitive Analysis	_____
4.9	Market Revenue Projections	_____
5.0	**Industry Analysis**	_____
5.1	Industry Leaders	_____
5.2	Industry Statistics	_____
5.3	Industry Trends	_____
5.4	Industry Key Terms	_____
6.0	**Strategy and Implementation Summary**	_____
6.1.0	Promotion Strategy	_____
6.1.1	Grand Opening	_____
6.1.2	Value Proposition	_____
6.1.3	Positioning Statement	_____
6.1.4	Distribution Strategy	_____
6.2	Competitive Advantage	_____
6.2.1	Branding Strategy	_____
6.3	Business SWOT Analysis	_____
6.4.0	Marketing Strategy	_____
6.4.1	Strategic Alliances	_____
6.4.2	Monitoring Marketing Results	_____
6.4.3	Word-of-Mouth Marketing	_____
6.5	Sales Strategy	_____
6.5.1	Customer Retention Strategy	_____
6.5.2	Sales Forecast	_____
6.5.3	Sales Program	_____
6.6	Merchandising Strategy	_____
6.7	Pricing Strategy	_____
6.8	Differentiation Strategies	_____
6.9	Milestone Tracking	_____
7.0	**Website Plan Summary**	_____
7.1	Website Marketing Strategy	_____
7.2	Development Requirements	_____
7.3	Sample Frequently Asked Questions	_____
8.0	**Operations**	_____
8.1	Security Measures	_____
9.0	**Management Summary**	_____
9.1	Owner Personal History	_____

Section	Description	Page
9.2	Management Team Gaps	_____
9.2.1	Management Matrix	_____
9.2.2	Outsourcing Matrix	_____
9.3	Employee Requirements	_____
9.4	Job Descriptions	_____
9.4.1	Job Description Format	_____
9.5	Personnel Plan	_____
9.6	Staffing Plan	_____
10.0	**Business Risk Factors**	_____
10.1	Business Risk Reduction Strategies	_____
10.2	Reduce Customer Perceived Risk Strategies	_____
11.0	**Financial Plan**	_____
11.1	Important Assumptions	_____
11.2	Break-even Analysis	_____
11.3	Projected Profit and Loss	_____
11.4	Projected Cash Flow	_____
11.5	Projected Balance Sheet	_____
11.6	Business Ratios	_____
12.0	**Business Plan Summary**	_____
13.0	**Potential Exit Strategies**	_____
	Appendix	_____
	Helpful Resources	_____
	Marketing Worksheets	_____

Business and Marketing Plan Instructions

1. If you purchased this Book via Amazon's Kindle or Print-on-Demand Systems, please send proof-of-purchase to Probusconsult2@Yahoo.com and we will email you the digital file.

2. Complete the Executive Summary section, as your final step, after you have completed the entire plan.

3. Feel free to edit the plan and make it more relevant to your strategic goals, objectives and business vision.

4. We have provided all of the formulas needed to prepare the financial plan. Just plug in the numbers that are based on your particular situation. Excel spreadsheets for the financials are available on the microsoft.com website and www.simplebizplanning.com/forms.htm http://office.microsoft.com/en-us/templates/

5. Throughout the plan, we have provided prompts or suggestions as to what values to enter into blank spaces, but use your best judgment and then delete the suggested values (?).

6. The plan also includes some separate worksheets for additional assistance in expanding some of the sections, if desired.

7. Additionally, some sections offer multiple choices and the word 'select' appears as a prompt to edit the contents of the plan.

8. Your feedback, referrals and business are always very much appreciated.

Thank you

Nat Chiaffarano, MBA
Progressive Business Consulting, Inc.
Pembroke Pines, FL 33027
ProBusConsult2@yahoo.com

"Progressive Business Plan for a Yoga Studio"

Copyright Notice

1.0 Executive Summary

Industry Overview

Within the United States, there are approximately 10,000 locations that operate as Yoga Studios. The popularity of yoga has increased substantially over the past ten years as more Americans have become concerned with their fitness. Each year, the industry generates more than 600 million of revenues. The excepted growth rate of the Yoga Studio industry is expected to remain in line with that of the general American economy.

Yoga teaching has become one of the fastest growing professions in North America. As many as 30 million people practice yoga in the United States alone. NAMASTA.com, the North American Studio Alliance, the organization for mind-body professionals, estimates that there are 70,000 yoga teachers in North America. NAMASTA is a member-supported community organization that helps professionals in the United States and Canada pursue their career. Its growth has paralleled that of yoga and the mind-body movement. Yoga has become increasingly popular as a low-impact, high calorie-burning exercise regiment, recommended by doctors and nutritionists nationwide. According to an April 2013 report published by leading industry and market research group IBISWorld Inc., the yoga and Pilates studio industry is one of the 10 fastest-growing industries in the U.S. The report specifies the studio industry, and does not include the sizable yoga apparel and accessories market. Even with this distinction, the industry has outpaced nearly every other in terms of recent growth and predicted growth. In fact, yoga and Pilates studios not only weathered the recent recession, but also managed to maintain a respectable average growth of 12.1 percent in the last 10 years. The industry is predicted to continue to grow at an average annual rate of 4.8 percent through the year 2017. The primary reason for such growth is that Americans are increasingly seeking ways to become and stay healthy, as well as find alternative ways to stay fit.

A 2008 "Yoga in America" study, released by *Yoga Journal* shows that Americans spend $5.7 billion a year on yoga classes and products, including equipment, clothing, vacations and media (DVDs, videos, books and magazines). This figure represents an increase of 87 percent compared to the previous study in 2004. Data for this survey were collected by the Harris Interactive Service Bureau on behalf of *Yoga Journal*. *Yoga Journal* commissioned RRC Associates, a research firm in Boulder, Colo., to perform the data analysis. The 2008 study indicates that 6.9% of U.S. adults, or 15.8 million people, practice yoga. Of current non-practitioners, nearly 8%, or 18.3 million Americans, say they are very or extremely interested in yoga, triple the number from the 2004 study. And 4.1% of non-practitioners, or about 9.4 million people, say they will definitely try yoga within the next year.

Business Overview

_____ (company name) _____ (was/is in the process of being) formed for the purpose of bringing quality and affordable Yoga instruction and _____ (aerobic exercise?) classes to the _____ area. We will offer a range of Yoga styles and class levels to suit students ranging from beginners to experienced practitioners and teachers.

The purpose of this business plan is to raise $_____ (100,000?) for the development of a Yoga Studio while showcasing the expected financials and operations over the next three years. _____ (company name) will be a _____ (state) based corporation that will provide Yoga based physical fitness training to customers in its targeted market. The Company _____ (is/was) founded in _____ (year) by _____ (owner name).

Our Yoga Studio will enable people to expand their knowledge of Yoga and enjoy being with other people who share this common interest. It is our plan to incorporate the existing Yoga community into our studio to begin with a strong base of supporters. Our goal is to spread the word that Yoga is a fun, healthy and exciting way for people of all ages to spend their leisure time. Yoga offers many benefits that will attract people from many different backgrounds, age groups and interests.

_____ (company name) will provide customers with an expansive line of yoga classes, which seek to cleanse the body by performing postures in a yoga room. The owner anticipates that these services will generate approximately $_____ of revenue for the business on a daily basis. The Company will employ ___ (#) full time yoga instructors to provide these services. The Company will also generate revenues from the sale of bottled water, yoga mats, and apparel that complement the Company's core line of yoga instruction services.

The mission of the instructors at _____ (company name) is to assist students in the development of physical, mental, and spiritual well-being: a truly priceless health advantage. We will offer ___ (#) eight-week sessions of classes per year. Courses offered will include Anusara-style Hatha Yoga plus workshops in related topics. Our Yoga studio will feature well-trained, professional instructors, progressive teaching methods, a non-competitive and encouraging atmosphere, and a modern light-filled facility. The studio will also have a boutique that will sell workshop clothing and yoga training aides.

In order to succeed, _____ (company name) will have to do the following:
1. Enforce Yoga Alliance Certified instructional standards
2. Stay abreast of trends in the personal training industry.
3. Precisely assess the needs and wants of each participant.
4. Stay in touch with customers to secure profitable repeat business and referrals.
5. Offer special reduced rate programs to intensive Yoga participants.
6. Foster the development of long-term instructor-participant relationships.
7. Use entry level classes and reduced initial consultation fees to capture interest at an early stage.

Our company is unique in that we will give each participant our undivided attention. We will listen to their needs, draft a needs analysis worksheet, which precisely documents those needs and wants, and then work with the participant to create the Yoga instruction program that exceeds their expectations.

Business Plan Objective

The purpose of this document is to provide a strategic business plan for our company. The plan has been adjusted to reflect the particular strengths and weaknesses of _____ (company name). Actual financial performance will be tracked closely and the business plan will be adjusted when necessary to ensure that full profit potential is realized.

Business Structure

The business _____ (will be/was) incorporated on _____ (date) as a _____ (Corporation/LLC), and intends to register for Sub-chapter 'S' status for federal tax purposes. This will effectively shield the owner(s) from personal liability and double taxation. The company was started by _____ (business owner name), who is the majority owner and a past _____ (indicate relevant business experience or achievements).

Business Goals

Our business goal is to continue to develop the _____ (company name) brand name. To do so, we plan to execute on the following:

1. Offer quality Yoga instruction at a competitive price.
2. Focus on quality controls and ongoing operational excellence.
3. Develop long-term participant relationships that generate referrals and repeat business.
4. Develop multiple revenue streams that maximize the utilization of our assets and core competencies.

Location

_____ (company name) will be located in the _____ (complex name) on _____ (street address) in _____ (city), ____ (state). The _____ (purchased/leased) space is easily accessible and provides ample parking for ____ (#) customers and staff. The location is attractive due to the area demographics, which reflect our target customer profile. The facilities will include _____ (#) Yoga training rooms, offices for the principals and bookkeeper, an inventory/prop storage area, locker/dressing area, snack bar area. Pro Shop and a reception area.

Products and Services

____ (company name) will provide a broad number of classes that pertain to training the body via yoga and related stretching practices. The business will generate income from the ongoing fees associated with yoga classes at the studio while concurrently generating secondary revenues through the sale of yoga mats and related accessories used during the course of yoga training. The Company will offer classes and personal instruction for this type of physical fitness activity. The business will generate its primary revenues from the teaching of Yoga to the general public.

Marketing Plan

With the help of an aggressive marketing plan, _____ (company name) expects to experience steady growth. _____ (company name) plans to attract its customers through the use of local newspaper advertisements, circulating flyers to surrounding businesses and major employers, a systematic series of direct mailings, news releases in local newspapers, a website, online directories, charitable demonstrations, networking with local organizations and limited Yellow Page and radio ads.

Mission Statement   (optional)
Our Mission is to address the following customer pain points or unmet needs and wants, which will define the opportunity for our business: _____
In order to satisfy these unmet needs and wants, we will propose the following unique solutions, which will create better value for our customers:

_____

The Management Team
The Company was founded by ____ (owner name). ____ (He/She) has more than ____ (#) years of experience in the personal training industry. Through his expertise, he will be able to bring the operations of the business to profitability within its first year of operations. ____ (owner name) has a _____ degree from ____ (institution name) and a ____ background within the _____ (personal training?) industry, having spent ____ (#) years with ____ (former employer name or type of business). During this tenure, ____ (he/she) helped grow the business from $_____ in yearly revenue to over $___. _____ (co-owner name) has a ____ background, and while employed by __ was able to increase operating profit by __ percent. These acquired skills, work experiences and educational backgrounds will play a big role in the success of our Yoga Studio. Additionally, our president, _____ (name), has an extensive knowledge of the _____ area and has identified a niche market retail opportunity to make this venture highly successful, combining his ____ (#) years of work experience in a variety of businesses. _____ (owner name) will manage all aspects of the business to ensure effective customer responsiveness while monitoring day-to-day operations. Qualified and trained associates personally trained by _____ (owner name) in customer service skills will provide additional support services. Support staff will be added as seasonal or extended hours mandate.

Past Successful Accomplishments
_____ (company name) is uniquely qualified to succeed due to the following past successes:
1. **Entrepreneurial Track Record**: The owners and management team have helped to launch numerous successful ventures, including a _____.

2. **Key Milestones Achieved**: The founders have invested $___ to-date to staff the company, build the core technology, acquire starting inventory, test market the _____ (product/service), realize sales of $_____ and launch the website.

Start-up Funding
_____ (owner name) will financially back the new business venture with an initial

investment of $ _____ , and will be the principal owner. Additional funding in the amount of $ _____ will be sought from _____ , a local commercial bank. This money will be needed to start the company. This loan will provide start up capital, financing for a selected site lease, remodeling renovations, inventory supplies, pay for permits and licensing, employee training, purchase equipment and cover expenses during the first year of operation. The expected start-up date for this business will be _____ (date).

Financial Projections

_____ (company name) is forecasted to gross in excess of $_____ in sales in its first year of operation, ending _____ (month/ year). Second year operations will produce a net profit of $_____ . This will be generated from an investment of $_____ in initial capital. It is expected that payback of our total invested capital will be realized in less than _____ (#) months of operation. It is further forecasted that cash flow becomes positive from operations in year _____ (two?). We project that our net profits will increase from $_____ to over $ _____ over the next three years.

Financial Profile Summary

	2018	2019	2020
Total Revenue			
Expenses			
Gross Margin			
Operating Income			
Net Income			
EBITDA			

EBITDA = Revenue - Expenses (excluding tax, interest, depreciation and amortization) EBITDA is essentially net income with interest, taxes, depreciation, and amortization added back to it, and can be used to analyze and compare profitability between companies and industries because it eliminates the effects of financing and accounting decisions.
Gross Margin (%) = (Revenue - Cost of Goods Sold) / Revenue
Net Income = Total revenue - Cost of sales - Other expenses - Tax

Expansion Plan

_____ (company name) will continue to expand through organic means including increasing the Company's advertising budget via the reinvestment into the after-tax cash flows of the business. Additionally, if the business is highly successful then the Company may seek to establish additional Yoga Studio locations after the third year of operations.

Exit Strategy

If the business is very successful, ____ (owner name) may seek to sell the business to a third party for a significant earnings multiple. Most likely, the Company will hire a qualified business broker to sell the business on behalf of ____ (company name). Based on historical numbers, the business could generate a sales premium of up to 4 times earnings.

Summary

Through a combination of a proven business model and a strong management team to guide the organization, _____ (company name) will be a long lasting, profitable business. We believe our ability to create future product and service opportunities and growth will only be limited by our imagination and our ability to attract talented people who understand the concept of branding.

1.1 Key Strategic Objectives   (select)

The following strategic objectives will specify quantifiable results and involve activities that can be easily tracked. They will also be realistic, tied to specific marketing strategies and serve as a good benchmark to evaluate our marketing plan success.

1. To create a company whose primary goal is to exceed customer expectations and create a memorable learning experience.
2. To develop a cash flow that is capable of paying all salaries, as well as grow the business, by the end of the _____ (first?) year.
3. To be an active networking participant and productive member of the community by _____ (date).
4. Create over _____ (60?) % of business revenues from repeat customers by _____ (date).
5. Achieve an overall customer satisfaction rate of ____ (100?) % by _____ (date).
6. Get a business website designed, built and operational by _____ (date), which will include an online shopping cart.
7. Achieve total sales revenues of $_____ in _____ (year).
8. Realize gross margins higher than _____ (65?) percent by _____ (date).
9. Achieve net income more than ___ (10?) percent of net sales by the ____ (#) year.
10. Increase overall sales by _____ (20?) percent from prior year through superior service and word-of-mouth referrals.
11. Reduce the cost of new customer acquisition by ___ % to $ ___ by _____ (date).
12. Turn in profits from the _____ (#) month of operations.
13. Expand operations to include all of the _____ (city) area, including _____, _____ and _____.
14. Provide employees with continuing training, benefits and incentives to reduce the employee turnover rate to _____%.
15. Provide Yoga training for _____ (#) participants at all levels of Yoga proficiency by___ (date).
16. Acquire ____ (#) customers by the end of the first year of operation.
17. Achieve sales in excess of $_____ from the product sales boutique.
18. Increase customer base by ___% by the end of the second year of operation.

1.2   Mission Statement   (select)

Our Mission Statement is a written statement that spells out our organization's overall goal, provides a sense of direction and acts as a guide to decision making for all levels of management. In developing the following mission statement we will encourage input from employees, volunteers, and other stakeholders, and publicize it broadly in our website and other marketing materials.

The mission of ___(company name) is to create a Yoga Studio where people can learn Yoga, make new friends, have fun, feel comfortable and develop a healthier lifestyle. Our mission is to become the recognized leader in its targeted market for providing superior Yoga training services.

Our mission is to enrich our clients' lifestyle through movement and body awareness, uniting mind, body and spirit in a positive, holistic environment. Our mission is to become the recognized local leader in its targeted market for yoga instruction services and classes. The mission of _____ (company name) is to give every student, a place to practice Anusara. It is our intention to keep the teaching of Anusara as close to the way we have been taught as possible.

Our mission is to become a Yoga Studio that offers professional and rigorous training for people interested in Yoga, and provide a totally comfortable ambience for social interaction. Our goal is to focus on developing the discipline, strength, composure, self-confidence, and creativity that every individual needs to succeed in life.

Our goal is to offer a varied Yoga program with price options for all levels of interest and to realize 100% participant satisfaction, and generate long-term profits through referrals and repeat business. Our goal is to set ourselves apart from the competition by making customer satisfaction our number one priority and to provide customer service that is responsive, informed and respectful. Our goal is to provide our instructors with access to continual training so that our participants will have exposure to the latest Yoga techniques and trends. Our goal is to help every student to open and develop their unique gift at their own pace. Our goal is to provide an environment that fosters participant artistic and social growth, while allowing participants to share their accomplishments with others and build their own self-esteem in the process.

1.2.1   Mantra

We will create a mantra for our organization that is three or four words long. Its purpose will be to help employees truly understand why the organization exists. Our mantra will serve as a framework through which to make decisions about product and business direction. It will boil the key drivers of our company down to a sentence that defines our most important areas of focus and resemble a statement of purpose or significance. Examples: To create harmony and balance in our lives.
Our Mantra is _____

1.2.2   Core Values Statement

The following Core Values will help to define our organization, guide our behavior, underpin operational activity and shape the strategies we will pursue in the face of various challenges and opportunities. We will fulfill our mission through our commitment to:

Being respectful and ethical.
Building enduring partnerships and relationships with customers.
Seeking innovation in our industry.
Practicing accountability to our colleagues and stakeholders.
Pursuing continuous learning as individuals and as a business entity.
Performing tasks on time to satisfy the needs of our internal and external clients.
Taking active part in the organization to meet the objectives and the establishment of continuous and lasting relationships.
Offering professional treatment to our clients, employees, shareholders, and the community.
Continuing pursuit of new technologies for the development of the projects that add value for our clients, employees, shareholders, and the community.
Personal and professional improvement through education.
Teamwork to achieve our goals.
Honesty and integrity in all areas of our professional relationships.
Loyalty to the team and dedication to achieving our mission.

1.3 Vision Statement   (select)

The following Vision Statement will communicate both the purpose and values of our organization. For employees, it will give direction about how they are expected to behave and inspires them to give their best. Shared with customers, it will shape customers' understanding of why they should work with our organization.

_____ (company name) will strive to become one of the most respected and favored Yoga Studios in the area. It is our desire to become a landmark business in _____ (city), ____ (state), and become known not only for the quality of our products and services, but also for our community and charity involvement. _____ (company name) is dedicated to operating with a constant enthusiasm for learning about the Yoga Studio business, being receptive to implementing new ideas, and maintaining a willingness to adapt to changing market needs and wants. To be an active and vocal member of the community, and to provide continual reinvestment through participation in community activities and financial contributions.

In five years,_____ (company name) will be an area leader in the Yoga Studio industry, and plans will be developed and implemented to pursue national business through the franchising of our business model concept.

1.4   Keys to Success   (select)

In broad terms, the success factors relate to providing what our clients want, and doing what is necessary to be better than our competitors. The following critical success factors are areas in which our organization must excel in order to operate successfully and achieve our objectives:

1. Service participants' needs with personalized instruction.
2. Launch a website to showcase photos of our participants, provide helpful information and benefit from online e-commerce.
3. Promote the health benefits and social aspects of Pilates.
4. Conduct a highly targeted and cost-effective advertising campaign.
5. Institute a program of profit sharing among all employees to reduce employee turnover and improve productivity.
6. Control costs at all times without exception.
7. Institute management processes and controls to insure the consistent replication of operations.
9. Recruit employees with a passion for delivering exceptional instructional services.
10. Institute an employee training to insure the best teaching techniques are consistently practiced.
11. Network aggressively within the community, as word of mouth will be our most powerful advertising asset.
12. The ability to operate across a range of markets to reduce the impact of local demand conditions.
13. The flexibility to respond to changing customer buying habits and needs.
14. The ability to offer clients a diverse range of Yoga packages.
16. Stay abreast of new Yoga teaching concepts.
17. Raising the studio's community profile through outreach programs.
18. Building brand awareness which will drive customers to increase their usage of our services and make referrals.
19. Provide a forum for people with diverse interests, backgrounds and ages to socialize.
20. Installation of an automatic tuition billing system to increase participant retention and cash flow.
21. Business planning with the flexibility to make changes based on gaining new insightful perspectives as we proceed.
22. Building trust by circulating and adhering to our Code of Ethics.
23. Pursue Yoga certification.
24. Perform a thorough review at the U.S. Patent and Trademark Office to see if anyone else is using or could begin using the desired name for the yoga studio.
25. Work with a handful of part-time Yoga instructors to fill gaps in the studio's class menu. an be scheduled based on participant demand. (Make sure that instructors understand that they are contractors who work based on enrollment demands rather than as full-time workers.)
26. Investigate class fees and course packages at competing studios before creating a price list.

27. Keep studio rent and other costs in mind to find the right prices for courses.
28. Schedule Yoga classes at times when prospective participants will be available. (Work with instructors to create a schedule featuring night, weekend and lunch hour courses to reach participants of all backgrounds.)
29. Generate additional revenue for Yoga Studio by selling apparel, mats, equipment, foam blocks and belts.
30. Design a multi-faceted advertising campaign that will reach the targeted market at minimal cost.
31. Start the Yoga Studio from home before opening a new location to create revenue sources.
32. Encourage friends, neighbors and coworkers to take free introductory courses to showcase the course quality of the new studio.
33. Counsel students who have specific health concerns prior to classes as to how to modify their practice to avoid injury.
34. Develop a Teacher Employment Contract with your lawyer that includes the following important contract provisions: Duties, Compensation, Type of Hire, Breach, Term, Termination and Covenant Not to Compete.
35. Consider profit-sharing based compensation programs or a cooperatively owned studio to reduce fixed salary pressures.
36. Choose a location with good visibility.
37. Keep the studio spotless, including mats, equipment, floor, bathrooms, and all places your clients go within your studio.
38. When pursuing the development of a new revenue stream, always have a back-up plan in the event it does not succeed.
39. Teach the entire empowering full-faceted system of yoga that can serve everyone's needs.
40. Include resources that educate and make the value of this powerful system ridiculously clear.
41. Ditch the overhead associated with a dedicated, full-time yoga studio and start with a part-time (before and after business work hours) space-sharing arrangement, such as with an indoor cycling studio.
Source:
http://yogadork.com/2015/01/20/get-a-life-yoga-kill-the-studio-paradigm/
42. Profit from the costly lessons learned by others.
Sources:
www.shape.com/lifestyle/mind-and-body/beginner-s-guide-starting-your-own-fitness-studio
http://blog.rateyourburn.com/blog/post/2013/08/08/10-mistakes-studios-make-that-hurt-their-instructors-1.aspx
http://blog.rateyourburn.com/blog/post/2013/03/19/15-tips-for-running-a-successful-fitness-studio-business-1.aspx
www.yogajournal.com/category/teach/tools-for-teachers/business-of-yoga/
43. Not only keep the studio clean and disinfected, but also make it smell clean.
44. Create a studio where people want to hang out (cafe) and build relationships (share profiles) and experience a new lifestyle (field trips) and build a team spirit (competitions).

45. Get to know the needs of your core clients and add programs that satisfy their needs. Examples: weight loss, pain management, natal, rehab, spiritual, etc.

46. We will build a nurturing community of shared interests by writing yoga themed articles for publications and news services, such as the Huffington Post, and posting instructional photos and videos on Instagram and YouTube.

47. Demonstrate a clear and consistent intention of style and offer that through classes, marketing materials, studio design and social media.

48. Make effective use of social media by posting relevant web images that have something to do with the studio.
     Source:
     www.shape.com/lifestyle/mind-and-body/beginner-s-guide-starting-your-own-fitness-studio

49. Help your yoga instructors to be the best that they can possibly be, as this will positively reflect upon your studio's brand image.
     Resource: http://seattleyoganews.com/business-yoga-teacher-salary/

50. Offer optional discounted packages of six- or eight-week programs, versus the pay per visit rate, aimed at specific clients, such as "Yoga for new mothers" to make students with common objectives, feel like they are committed to the complete multi-week series.

51. To draw new students and retain them, offer a clearly stated, 30-day introductory deal at an irresistible price, such as $30 for 30 days of unlimited classes.

52. A key differentiator in a yoga studio is the engaging personality of the instructor.

53. Conduct workshops and sell designer apparel to realize the real money and establish the studio as a unique brand.
     Source: http://blog.penelopetrunk.com/2012/11/27/secrets-of-successful-yoga-studios-and-other-ways-to-think-of-ideas-that-suck/

54. Develop other revenue streams, such as corporate wellness programs, massage therapies and weight loss programs.
     Source:
     www.elephantjournal.com/2012/08/the-business-of-yoga-the-successful-studio/

55. Focus on building a connection to the local community.

56. Resist the temptation to tinker constantly with the class schedule.

57. Choose a location with easy access rather than expensive high visibility because business is driven by word-of-mouth recommendations.
     Source:
     https://yogaisforlovers.wordpress.com/2012/11/25/why-do-some-yoga-studios-fail/

58. Create a sense of community around the studio to provide the feeling of belonging to a group with a healthful habit theme.

2.0   Company Summary

_____ (company name) is a start-up _____ (Corporation/Limited Liability Company) consisting of _____ (#) principle officers with combined _____ industry experience of _____ (#) years.
Resource:
http://www.yogaeducationinstitute.com/Yoga-Business-Success.pdf

The company was formed to offer a wide range of Yoga instruction and to capitalize on the increasing popularity of Yoga as a _____ (stress reduction technique?). _____ (company name) will offer private Yoga instruction, group classes, aerobic exercise classes and corporate teamwork workshops. We plan to appeal to people of all age groups, abilities and backgrounds looking for creative self-expression, a healthier lifestyle, enjoyable forms of exercise and/or social networking opportunities.

A total of ___ (25?) classes will be offered by a team of ___ (10?) instructors and the business will be open _____ (seven?) days a week, which means a variety of classes will be available. There will be a beginning yoga class, which is a multi-week class. Its purpose will be to bring new and experienced students to the yoga mat to learn about alignment and movement before moving on to full classes. We will offer kids' yoga once a week. We' will offer a chair yoga for people who have limitations getting down on the floor. We will have a hot power class for people who love that grind and power push. Other classes will include a weekend warrior class on Saturday and a soulful Sunday class on Sundays. We will also offer a free community yoga class each month to drive our word-of-mouth advertising campaign. I

_____ (company name) will offer Anusara-style Hatha Yoga plus workshops in related yoga topics. We will feature well-trained, professional instructors, progressive teaching methods, a non-competitive and encouraging atmosphere, and a beautiful light-filled facility. ____ (company name) will be located in the commercial downtown section of ___ (city). Our goal is to build a large base of yoga students from the thousands of office workers that are employed in the area. Besides the training, ____ (company name) will also have a boutique that will sell workshop clothing and yoga training aides.

The owner of the company will be investing a significant amount of ____ (his/her) own capital into the company and will also be seeking a loan to cover start-up costs and future growth.

Our yoga studio will focus on building relationships with our students in the following ways:
1.   Instructors will introduce themselves at the start of new classes, including their backgrounds, family status, interests and yoga philosophy.
2.   Students will be asked to talk about themselves, including their other interests, profession and what they hope to realize by attending yoga classes.
3.   Students will be asked to put their name tags on the front right edge of their mats

so that student names can be learned by instructors.

4.   Students will be asked to fill out a 'Student Profile Sheet', which instructors will use to help better connect with their students.

_____ (company name) will be located in a _____ (purchased/rented) _____ (suite/complex) in the _____ on _____ (address) in _____ (city), _____ (state). The facilities will include a reception area, admin offices for the owner and bookkeeper, Yoga floor training area, storage closet, snack bar, and a dressing area.

The company plans to use its existing contacts and customer base to generate short-term sales. Its long-term profitability will rely on focusing on participant referrals, networking within community organizations and a comprehensive marketing program that includes public relations activities. Sales are expected to reach $_____ within the first year and to grow at a conservative rate of _____ (15?) percent during the next two to five years.

Facilities Renovations

The necessary renovations are itemized as follows: Estimate

Partition of space into functional training areas.   _____

Install new flooring.   _____

Mirror wall installation   _____

Build dressing rooms   _____

Build snack bar area   _____

Painting and other general cosmetic repairs   _____

Install professional sound system.   _____

Update air conditioning system.   _____

Other _____   _____

Total: _____

Operations

_____ (company name) will open for business on _____ (date) and will maintain the following business hours:

Monday through Thursday:	_____	(10 to 6 ?)
Friday:	_____	(11 to 9 ?)
Saturday:	_____	(10 to 6 ?)
Sunday:	_____	(Closed ?)

Note: Most yoga studios are busiest at lunchtime, from 5-9 in the evening, sometimes in the early morning and often all day on the weekends.

The company will invest in customer relationship management software (CRM) and a point of sales (POS) system to track sales and collect customer information, including names, email addresses, key reminder dates and preferences. This information will be used with email, e-newsletter and direct mail campaigns to build personalized fulfillment programs, establish customer loyalty and drive revenue growth.

2.0.1   Traction (optional)

We will include this section because investors expect to see some traction, both before and after a funding event and investors tend to judge past results as a good indicator of future projections. It will also show that we can manage our operations and develop a business model capable of funding inventory purchases. Traction will be the best form of market research.

Period	_____
Product/Service Focus	_____
Our Sales to Date:	_____
Our Number of Users to Date:	_____
Number of Repeat Users	_____
Number of Pending Orders:	_____
Value of Pending Orders:	_____
Reorder Cycle:	_____
Key Reference Sites	_____
Mailing List Subscriptions	_____
Competitions/Awards Won	_____
Notable Product Reviews	_____
Actual Percent Gross Profit Margin	_____
Industry Average: GPM	_____
Actual B/(W) Industry Average	_____

Note: Percent Gross Profit Margin equals the sales receipts less the cost of goods sold divided by sales receipts multiplied by 100.

2.1   Company Ownership

_____ (company name) is a _____ (Sole-proprietorship /Corporation/Limited Liability Corporation (LLC)) and is registered to the principal owner, _____ (owner name). The company was formed in _____ (month) of _____ (year).
Resource: www.mycorporation.com

It will be registered as a Subchapter S to avoid double taxation, with ownership allocated as follows: _____ (owner name) _____ % and _____ (owner name) _____ %.

The owner is a _____ (year) graduate of _____ (institution name), in _____ (city, _____ (state), with a _____ degree. He/she has _____ years of executive experience in the _____ (Pilates?) industry as a _____, performing the following roles:
_____.

His/her major accomplishments include: _____.

Ownership Breakdown:

Shareholder Name	Responsibilities	Number and Class of Shares	Percent Ownership

The remainder of the issued and outstanding common shares are retained by the Company for __ (future distribution / allocation under the Company's employee stock option plan).

Shareholder Loans

The Company currently has outstanding shareholder loans in the aggregate sum of $_____. The following table sets out the details of the shareholder loans.

Shareholder Name	Loan Amount	Loan Date	Balance Outstanding

Directors

The Company's Board of Directors, which is made up of highly qualified business and industry professionals, will be a valuable asset to the Company and be instrumental to its development. The following persons will make up the Board of Directors of the Company:

Name of Person	Educational Background	Past Industry Experience	Other Companies Served

2.2 Company Licensing and Liability Protection

The business will consider the need to acquire the following types of insurances. This will require extensive comparison shopping, through several insurance brokers, listed with our state's insurance department:

Accident & Liability Insurance - covers a Yoga teacher or Yoga Studio, for accidental bodily injury or property damage incurred by your clients or visitors.

Participant Liability Insurance - in class or participating in a recital, your Yoga participants, volunteers, staff and owners will be covered.

Property Insurance - Coverage arising from third party liability.

Professional Liability Insurance - coverage applies when a dissatisfied client claims negligence while providing Yoga instruction.

Suggested General Liability Insurance Coverage

Basic Coverage for Yoga Instructors	$2,000,000 per occurrence
	$4,000,000 aggregate limit

Miscellaneous Professional Liability for Yoga Instructors
Protects against bodily injury arising out of rendering or failing to render services.

Personal Injury Liability for Yoga Instructors
Protects you against suits involving libel, slander, or wrongful invasion of privacy.

Sexual Abuse Liability for Yoga Instructors	$100,000 per occurrence
	$300,000 aggregate limit
Products Liability for Yoga Instructors	$1,000,000 aggregate limit

Other Insurance Coverages Include:
1. Workman's Compensation,
2. Business Policy: Property & Liability Insurance
3. Health insurance.
4. Commercial Vehicle Insurance
5. Business Interruption Insurance
6. Disability Insurance
7. Personal & Advertising Injury
8. Medical Expense Payments
9. Damage to Premises rented to you (Covers fire damage to building you lease if proven negligent)

Cost Estimates: $4.00 per participant (minimum of $450 per year)

Workman's compensation covers employees in case of harm attributed to the workplace. The property and liability insurance protects the building from theft, fire, natural disasters, and being sued by a third party. Employee health insurance will be provided for the full-time employees. Professional Liability or Errors and Omissions Insurance is usually needed if a business deal with contracts.

Note: Yoga Instructors, like all personal fitness professionals, need high quality, affordable, professional liability insurance. The Yoga Alliance protects Yoga instructors from liability claims with affordable coverage.

To help save on insurance cost and claims, management will do the following:
1. Stress employee safety in our employee handbook.
2. Screen employees with interview questionnaires and will institute pre-employment drug tests and comprehensive background checks.
3. Videotape our equipment and inventory for insurance purposes.
4. Create an operations manual that shares safe techniques.
5. Limit the responsibilities that we choose to accept in our contracts.
6. Consider the financial impact of assuming the exposure ourselves.
7. Establish loss prevention programs to reduce the hazards that cause losses.
8. Consider taking higher deductibles on anything but that which involves liability insurance because of third-party involvement.
9. Stop offering services that require expensive insurance coverage or require signed releases from clients using those services.
10. Improve employee training and initiate training sessions for safety.
11. Require Certificate of Insurance from all subcontractors.

12. Make staff responsible for a portion of any damages they cause.
13 We will investigate the setting-up of a partial self-insurance plan.
14. Convince underwriters that our past low claims are the result of our ongoing safety programs and there is reason to expect our claims will be lower than industry averages in the future.
15. At each renewal, we will develop a service agreement with our broker and get their commitment to our goals, such as a specific reduction in the number of incidents.
16. We will assemble a risk control team, with people from both sides of our business, and broker representatives will serve on the committee as well.
17. When an employee is involved in an accident, we will insist on getting to the root cause of the incident and do everything possible to prevent similar incidents from re-occurring.
18. At renewal, we will consult with our brokers to develop a cost-saving strategy and decide whether to bid out our coverage for competitive quotes or stick with our current carrier.
19. We will set-up a captive insurance program, as a risk management technique, where our business will form its own insurance company subsidiary to finance its retained losses in a formal structure.
20. Review named assets (autos and equipment), drivers and/or key employees identified on policies to make sure these assets and people are still with our company.
21. As a portion of our business changes, that is, closes, operations change, or outsourcing occurs, we will eliminate unnecessary coverage.
22. We will make sure our workforce is correctly classified by our workers' compensation insurer and liability insurer because our premiums are based on the type of workers used.
23. We will become active in Trade Organizations or Professional Associations, because as a benefit of membership, our business may receive substantial insurance discounts.
24. We will adopt health specific changes to our work place, such as adopting a no smoking policy at our company and allow Yoga or weight loss classes to be held in our break room.
25. We will consider a partial reimbursement of health club membership as a benefit.
26. We will find out what employee training will reduce rates and get our employees involved in these programs.
27. We will have students sign a consent form, as such a form will disclose the risks and benefits of the yoga practice and allows the student to formally acknowledge his awareness of the disclosed risks.
28. We will consider a liability waiver, which goes beyond a mere disclosure of benefits and risks by asking the signer to assume legal responsibility for these risks and also to promise not to sue if an injury results.
29. Our teachers will ask students about injuries and conditions before beginning class and then caution their students accordingly.
30. Our teachers will be mindful of students' pace and limitations so as not to create unnecessary injuries, discomfort, or an experience of invasion.

The required business insurance package will be provided by _____ (insurance carrier name). The business will open with a _____ (#) million-dollar liability insurance policy, with an annual premium cost of $ _____.

Note: We will seek at least $2 million of coverage per claim and at least $3 million in aggregate coverage per year. Aggregate coverage per year means we are covered up to the set amount for all incidents.

All required licenses to own and operate a small business of this type will be obtained through the local city and county government offices.

The Yoga Studio will need to acquire the following special licenses to operate:
- A sales tax license is required through the State Department of Revenue.
- A County and/or City Occupational License.
  Sign Permit
Note: A board issued license will be required to engage in physical therapy.

Note: In most states, you are legally required to obtain a business license, and a dba certificate. A business license is usually a flat tax assessment and a percentage of your gross income. A dba stands for Doing Business As, and it is the registration of your trade name if you have one. You will be required to register your trade name within 30 days of starting your business. Instead of registering a dba, you can simply form an LLC or Corporation and it will have the same effect, namely register your business name.

Yoga teacher insurance providers include:
IMA Group Inc.
Yoga Journal's Benefits Plus
Sport and Fitness Insurance Corporation
AYIO Insurance Center
InnerIdea
Idea Health and Fitness Association.
Beyogi Insurance   https://beyogi.com/partner/baron

Resources:
Workers Compensation Regulations
              http://www.dol.gov/owcp/dfec/regs/compliance/wc.htm#IL
New Hire Registration and Reporting
              www.homeworksolutions.com/new-hire-reporting-information/
State Tax Obligations
              www.sba.gov/content/learn-about-your-state-and-local-tax-obligations
Resource:
www/sba.gov/content/what-state-licenses-and-permits-does-your-business-need

Note: Check with your local County Clerk and state offices or Chamber of Commerce to make sure you follow all legal protocols for setting up and running your business.

Note: To find out about your local business licensing office, visit SBA.gov. This government website compiles information on business licenses and permits at the sta/ level.

Resources:

Insurance Information Institute	www.iii.org/individuals/business/
National License Directory	www.sba.gov/licenses-and-permits
Independent Insurance Agents & Brokers of America	www.iiaa.org
National Association of Surety Bond Producers	www.nasbp.org
Find Law	http://smallbusiness.findlaw.com/starting-business/starting-business-licenses-permits/starting-business-licenses-permits-guide.html
Business Licenses	www.iabusnet.org/business-licenses
Legal Zoom	www.legalzoom.com
Business Filings	www.bizfilings.com
Yoga Insurance	www.yogajournal.com/benefitsplus/
Namasta Alliance (Insurance)	www.namasta.com
Sports and Fitness Insurance Corp.	www.sportsfitness.com

2.3   Start-up To-Do Checklist

1.   Describe your business concept and model, with special emphasis on planned multiple revenue streams and services to be offered.
2.   Create Business Plan and Opening Menu of Products and Services.
3.   Determine our startup costs of Yoga Studio business, and operating capital and capital budget needs.
4.   Seek and evaluate alternative financing options.
5.   Do a name search: Check with County Clerk Office or Department of Revenue and Secretary of State to see if the proposed name of business is available.
6.   Decide on a legal structure for business.
       Common legal structure options include Sole Proprietorship, Partnership, Corporation or Limited Liability Corporation (LLC).
7.   Make sure you contact your State Department of Revenue, Secretary of State, and the Internal Revenue Service to secure EIN Number and file appropriate paperwork. Also consider filing for Sub-Chapter S status with the Federal government to avoid the double taxation of business profits.
8.   Protect name and logo with trademarks, if plan is to go national.
9.   Find a suitable location with proper zoning.
10.   Research necessary permits and requirements your local government imposes on your type of business. (Refer to: www.business.org)
11.   Call for initial inspections to determine what must be done to satisfy Fire Marshall, Health Inspector and Building Inspector requirements.
12.   Adjust our budget based on build-out requirements.
13.   Negotiate lease or property purchase contract.
14.   Obtain a building permit.

15. Obtain Federal Employee Identification Number (FEIN).
16. Obtain State Sales Tax ID/Exempt Certificate.
17. Open a Business Checking Account.
18. Obtain Merchant Credit Card Account.
19. Obtain City and County Business Licenses
20. Create a prioritized list for equipment, furniture and décor items.
21. Comparison shop and arrange for appropriate insurance coverage with product liability insurance, public liability insurance, commercial property insurance and worker's compensation insurance.
22. Locate and purchase all necessary equipment and furniture prior to final inspections.
23. Get contractor quotes for required alterations.
24 Manage the alterations process.
25. Obtain information and price quotes from possible supply distributors.
26. Set a tentative opening date.
27. Install 'Coming Soon' sign in front of building and begin word-of-mouth advertising campaign.
28. Document the preparation, project and payment process flows.
29. Create your accounting, purchasing, payroll, marketing, loss prevention, employee screening and other management systems.
30. Start the employee interview process based on established job descriptions and interview criteria.
31. Contact and interview the following service providers: uniform service, security service, trash service, utilities, telephone, credit card processing, bookkeeping, cleaning services, etc.
32. Schedule final inspections for premises.
33. Correct inspection problems and schedule another inspection.
34. Set a Grand Opening date after a month of regular operations to get the bugs out of the processes.
35. Make arrangements for website design.
36. Train staff.
37. Schedule a couple of practice sessions for friends and interested prospects.
38. Be accessible for direct customer feedback.
39. Distribute comment cards and surveys to solicit more constructive feedback.
40. Remain ready and willing to change your business concept and offerings to suit the needs of your actual customer base.

2.3.1   EMPLOYER RESPONSIBILITIES CHECKLIST

1. Apply for your SS-4 Federal Employer Identification Number (EIN) from the Internal Revenue Service. An EIN can be obtained via telephone, mail or online.
2. Register with the State's Department of Labor (DOL) as a new employer. State Employer Registration for Unemployment Insurance, Withholding, and Wage Reporting should be completed and sent to the address that appears on the form. This registration is required of all employers for the purpose of determining whether the applicants are subject to state unemployment

insurance taxes.

3.   Obtain Workers Compensation and Disability Insurance from an insurer. The insurance company will provide the required certificates that should be displayed.

4.   Order Federal Tax Deposit Coupons – Form 8109 – if you didn't order these when you received your EIN. To order, call the IRS at 1-800-829-1040; you will need to give your EIN. You may want to order some blanks sent for immediate use until the pre-printed ones are complete. Also ask for the current Federal Withholding Tax Tables (Circular A) – this will explain how to withhold and remit payroll taxes, and file reports.

5.   Order State Withholding Tax Payment Coupons. Also ask for the current Withholding Tax Tables.

6.   Have new employees complete an I-9 Employment Eligibility Verification form. You should have all employees complete this form prior to beginning work. Do not send it to Immigration and Naturalization Service – just keep it with other employee records in your files.

7.   Have employees complete aW-4 Employees Withholding Allowance Certificate.

2.4 Company Location

_____ (company name) will be located in the _____ residential area in ____ (city). The site is one of the densest and _____ (affluent?) markets in the state. Our storefront will be prime retail space in the _____ (northeast?) corner of the ____ Avenue building, facing ___, a main artery for vehicles and city buses coming and going from the complex. The store is centered within a cluster of ____ (#) residential _____ (buildings?).

_____ (company name) will be located in the _____ (complex name) in _____ (city), ___ (state). It is situated on a _____ (turnpike/street/avenue) just minutes from _____ (benchmark location), in the neighborhood of _____. It borders a large parking lot which is shared by all the businesses therein. Important considerations relative to studio location are competition, visibility, accessibility, signage, community growth trends, demographics, walk by foot traffic, and drive by traffic patterns. A visible, busy location will make the difference between a business that is stagnant and a business that thrives.

The location has the following advantages: (Select Choices)

1.   It is easy to locate and accessible to a number of major roadways.
2.   Easy access from public transportation.
3.   Ground level access.
4.   Good neighborhood visibility and traffic flow.
5.   Plentiful parking.
6.   Proximity to _____ and _____ income growth areas.
7.   Proximity to businesses in same affinity class with same ideal client profiles.
8.   Reasonable rent.
9.   Conveniently located to customer base in a high-traffic location.

10.   Proximity to the growing residential community of _____.
11.   Low crime rate with good police and fire protection.
12.   Excellent foot traffic
13.   Exposure to natural light.
14.   Zoning approved for a yoga studio.
15.   Near a health food store or Whole Foods Store.
16.   No unusual smells coming from neighboring businesses.

2.4.1   Company Facilities

_____ (company name) signed a _____ (#) year lease for _____ (#) square foot of space. The cost is very reasonable at $____/sq. foot. We also have the option of expanding into an additional _____ sq. ft. of space and subletting the space. A leasehold improvement allowance of $___ /sq. ft. would be given. Consolidated area maintenance fees would be $___/month initially. _____ (company name) has obtained a _____ (three) month option on this space effective _____ (date), the submission date of this business plan, and has deposited refundable first and last lease payments, plus a $ _____ security deposit with the leasing agent.

Note: A good rule of thumb is to figure on needing roughly 30 square feet for every practitioner. This estimate takes into account a two-by-six-foot mat and still allows for one to two extra feet per person

The facility will need to accommodate at least 20 students, which means there will be a l need a minimum of 700 square feet of space.

The facilities will incorporate the following room parameters into the layout:

		Percentage	Square Footage
1.	__ (#) Yoga Workshop Rooms	_____	_____
2.	__ (#) Practice/Training Rooms	_____	_____
3.	Storage Room	_____	_____
4.	Product Inventory Storage	_____	_____
5.	Staff Room	_____	_____
6.	Admin Office	_____	_____
7.	Restroom	_____	_____
8.	Snack Bar/Refreshment Area	_____	_____
9.	Reception/Check in Area	_____	_____
10.	Waiting Area	_____	_____
11.	Shoe Storage/Dressing Rooms	_____	_____
12.	Retail Boutique Shop	_____	_____
13.	Laundry Room	_____	_____
14.	Supplemental Services Room	_____	_____
Totals:		_____	_____

Resource: www.katicurtisdesign.com/blog/2010/06/26/yoga-studio-interior-design-programming-and-planning.html

Note: Supplemental Services may include massage, acupuncture, chiropractic, therapy, Pilates, self-defense, etc.

2.4.2   Facilities Design

We plan to build a yoga studio that uses the following elements to create an environment of peace, positive energy, and joy:

1.   Sound System
2.   Hardwood, Bamboo, Cork or Laminate Flooring
3.   Mirrored Wall
4.   Reception Counter
5.   Dressing Room Lockers
6.   Natural light access
7.   Ambient lighting
8.   Unobstructed view of the teacher.
9.   Keep walls available for posture assistance
10.   Consistent Studio and Logo Color and Design Scheme
11.   Integrate color scheme with yoga equipment such as mats, bolsters, equipment.
12.   Introduce a subtle scent is good to cover up body odor.
13.   Air and Water Filtration Systems

Resources:
http://www.yogabaron.com/yoga-studio-design
https://www.pinterest.com/explore/yoga-studio-design/
http://www.homestratosphere.com/yoga-studio-design-tips/

2.5   Start-up Summary

The start-up costs for the Yoga Studio business will be financed through a combination of an owner investment of $ _____ and a short-term bank loan of $ _____.
The total start-up costs for this company are approximately $ _____ and can be broken down in the following major categories:

1.   Major Equipment $ _____
2.   Software $_____
3.   Furniture, Work Tables and Fixtures $_____
4.   Inventory $_____
5.   Working Capital $_____
       For day-to-day operations, including payroll, etc.
6.   Renovations/Buildout $ _____
       Includes architect, lighting update, flooring, etc.

7.	Marketing/Advertising Expenses		$ _____
	Includes sales brochures, direct mail, opening expenses.		
8.	Rent and Utility Deposits		$ _____
9.	Contingency Fund		$ _____
10.	Other		$ _____
	Includes training, legal expenses, etc.		
Totals:			$ _____

Notes: Must figure on needing roughly 21 square feet for every practitioner. This estimate takes into account a two-by-six-foot mat and still allows for one to two extra feet per person.

Anticipate spending up to a third of your revenue on rent in the first year, and a quarter or less in subsequent years.

Note: Average Startup Costs
  Lease - 800-1000 sq ft studio - $3000/mo
  Yoga Mats - = $1000
  Commercial space renovation - $20,000
  Advertising - $10,000
  Sound System - $1,000
  Utilities - $100
  Working Capital Reserves - $40,000 (approximately 1 year with zero income)
Total estimated startup costs - $75,000

The company will require $_____ in initial cash reserves and additional $_____ in assets. The start-up costs are to be financed by the equity contributions of the owner in the amount of $ _____ , as well as by a _____ (#) year commercial loan in the amount of $ _____. The funds will be repaid through earnings.
These start-up expenses and funding requirements are summarized in the tables below.

2.5.1   Inventory

Inventory:	Supplier	Qty	Unit Cost	Total
Beverages/Snacks				
Journals				
Cleaning Supplies				
Bathroom Supplies				
Candles				
Copy Paper				
Marketing Materials				
Business Forms				
Intake Form				
Office Supplies				
Computer Supplies				
Apparel				

DVDs/Videos/Books	_____
Exercise Mats	_____
Straps	_____
Rollers	_____
Bolsters	_____
Misc. Supplies	_____
Totals:	_____

Note: Business forms include; collateral and support documentation, promotional materials, invoice form templates, liability release form templates, workshop flier templates, attendance tracking sheets, and contract templates.

Resource: www.yogaeducationinstitute.com/Yoga-Business-Success.pdf
              Pages 42 - 44.

2.5.2   Supply Sourcing

Initially, _____ (company name) will purchase all of its equipment from _____ and supplies from _____, the _____ (second/third?) largest supplier in _____ (state), because of the discount given for bulk purchases. However, we will also maintain back-up relationships with two smaller suppliers, namely _____ and _____. These two suppliers have competitive prices on certain products.

Resources:
Yoga Accessories   www.yogaaccessories.com/
Lululemon   www.lululemon.com
              http://deniseleeyohn.com/bites/radical-differentiation-at-lululemon/

Note: Balanced Body, Gratz Pilates, Peak Yoga and Stott Yoga are some of the   major professional quality manufacturers of Yoga equipment.

2.5.3   Supplier Assessments

We will use the following form to compare and evaluate suppliers, because they will play a major role in our procurement strategies and significantly contribute to our profitability.

	Supplier #1	Supplier #2	Compare
Supplier Name			
Website			
Address			
Contacts			
Annual Sales			
Distribution Channels			
Memberships/Certifications			
Quality System			
Positioning			

Pricing Strategy	_____
Payment Terms	_____
Discounts	_____
Delivery Lead-time	_____
Return Policy	_____
Rebate Program	_____
Technical Support	_____
Core Competencies	_____
Primary Product	_____
Primary Service	_____
New Products/Services	_____
Innovative Applications/Uses	_____
Competitive Advantage	_____
Capital Intensity	_____
State of Technology	_____
Capacity Utilization	_____
Price Volatility	_____
Vertical Integration	_____
References	_____
Overall Rating	_____

2.5.4   Equipment Leasing

Equipment Leasing will be the smarter solution allowing our business to upgrade our equipment needs at the end of the term rather than being overly invested in outdated equipment through traditional bank financing and equipment purchase. We also intend to explore the following benefits of leasing some of the required equipment:

1.	Frees Up Capital for other uses.	2.	Tax Benefits
3.	Improves Balance Sheet	4.	Easy to add-on or trade-up
5.	Improves Cash Flow	6.	Preserves Credit Lines
7.	Protects against obsolescence	8.	Application Process Simpler

Our leasing strategy will also be shaped by the following factors:
1.   Estimated useful life of the equipment.
2.   How long our business plans to use the equipment.
3.   What our business intends to do with the equipment at the end of the lease.
4.   The tax situation of our business.
5.   The cash flow of our business.
6.   Our company's specific needs for future growth.

List Any Leases:

Leasing Company	Equipment Description	Monthly Payment	Lease Period	Final Disposition

Resource:

LeaseQ   www.leaseq.com
An online market place that connects businesses, equipment dealers, and leasing
companies to make selling and financing equipment fast and easy. The LeaseQ Platform
is a free, cloud based SaaS solution with a suite of on-demand software and data solutions
for the equipment leasing industry. Utilizes the Internet to provide business process
optimization (BPO) and information services that streamline the purchase and financing
of business equipment across a broad array of vertical industry segments.

Innovative Lease Services   http://www.ilslease.com/equipment-leasing/
This company was founded in 1986 and is headquartered in Carlsbad, California. It is
accredited by the Better Business Bureau, a long-standing member of the National
Equipment Finance Association and the National Association of Equipment Leasing
Brokers and is the official equipment financing partner of Biocom.

2.5.5   Funding Source Matrix

Funds Source	Amount	Interest Rate	Repayment Terms	Use

2.5.6   Distribution or Licensing Agreements (if any)

Note: These are some of the key factors that investors will use to determine if we have a
       competitive advantage that is not easily copied.

Licensor	License Rights	License Term	Fee or Royalty

2.5.7   Trademarks, Patents and Copyrights (if any)

Our trademark will be virtually our branding for life. Our choice of a name for our
business is very important. Not only will we brand our business and services forever, but
what may be worthless today will become our most valuable asset in the years to come.
A trademark search by our Lawyer will be a must, because to be told down the road that
we must give up our name because we did not bother to conduct a trademark search
would be a devastating blow to our business. It is also essential that the name that we
choose suit the expanding product or service offerings that we plan to introduce.
Note: These are some of the key factors that investors will use to determine if we have a
       competitive advantage that is not easily copied.

Resources:
Patents/Trademarks   www.uspto.gov
Copyright   www.copyright.gov

2.5.8   Innovation Strategy   (optional)

_____ (company name) will create an innovation strategy that is aligned with not only our firm's core mission and values, but also with our future technology, supplier, and growth strategies. The objective of our innovation strategy will be to create a sustainable competitive advantage. Our education and training systems will be designed to equip our staff with the foundations to learn and develop the broad range of skills needed for innovation in all of its forms, and with the flexibility to upgrade skills and adapt to changing market conditions. To foster an innovative workplace, we will ensure that employment policies facilitate efficient organizational change and encourage the expression of creativity, engage in mutually beneficial strategic alliances and allocate adequate funds for research and development. Our radical innovation strategies include _____ to achieve first mover status. Our incremental innovation strategies will include modifying the following _____ (products/services/processes) to give our customers added value for their money.
Resource:
https://hbr.org/2015/04/the-5-requirements-of-a-truly-innovative-company

2.5.9   Summary of Sources and Use of Funds

Sources:
Owner's Equity Investment $ _____
Requested Bank Loans $ _____
Total: $ _____

Uses:
Capital Equipment $ _____
Beginning Inventory $ _____
Start-up Costs $ _____
Working Capital $ _____
Total: $ _____

2.5.9.1   Funding to Date   (optional)

To date, _____'s (company name) founders have invested $_____ in _____ (company name), with which we have accomplished the following:

1.   _____ (Designed/Built) the company's website
2.   Developed content, in the form of ____ (#) articles, for the website.
3.   Hired and trained our core staff of ___(#) full-time people and ____ (#) part-time people.
4.   Generated brand awareness by driving ____ (#) visitors to our website in a ____(#) month period.
5.   Successfully _____ (Developed/Test Marketed) ____ (#) new _____ (products/services), which compete on the basis of _____.
6.   _____ (Purchased/Developed) and installed the software needed to _____ (manage _____ operations?)
7.   Purchased $ _____ worth of _____ (supplies)
8.   Purchased $ _____ worth of _____ equipment.

2.6   Start-up Requirements

Start-up Expenses:		Estimates
Legal	_____	400
Accountant	_____	300
Accounting Software Package	_____	300
Licenses & Permits	_____	300
Office Supplies	_____	300
Sales Brochures	_____	300
Direct Mailing	_____	500
Other Marketing Materials	_____	2000
Logo Design		500
Advertising (2 months)	_____	2000
Consultants	_____	1000
Insurance	_____	1200
Rent (2 months security)	_____	3000
Rent Deposit	_____	1500
Utility Deposit		600
DSL Installation/Activation	_____	100
Telephone System Installation		200
Telephone Deposit	_____	200
Expensed Equipment	_____	1000
Website Design/Hosting		2000
Computer/Printer	_____	
Marketing Plan/Software		
Used Office Equipment/Furniture		2000
Display Cases	_____	
Studio Planner/Design	_____	1000
Organization Memberships	_____	300
Facility Renovations/Buildout	_____	5000
Installation Expenses	_____	

Training Materials	_____		
Signs	_____		
Other	_____		
Total Start-up Expenses	_____	**(A)**	

Start-up Assets:

Cash Balance Required	_____	(T)	5000
Start-up Equipment	_____		
Start-up Inventory	_____		
Other Current Assets	_____		
Long-term Assets	_____		
Total Assets	_____	**(B)**	
Total Requirements	_____	(A+B)	

Start-up Funding

Start-up Expenses to Fund	_____	(A)
Start-ups Assets to Fund	_____	(B)
Total Funding Required:	_____	**(A+B)**

Assets

Non-cash Assets from Start-up	_____	
Cash Requirements from Start-up	_____	(T)
Additional Cash Raised	_____	(S)
Cash Balance on Starting Date	_____	(T+S=U)
Total Assets:	_____	**(B)**

Liabilities and Capital

Short-term Liabilities:

Current Borrowing	_____	
Unpaid Expenses	_____	
Accounts Payable	_____	
Interest-free Short-term Loans	_____	
Other Short-term Loans	_____	
Total Short-term Liabilities	_____	**(Z)**

Long-term Liabilities:

Commercial Bank Loan	_____	
Other Long-term Liabilities	_____	
Total Long-term Liabilities	_____	**(Y)**
Total Liabilities	_____	**(Z+Y = C)**

Capital

Planned Investment

Owner	_____
Family	_____
Other	_____

Additional Investment Requirement _____

Total Planned Investment _____ **(F)**

Loss at Start-up (Start-up Expenses) **(-)**_____ **(A)**

Total Capital **(=)**_____ **(F+A=D)**

Total Capital and Liabilities _____ **(C+D)**

Total Funding _____ (C+F)

2.6.1 Capital Equipment List

Equipment Type	Model No.	New/ Used	Lifespan	Quantity	Unit Cost	Total Cost
Computer System						1000
Fax Machine						200
Digital Camera						500
Copy Machine						600
Answering Machine						200
Postage Meter						
Sound System						
Recording Equipment						
Lighting Equipment						
Yoga Props						
Foam Rollers						
Rotational Disks						
Flex-Bands®						
Yoga Floor Mats						
Glassless Mirrors						
Security System						
Lockers						
Surge Protector						
Accounting Software						
Microsoft Office Software						
Management/Scheduling Software						
Electronic Scale						
Props						
Blender						
Refrigerator						
Microwave						
Glue Gun						
Phone System						
Trophy Display Case						
Merchandise Display Cases						
Cash Register						
Calculator						
Vending Machines						
Other						
Total Capital Equipment						

Note: Equipment costs are dependent on whether purchased new or used or leased. All items that are assets to be used for more than one year will be considered a long-term asset and will be depreciated using the straight-line method.

2.7 SBA Loan Key Requirements

In order to be considered for an SBA loan, we must meet the basic requirements:
1. Must have been turned down for a loan by a bank or other lender to qualify for most SBA Business Loan Programs. 2. Required to submit a guaranty, both personal and business, to qualify for the loans. 3. Must operate for profit; be engaged in, or propose to do business in, the United States or its possessions; 4. Have reasonable owner equity to invest; 5. Use alternative financial resources first including personal assets.

All businesses must meet eligibility criteria to be considered for financing under the SBA's 7(a) Loan Program, including: size; type of business; operating in the U.S. or its possessions; use of available of funds from other sources; use of proceeds; and repayment. The repayment term of an SBA loan is between five and 25 years, depending on the lift of the assets being financed and the cash needs of the business.
Working capital loans (accounts receivable and inventory) should be repaid in five to 10 years. The SBA also has short-term loan guarantee programs with shorter repayment terms.

A Business Owner Cannot Use an SBA Loan:

To purchase real estate where the participant has issued a forward commitment to the developer or where the real estate will be held primarily for investment purposes. To finance floor plan needs. To make payments to owners or to pay delinquent withholding taxes. To pay existing debt, unless it can be shown that the refinancing will benefit the small business and that the need to refinance is not indicative of poor management.

SBA Loan Programs:
Low Doc: www.sba.gov/financing/lendinvest/lowdoc.html
SBA Express   www.sba,gov/financing/lendinvest/sbaexpress.html
Basic 7(a) Loan Guarantee Program
> For businesses unable to obtain loans through standard loan programs. Funds can be used for general business purposes, including working capital, leasehold improvements and debt refinancing.
> www.sba.gov/financing/sbaloan/7a.html

Certified Development Company 504 Loan Program
> Used for fixed asset financing such as purchase of real estate or machinery.
> www. Sba.gov/gopher/Local-Information/Certified-Development-Companies/

MicroLoan 7(m) Loan Program
> Provides short-term loans up to $35,000.00 for working capital or

purchase of fixtures.
www.sba.gov/financing/sbaloan/microloans.html

2.7.1   Other Financing Options

1.   Grants:
Health care grants, along with education grants, represent the largest percentage of grant giving in the United States. The federal government, state, county and city governments, as well as private and corporate foundations all award grants. The largest percentage of grants are awarded to non-profit organizations, health care agencies, colleges and universities, local government agencies, tribal institutions, and studios. For-profit organizations are generally not eligible for grants unless they are conducting research or creating a significant number of jobs.

A.   Contact your state licensing office.
B.   Foundation Grants to Individuals: www.fdncenter.org
C.   US Grants   www.grants.gov
D.   Foundation Center   www.foundationcemter.org
E.   The Grantsmanship Center   www.tgci.com
F.   Contact Local Chamber of Commerce
G.   The Catalog of Federal Domestic Assistance is a major provider of
             business grant money.
H.   The Federal Register is a good source to keep current with the continually changing federal grants offered.
I.   FedBizOpps is a resource, as all federal agencies must use FedBizOpps to notify the public about contract opportunities worth over $25,000.
J.   Fundsnet Services   http://www.fundsnetservices.com/
K.   SBA Women Business Center
       www.sba.gov/content/womens-business-center-grant-opportunities

Local Business Grants
Check with local businesses for grant opportunities and eligibility requirements. For example, Bank of America sponsors community grants for businesses that endeavor to improve the community, protect the environment or preserve the neighborhood.
Resource:
www.bankofamerica.com/foundation/index.cfm?template=fd_localgrants

Green Technology Grants
If you install green technology in the business as a way to reduce waste and make the business more energy efficient, you may be eligible for grant funding. Check your state's Economic Development Commission. This grant program was developed as part of the American Recovery and Reinvestment Act.
Resource: www.recovery.gov/Opportunities/Pages/Opportunities.aspx

2.	Friends and Family Lending	www.virginmoney.com
3.	Peer-to-Peer Lending	www.lendingclub.com
4.	National Business Incubator Association	www.nbia.org/
5.	Women's Business Associations	www.nawbo.org/
6.	Minority Business Development Agency	www.mbda.gov/
7.	Social Networking Loans	www.prosper.com (kiva.com)
8.	Extended Credit Terms from Suppliers	(30/60/90 days)
9.	Prepayment from customer	To cover cost of goods
10.	Accounts Receivable Financing	Factoring
12.	Angel Investors	www.angelcapitalassociation.com

13. Seller Financing when purchasing an existing Yoga Studio.

14.	Business Funding Directory	www.businessfinance.com
15.	FinanceNet	www.financenet.gov
16.	SBA Financing	www.sbaonline.sba.gov

17. Private Investors

18. Use retirement funds to open a business without taxes or penalty. First, establish a C-corporation for the new business. Next, the C-corporation establishes a new retirement plan. Then, the owner's current retirement funds are rolled over into the C-corporation's new plan. And last, the new retirement plan invests in stock of the C-corporation. Warning: Check with your accountant or financial planner. Resource: http://www.benetrends.com/

19. Business Plan Competition Prizes
www.nytimes.com/interactive/2009/11/11/business/smallbusiness/Competitions-table.html?ref=smallbusiness

| 20. | Tech Stars | www.techstars.org |
| 21. | Capital Source | www.capitalsource.com |

www.msl.com/index.cfm?event=page.sba504
Participates in the SBA's 504 loan program. This program is for the purchase of fixed assets such as commercial real estate and machinery and equipment of a capital nature, which are defined as assets that have a minimum useful life of ten years. Proceeds cannot be used for working capital.

| 22. | Commercial Loan Applications | www.c-loans.com/onlineapp/ |

23. Sharing assets, marketing expense and resources with other non-competing businesses.

24.	Angel Investors	www.angelcapitaleducation.org
25.	The Receivables Exchange	http://receivablesxchange.com/
26.	Micro-Loans	www.accionusa.org/

27. Bootstrap Methods: Personal Savings/Credit Card/Second Mortgages

| 28. | Community-based Crowd-funding | www.profounder.com |
| | | www.peerbackers.com |

A funding option designed to link small businesses and entrepreneurs with pools of prospective investors. Crowdfunding lenders are often repaid with goods or services.

| 29. | On Deck Capital | www.ondeckcapital.com/ |

Created the Short-term Business Loan (up to $100,000.00) for small businesses to get quick access to capital that fits their cash flow, with convenient daily payments.

30. Royalty Lending   www.launch-capital.com/

    With royalty lending, financing is granted in return for future revenue or company performance, and payback can prove exceedingly expensive if a company flourishes.

31. Stock Loans   Southern Lending Solutions, Atlanta. GA.

                            Custom Commercial Finance, Bartlesville, OK

    A stock loan is based on the quality of stocks, Treasuries and other kinds of investments in a businessperson's personal portfolio. Possession of the company's stock is transferred to the lender's custodial bank during the loan period.

32. Lender Compatibility Searcher   www.BoeFly.com

33. Strategic Investors

    Strategic investing is more for a large company that identifies promising technologies, and for whatever reason, that company may not want to build up the research and development department in-house to produce that product, so they buy a percentage of the company with the existing technology.

34. Bartering

35. Small Business Investment Companies   www.sba.gov/INV

36. Cash-Value Life Insurance

37. Employee Stock Option Plans   www.nceo.org

38. Venture Capitalists   www.nvca.org

39. Initial Public Offering (IPO)

40. Meet investors through online sites, including LinkedIn (group discussions), Facebook (BranchOut sorts Facebook connections by profession), and CapLinked (enables search for investment-related professionals by industry and role).

41. SBA Community Advantage Approved Lenders

           www.sba.gov/content/community-advantage-approved-lenders

42. Small Business Lending Specialists

    https://www.wellsfargo.com/biz/loans_lines/compare_lines

    http://www.bankofamerica.com/small_business/business_financing/

    https://online.citibank.com/US/JRS/pands/detail.do?ID=CitiBizOverview

    https://www.chase.com/ccp/index.jsp?pg_name=ccpmapp/smallbusiness/home/pa
        ge/bb_business_bBanking_programs

43. Startup America Partnership   www.s.co/about

    Based on a simple premise: young companies that grow create jobs. Once startups apply and become a Startup America Firm, they can access and manage many types of resources through a personalized dashboard.

44. United States Economic Development Administration   www.eda.gov/

45. Small Business Loans   http://www.iabusnet.org/small-business-loans

46. Tax Increment Financing (TIF)

    A public financing method that is used for subsidizing redevelopment, infrastructure, and other community-improvement projects. TIF is a method to use future gains in taxes to subsidize current improvements, which are projected to create the conditions for said gains. The completion of a public project often results in an increase in the value of surrounding real estate, which generates additional tax revenue. Tax Increment Financing dedicates tax increments within a certain defined district to finance the debt that is issued to pay for the project. TIF is often designed to channel funding toward improvements in distressed, underdeveloped, or underutilized parts of a jurisdiction.

47. Gust   https://gust.com/entrepreneurs
Provides the global platform for the sourcing and management of early-stage investments. Gust enables skilled entrepreneurs to collaborate with the smartest investors by virtually supporting all aspects of the investment relationship, from initial pitch to successful exit.

48. Goldman Sachs 10,000 Small Businesses   http://sites.hccs.edu/10ksb/
49. Earnest Loans   www.meetearnest.com
50. Biz2Credit   www.biz2credit.com
51. Funding Circle   www.fundingcircle.com
A peer-to-peer lending service which allows savers to lend money directly to small and medium sized businesses

52. Lending Club   www.lendingclub.com
53. Equity-based Crowdfunding www.Indiegogo.com   www.StartEngine.com
www.SeedInvest.com

54. National Funding   www.nationalfunding.com
Their customers can to get working capital, merchant cash advances, credit card processing, and, equipment leasing.

55. Quick Bridge Funding   www.quickbridgefunding.com
Offers a flexible and timely financing program to help assist small and medium sized businesses achieve their goals.

56. Kabbage   www.kabbage.com
The industry leader in providing working capital online.

Resources: www.sba.gov/category/navigation-structure/starting-managing-business/starting-business/local-resources

http://usgovinfo.about.com/od/moneymatters/a/Finding-Business-Loans-Grants-Incentives-And-Financing.htm

3.0 Products and Services

In this section, we will not only list all of our planned products and services, but also describe how our proposed products and services will be differentiated from those of our competitors and solve a real problem or fill an unmet need in the marketplace.

As stated in the executive summary, the primary revenue center for the business will come from ongoing yoga classes hosted at the Company's retail storefront location. For each yoga session, Management intends on charging a fee of approximately $ _____. The average yoga class will have five to ten students. Classes will be held five to six times per day. The business will also generate sales through the sale of yoga mats and other products as they related to yoga training.

Yoga Instruction and Classes

The Company will offer several styles of yoga classes, including: Gentle Kripalu, Classic Hatha, Vinyasa Flow, Power Vinyasa and the Ashtanga Yoga Series. These styles represent different approaches to yoga with varying levels of technical difficulty and strenuousness. The Company's eclectic continuum of yoga classes will allow our Yoga Studio and its instructors to continuously challenge students both physically and mentally as they deepen their practice and achieve proficiency. ____ (company name) will allow each of its teachers/instructors to use their experience, training and creativity to inform the direction of their classes, rather than dictate how each class must be taught. From the instructors' perspective, they get the freedom to be themselves while sharing their unique passion for yoga. From the students' perspective, the Company offers a variety of classes and interpretations helping to keep their practice evolving.

1.   Yoga Beginner

An introductory class for students who are new to Yoga. This class focuses on poses to stretch and strengthen the legs, back, and shoulders. Emphasis is given to the basic alignment of the standing poses.

2.   Fundamentals of Vinyasa Yoga

This class will prepare students for a vigorous flow style of yoga (Vinyasa) that synchronizes breath with movement. It will offer a balance of strength, flexibility, and endurance to challenge the fitness enthusiast. The course will begin with instruction on the alignment of the poses and move toward linking all the poses together in a continuous flow by the end of the session.

3.   Gentle Yoga

A class designed for those who prefer a class less vigorous than Yoga 1. It includes gentle stretches and breathing as well as simple movements designed to systematically increase the range of motion of every major joint and increase energy. This class is ideal for students with chronic symptoms such as muscle/joint pain, stiffness, weakness, or fatigue.

4.   Yoga Continuing Beginner

This is a continuation class for Yoga 1. The emphasis of this course is on refining and building endurance in Yoga 1 and Yoga 2 standing poses. It does not include the shoulder stand. The basic Anusara Yoga principles of alignment are presented. This class is suitable for students who have practiced other styles of yoga, but it is not suitable for those who have never studied yoga before.

5.   Yoga Intermediate
This class focuses on refining the standing poses and learning basic sitting postures, simple back bending poses, and the shoulder stand using the Anusara Yoga principles of alignment.

6.   Yoga Advanced
This class continues with refinements to poses studied in Yoga 2 and introduces full arm balance (handstand), headstand, and forearm balance. Additional back bend poses are also included. Regular yoga practice outside of class is strongly encouraged. Permission of the instructor is required.

Other Yoga Class Descriptions Include:
Short Form Ashtanga (S.F.A.)– This ancient practice of yoga uses pose repetition. This shifts the focus away from learning new poses and allows students to focus on improving postures, transitioning between poses, and pairing breath with movement. All levels.

Lunar Flow – Cutting-Edge Vinyasa. The class is created for the students that do not limit themselves only to the working-out benefits of Yoga but are also looking for a "working-in" approach, including few minutes of Meditation. The class will have a dynamic but still subtle flow of postures. Very energetic but relaxing at the same time.

Yin Yoga – Deep Tissue Yoga. This class starts with a set of warm up poses, and then moves into longer holding postures whose practice targets the deeper tissues rather than the muscular tissues. Yin Yoga is a perfect complement to EDY and Ashtanga and is suitable for all.

Vinyasa Flow
Vinyasa Flow is a flowing series of postures that move at a more moderate tempo. Classes begin with warm up movements and breath awareness to prepare you for the heart of each class, a sequence of postures that stretch, strengthen, and balance your body. Levels 1/2 beginner to intermediate. Levels 2/3 intermediate to advanced.

Slow Flow
This class is a slower flowing series of postures. Classes begin with warm up movements and breath awareness to prepare you for the heart of each class, a sequence of postures that stretch, strengthen, and balance your body.

Prana Flow
Prana Flow is an energetic, creative, full-spectrum approach to embodying the flow of yoga cultivated by Shiva Rea and the Global Vinyasa Collective of Teachers. Students of all levels are empowered to experience prana – the universal source of breath, life-energy

and conscious intelligence – as the navigating source of yoga practice and vital living. Practitioners learn classical and innovative approaches to vinyasa yoga and the state of flow drawn from Krishnamacharya's teachings, Tantra, Ayurveda, Bhakti, Somatics and Shiva's teaching experience from the last fifteen years.

Deep Stretch Yoga

This is a wonderful Yoga class for de-stressing! A quiet practice that targets the deeper tissues that lay beneath the muscle layer. Beginning with Pratapana (gentle simple movements) to warm up the body we will move into various postures and use the resource of breath as we explore our edge and free congested energy. This deep stretch class will improve joint flexibility, re-lubricate the joints, and foster a quiet, meditative state. This is the perfect complement to a more active yoga practice. Open to everyone.

Restorative Yoga

This gentle style of yoga uses soothing and well-supported poses to provide us the opportunity to linger quietly for a few moments and savor the peace within us. Through forward bends (to release the low back and quiet the mind), back bends (to energize you, to open the chest and stimulate your spine), twists (to wring out the internal organs, freeing up stagnant energy), inversions (to balance your hormone and lymphatic systems), and hip openers (to improve the way you walk, sit, stand, etc.), you will start to release blockages, both muscular and energetic, while your nervous system gets a bubble bath. This class is open to all levels, including beginner's.

Kundalini/Vinyasa

Kundalini yoga is called the yoga of awareness because it directly affects ones' consciousness, develops intuition, increases self-knowledge, and unleashes the unlimited creative potential that exists within every human being. Everyone is welcome in this energetic yoga class that combines Kundalini Yoga and Vinyasa (Flow) Yoga. We'll connect movement and breath with an active mix of flowing postures and standing postures, combined with the cleansing effects of Kundalini yoga practices. Bri uses uplifting music, targeted breath work and specific movements to help students awaken the creative energy within themselves for their unique personal transformation and growth. A unique and inspiring combination.

Anusara Yoga

Anusara means "flowing with Grace." A heart-oriented and spiritually inspiring style of yoga, Anusara is grounded in the Universal Principles of Alignment for both the inner and the outer body. It is a uniquely integrated style of hatha yoga in which the artistic glory of the human heart blends magically with the scientific principles of biomechanics. Through vigorous poses, specific alignment, keen self-awareness, and attention to energy, Anusara students will find themselves tapped into a river of Grace. All levels welcome.

Anjali Restorative Yoga

Anjali Restorative Yoga is a deeply restful practice where the practitioner is guided through a series of meditations and thoughtful visualizations while the body is held and supported by bolsters, pillows, and blankets. By resting deeply, the body engages its natural ability to heal and rest. The effect is profoundly nurturing, thoughtful, and balancing.

Ashtanga Vinyasa

A dynamic and invigorating yoga, this class honors the system of yoga by Sri K.Pattabhi Jois in Mysore, India. This method of yoga involves synchronizing the breath with an organically progressive series of postures, known as asanas, which allow the body to produce an intense internal hear and, in turn, produce detoxifying sweat. Once will find improved circulation, a light and strong body, and a calm mind with regular practice.

Baptiste Yoga

A potent physical yoga practice, meditation practice and active self-inquiry are used as tools of transformation – encouraging participants to reclaim their full potential, discover creativity, awaken passion, and create authenticity, confidence and new possibilities. This is a heated power yoga experience. Temperatures inside the building reach up to 90 degrees during sessions, providing yogis with a challenging and strengthening workout.

Broga Yoga

A growing global fitness trend that has Yoga instructors now catering to men with classes that emphasize strength over stretching and offering everything from craft beer after class to man-only retreats away from the fairer sex.   The Massachusetts-based Broga yoga empire, which holds a copyright on the man-tastic portmanteau, claims to have more than 12,000 students and 500 teachers, boasting classes online and all over the world.

Jock Yoga

A fast-paced, full-body workout that aims for tight hips and strong upper bodies. For an hour or more, students flow through dozens of tricep push-ups, complicated arm balances and inverted acrobatics, leaving with stronger abs and a sense of calm.

Power Yoga

This form of yoga is focused more on strength training.

Hot Yoga

Yoga in a hot studio (of 100 degrees), has added benefits, as sweating during a session helps rid the body of toxins and opens up blood vessels to allow blood to move throughout the body.

SUP Yoga

A form of Yoga that requires intense concentration where yogis challenge their inner self to find balance posing on the water. The whole idea is to get people on water to practice their balance even more than what they would on land. The class will begin with an hour of paddle boarding to get people used to balancing on the water, followed by an hour of yoga on the paddle board. Participants are constantly having to be aware of their body in correlation of the water, and the wind, and the sun.   SUP (Stand up paddleboard) is a practice that combines core training with sup with a harmonious experience in nature. It can be practiced in the ocean, on a lake, in a cove, as long as the space is safe and adapted for a yoga practice.

Examples: www.yoga-water.com

Specialty Workshops
Example: Yoga as the Art of Self-Love: Integrating the Timeless Teachings of the
Yoga Sūtra into our Practice

In this ____ (#)-hour workshop, _____ (presenter name) will present some of the most practical, core teachings of the Yoga Sūtra in simple and practical language. Students will be introduced to the most important facet of the Yoga Sūtra: Patañjali's model of the 'mind-cycle,' which can: - Help us to see how we limit our experience of joy by investing mental and emotional energy into delimiting cycles of thought - Show us how our practice can be used to expose and to dissolve habitual, unconscious patterns that are the cause of all suffering. Students will be given simple yet empowering meditation practices, that, when added to a daily āsana routine, are meant to reveal the magnanimity of the Immortal Self which joyfully resides behind the 'whirling of the mind'.
Resource:
www.yogabycandace.com/blog/2016/12/30/yoga-teacher-talk-how-to-host-a-yoga-workshop

Meditation Workshops
We will offer a "Learn How to Meditate Workshop" one evening per _____ (week/month?). We will become experts in logistic planning for specialty seminars.
Resource: https://zenplanner.com/planning-for-fitness-seminars/

Space Rentals
We will consider renting out our studio to other small business owners like self-defense instructors and martial arts teachers.

Class Photography
We will contract with a local photographer to take student and class photos on a commission basis.

Yoga Therapy
Our Yoga Therapy will involve systematically using breath and movement to strengthen, stretch and stabilize the muscular-skeletal system, smooth and deepen respiratory rhythms, improve circulation, balance internal physiology and emotions and in general, target natural recuperative powers to specific systems of the body. All as part of a specific practice for an individual. May also involve examining behaviors and attitudes that contribute to undesirable conditions and then cultivating a practice to support movement in the desired direction.

Yoga Teacher Training Program
We will set-up a program for those interested in taking their yoga practice to the next level and taking a yoga teacher training and yoga certification program. We will offer an introductory 200-hour yoga teacher training and an advanced 500-hour series.
Teacher training programs are usually the most lucrative revenue source a studio can

have. Expected revenue will vary based on how experienced or well-known our instructors are, and whether our program is a specialty program or a general 200-hour program. On average, general programs run between $2,000 – 4,000 per student. Specialty training programs, like Pre-Natal Yoga, Kid's Yoga, or Yoga Nidra run from $400 -$1,500 per student.

To start our training program, we will need to apply with the Yoga Alliance for our Registered Yoga School (RYS) designation. The Yoga Alliance review process is designed to ensure a standard curriculum that is taught by Experienced Registered Yoga Teachers (E-RYT). Only teachers who complete a program at an RYS school can go on to be certified as a Registered Yoga Teacher (RYT) with the Yoga Alliance. For that reason, the RYS designation will be crucial to our program's success.

Source: www.causely.com/sweatangels/blog/double-reveue-at-your-yoga-studio-
                    by-launching-a-teacher-training-program
Resource: www.yogaalliance.org/Credentialing/CredentialsforSchools
Example: http://www.sivayogastudios.com/teacher-trainings.html

Yoga Retreats

We will organize yoga retreats to an ashram, which is a secluded place where the principles of yoga and meditation are taught and practiced. The word Ashram describes a house where a true Guru is living and teaching God-seekers seeking spiritual advice and help.

The following types of classes will be made available:

Group class

This is a great place for beginners to start, and a fun, social way to continue Yoga practice. These classes will have a manageable participant-teacher ratio (10-15 participants) so the instructor can monitor each individual's form and progress. Classes will be designed for beginner, intermediate and advanced participants.

Private one-on-one session

A personal training session will be the most effective way to learn, practice and perfect the participant's Yoga performance. The instructor will devote undivided attention to the participant's specific needs and develops a custom program for optimum results.

Other Services

Family Yoga Classes

With wide age ranges and levels of ability, this class will be fun and especially rewarding for all members of the family. Family Yoga will teach simple routines, games and partner poses the whole family will enjoy. Invigorating poses as well as calming restorative poses will be taught, with emphasis on alignment, symmetry and technique.

Mobile Private Sessions

These sessions provide personalized instruction in the privacy, convenience and comfort of the participant's home or office, according to their schedule of availability. We will assemble the portable flooring materials and sound system to make these at-home sessions possible, and compensate instructors on a pay-for-performance basis.

Corporate Team Building/Training Programs
Our Corporate Yoga Programs are designed to develop effective work teams by enhancing communication, relationships, self-esteem, cooperation and social awareness among all team members. Corporate members will strengthen key business skills as they listen, learn, persevere, perform and encourage each other in a relaxed, nurturing and fun-filled environment.

To help sell our services to corporations, we will focus on the following benefits that yoga has for their employees:
A.   Increases employee satisfaction, productivity and morale.
B.   Reduces employee fatigue, stress and anxiety
C.   Improves employees' ability to concentrate and focus
D.   Strengthens the immune system and reduces employee sick days
E.   Promotes camaraderie and team building between employees.

Corporate Wellness Programs
The current boom in corporate yoga can be traced back 25 years to when companies began adopting wellness programs to lower health care costs. At about that time, the Surgeon General issued a warning saying inactivity was as big a health risk as smoking cigarettes. Many companies have jumped at the opportunity to establish fitness programs as part of a wellness initiative and began subsidizing gyms, which offered yoga as a "lite" exercise option. Companies understand that they have to address employees' health and well-being. Employees need time to relax, and a lot of people are gravitating towards yoga as a way to manage stress. According to researchers from the Stress Reduction Clinic at the University of Massachusetts Medical Center in Worcester, yoga in conjunction with meditation can indeed relieve stress and improve work performance.

Birthday Parties
We will create multiple birthday party celebration packages that can either be experienced at our studio or at the client's location. The party will feature the services of a mobile instructor, who is also capable of presenting a mini-Yoga session to the party attendees. These parties will also give us the opportunity to market to all of the party guests.

Yoga Therapy
Our Yoga Therapy program will focus on injury prevention and recovery due to the focus on relaxation and slower movement patterns. Our Yoga Therapy program will help with the following types of conditions:
    Orthopedic injuries (knee pain, shoulder pain, back pain)
    Chronic pain, Fibromyalgia, Osteoporosis, Arthritis
    Anxiety, Depression, sleep disorders.

Products
Sales of Ancillary Products

In addition to providing Yoga instruction services, the Company will also sell bottled water and apparel as complimentary items. Management expects that 5% to 10% of the Company's aggregate revenues will come from this revenue center.

1.	Healthy Snacks and Beverages	2.	Instructional DVDs / Videos
3.	Custom Studio Logowear	4.	Bottled Water
5.	Mats	6.	Athletic/Yoga Apparel
7.	Balancing balls	8.	Belts and weights
9.	Instructional manuals	10.	Inspirational books
11.	Nutritional Supplements	12.	Yoga Mat Wipes

We will create an ecommerce sales platform to also sell these products online.
Resource:
www.shopify.com
https://www.shopify.com/success-stories/mukhayoga
https://ecommerce.shopify.com/c/ecommerce-marketing/t/do-you-need-of-yoga-studio-software-systems-228848

3.0.1   The Benefits of Our Services

Our clients will potentially experience the following benefits from our yoga programs:
1. Sleep improves
2. Immunity increases
3. Pain decreases
4. Posture improves
5. Weight normalizes
6. Muscular flexibility increase
7. Energy level increases
8. Endocrine function normalizes
9. Gastrointestinal function normalizes

3.1   Alternative Service Options

1.	Fitness Classes	2.	Weight Management Classes
3.	Fitness Equipment Room	4.	Pre/Post-natal Certified Train
5.	Pilates Classes	6.	Model Training Workshop
7.	Birthday Parties: Onsite and At-Home	8.	After studio Programs
9.	Digital Recording of sessions	10.	Physical Therapy Sessions
11.	Injury Prevention Classes	12.	Martial Arts
13.	Bootcamp	14.	Sculpt

3.2   Alternative Revenue Streams

1.	DVD Productions	2.	Newsletter Classified Ads
3.	Café/Healthy Snack Bar Sales	4.	Vending Machine Sales
5.	Affiliate Program Sales	6.	Seminar Presentation Fees
7.	Yoga Party Ticket Sales	8.	Singles Event Ticket Sales
9.	Cultural Exchange Programs	10.	Videography
11.	Corporate Workshop Programs	12.	Nutrition Counseling

3.3 Production of Products and Services

We will use the following methods to locate the best suppliers for our business:

- Attend trade shows to spot upcoming trends, realize networking
opportunities and compare prices.

- Subscribe to appropriate trade magazines, journals, newsletter and blogs.

Yoga Journal   www.yogajournal.com/for_teachers/2616

Yogi Times   www.yogitimes.com

The Yoga Lunchbox   http://theyogalunchbox.co.nz/about-2/
Offers an online meeting place for yoga teachers and students to come together to share their experiences with each other, creating a platform for community learning where everyone's contribution is valued.

- Join our trade association to make valuable contacts, get listed in any online
directories, and secure training and marketing materials.

North American Studio Alliance   www.namasta.com
NAMASTA is the trade organization that caters to the business needs of Yoga professionals. NAMASTA's membership benefits include access to liability insurance for Yoga Instructors starting from $95/year, an alternative health care benefit, discounts on Yogamats and important business services.

The Yoga Alliance   http://yogaalliance.org//index.html
A nonprofit standards organization for yoga teachers and schools.

Yoga Teacher's Association   www.ytayoga.com/
A non-profit, educational organization dedicated to continuing and improving the quality of Hatha Yoga teaching in accordance with the high standards of the Hatha Yoga Pradipika and as developed by great yoga masters. Based in Westchester, N.Y., the YTA serves members from the tri-state area.

American Yoga Association   www.americanyogaassociation.org/
A nonprofit, federally tax-exempt, educational organization. Their goal is to provide the highest quality Yoga instruction and educational resources to anyone interested in Yoga. Provides educational services to program developers in

various health-related fields, and journalists preparing articles and special reports on Yoga-related topics.

Resources: www.marketingsource.com/associations/
  "National Trade and Professional Associations of the U.S." Buck Downs

3.4   Competitive Comparison

The Yoga Studio business is competitive, as the barriers to entry and exit in this market are relatively low. This a luxury service industry with a large number of firms. Buyers have a significant amount of power since they have a number of companies to choose from. Yoga Studio companies must compete on quality of instruction, uniqueness of programs and packages, building of customer relationships, educating clients as to the benefits of their services and the price/value equation.

_____ (company name) believes that it can improve on the quality and diversity of programs in this industry by instituting management control procedures and pay-for-performance compensation practices that will assure a consistently superior service.

The company will be competitive in price and will maintain close relationships with its participants to realize their lifetime value to the business. Through these steps, _____ (company name) will be able to build up a brand reputation for better quality service at competitive prices than its competitors.

We will also reinvest major dollars every year in professional and educational training materials and seminars. We will attend seminars and club venues to bring participants the finest selection of Yoga related products and services, and industry trend information. We will also offer our participants a Satisfaction Guarantee.

3.5   Sales Literature

_____ (company name) has developed sales literature that illustrates a professional organization with vision. _____ (company name) plans to constantly refine its marketing mix through a number of different literature packets. These include the following:
  - direct mail with introduction letter and product price sheet.
  - product information brochures
  - press releases
  - new product/service information literature
  - email marketing campaigns
  - website content
  - corporate brochures

A copy of our informational brochure is attached in the appendix of this document. This brochure will be available to provide referral sources, leave at seminars, and use for direct mail purposes.

3.6 Fulfillment

The key fulfillment and delivery of services will be provided by our director/owner, and certified store associates. The real core value is the industry expertise of the founder, and staff experience and company training programs.

3.7 Technology

___(company name) will employ and maintain the latest technology to enhance its office management, inventory management, payment processing, customer profiling and record keeping systems. We will also use a Cash Register POS system to manage our studio. Each item that gets sold will be deducted from our inventory list. Additionally, tracking items in our studio will easily be managed with handheld inventory devices that integrate with Cash Register system. Our point of sale system will include a small form factor computer, cash drawer, receipt printer and laser bar code scanner or tabletop scanner. An optional pole display will be easily added, which will inform our customers how much they are paying so they are likely to have the cash out quickly. A laser bar code scanner will aggressively scan bar codes that might be on bags or around bottles and quickly add the item to the invoice. All these devices help to reduce the time it takes to process a customer.

Top Key Players in the Yoga Studio Software Market Include:

Acuity Scheduling	Skedda
Bookeo	Reservio
Punchpass	Retreat Guru
Karmasoft	Eversports Software
iClassPro	

Source:
https://hugopress.com/yoga-studio-software-market/6227974

MINDBODY, Inc.   **www.mindbodyonline.com/en/products/**
MINDBODY Business Management Software offers online classes, event, and appointment scheduling, total client management, strategic marketing and ecommerce solutions for our type of business.

Zen Planner   **www.zenplanner.com**
Their all-in-one software includes easy-to-use tools for membership management, scheduling and integrated payment processing, as well as automated email and website templates that help users keep in touch with members.

Mobile POS Systems
Vend   **www.vendhq.com/**

A retail POS software, inventory management, ecommerce & customer loyalty for iPad, Mac and PC. Easily manage & grow your business in the cloud.

Shopkeep **www.shopkeep.com**
Charges a monthly fee of $49 per register. It customizes service for retail, quick service, restaurants and bars with features including inventory monitoring, staff management and customer marketing. Administrators can monitor business stats through an online back-end, which also syncs with an iOS app for iPhone. Shopkeep's system can also be integrated with MailChimp to manage emails to a customer listserv and Quickbooks accounting software for an additional fee.

LevelUp **www.thelevelup.com/**
LevelUp charges a 1.95% rate for every transaction, as well as $50 per scanner, which plugs into most POS systems or the $100 LevelUp Tablet. The scanner reads a QR code displayed on a customer's smartphone or uses near field communication technology to allow the customer to pay with the likes of ApplePay or Google Wallet. LevelUp reminds customers when they have not visited the businesses after a set period of time and provides a rewards program. Customers also have the option of leaving feedback for the owner through the LevelUp app.

Revel **http://revelsystems.com/**
An award-winning iPad Point of Sale solution for single and multi-location businesses.

Mobile Phone Credit Card Reader https://squareup.com/
Square, Inc. is a financial services, merchant services aggregator and mobile payments company based in San Francisco, California. The company markets several software and hardware products and services, including Square Register and Square Order. Square Register allows individuals and merchants in the United States, Canada, and Japan to accept offline debit and credit cards on their iOS or Android smartphone or tablet computer. The app supports manually entering the card details or swiping the card through the Square Reader, a small plastic device which plugs into the audio jack of a supported smartphone or tablet and reads the magnetic stripe. On the iPad version of the Square Register app, the interface resembles a traditional cash register.

Google Wallet https://www.google.com/wallet/
A mobile payment system developed by Google that allows its users to store debit cards, credit cards, loyalty cards, and gift cards among other things, as well as redeeming sales promotions on their mobile phone. Google Wallet can be used NFC to make secure payments fast and convenient by simply tapping the phone on any PayPass-enabled terminal at checkout.

Apple Pay http://www.apple.com/apple-pay/
A mobile payment and digital wallet service by Apple Inc. that lets users make payments using the iPhone 6, iPhone 6 Plus, Apple Watch-compatible devices (iPhone 5and later models), iPad Air 2, and iPad Mini 3. Apple Pay does not require Apple-specific contactless payment terminals and will work with Visa's PayWave,

MasterCard's PayPass, and American Express's ExpressPay terminals. The service has begun initially only for use in the US, with international roll-out planned for the future. Resource:
www.wired.com/2016/01/shadow-apple-pay-google-wallet-expands-online-reach/

WePay   https://www.wepay.com/
An online payment service provider in the United States. WePay's payment API focuses exclusively on platform businesses such as crowdfunding sites, marketplaces and small business software. Through this API, WePay allows these platforms to access its payments capabilities and process credit cards for the platform's users.

Chirpify
Connects a user's PayPal account with their Twitter account in order to enable payments through tweeting.

Article: www.prnewswire.com/news-releases/tips-to-leverage-mobile-payments-in-your-marketing-strategy-300155855.html

POS Prophet Systems   www.softwareadvice.com/retail/pos-prophet-systems-profile/
This system includes the following applications: inventory management, retail accounting, POS, CRM, and e-commerce. Ideal for both start-ups and medium-sized retailers. Must be deployed on-premise on a Windows-based system. POS Prophet Systems can be paid for in monthly installments or in one up-front payment. The system also includes QuickBooks and Peachtree integration.

3.8   Future Products and Services

_____ (company name) will continually expand our offering of products and services based on Yoga Studio industry trends and changing client needs. We will not only solicit feedback via surveys and comments cards from clients on what they need in the future, but will also work to develop strong relationships with all of our clients and vendors.

We plan to offer a couples Yoga lesson program on Sunday afternoons that includes a light boxed lunch as a packaged deal. We also plan to install a smoothie and juice bar under the guidance of a nutritionist.

We also plan to offer our own Yoga DVD productions using a two-camera production system with editing. We will also sell digital recordings of our instruction classes to interested consumers.

We plan to develop special Yoga classes for the workplace to boost productivity, reduce sick days, increase mental clarity and focus, combat fatigue, improve memory, strengthen the muscles, fight stress and increase workplace satisfaction. We will help corporations to offer yoga classes in their workplace surroundings.

We will develop and organize two-day corporate team-building retreats that include "active relaxation" yoga, as well as hikes, sports and croquet tournaments.

We plan to create a mobile yoga studio. We will go to our students rather than have the students come to us. We will market our innovative service as a mobile yoga studio for corporations, nursing homes, schools, and anywhere that will accommodate our requirements. We also plan to add life-recovery yoga classes for students struggling with addictions, and special classes for students with multiple sclerosis.

We also plan to add an organic café, separate bookstore, and a wellness center.

Pop-up Yoga Studios
We will rent temporary pop-up retail spaces to test the market for new yoga studio locations and to generate a secondary revenue stream.
Source:
www.inforum.com/business/small-business/4377457-new-yoga-studio-now-open-downtown-fargo
Example:
https://www.danilynnyoga.com/
Resources:
www.popuprepublic.com
www.thestorefront.com

After-school Yoga Program
We plan to develop an after-school yoga program that helps children to do better in school. We will do the research to determine how the yoga class will help young people to de-stress and calm down, shed some of that nervous energy and be better able to focus on their studies. We know that parents are always looking for quality after-school enrichment programs for their children, and we will facilitate after-school transportation to our facility. We may also look to form an alliance with a business that offers a tutoring program.
Resource: http://www.thirdeyeyogastudio.com/success_stories/

Mobile Yoga Service
We will offer our mobile yoga service to local businesses and non-profit organizations, because most companies have conference room or cafeteria space large enough to hold a yoga class once a few tables and chairs are moved out of the way. Because yoga can happen anywhere, we will seek to hold affordable classes in community centers, parks, art galleries, school gyms, and even restaurants. These classes will focus on the health and productivity benefits of yoga, and will also help to build visibility for these hosting businesses. The objective will be to help these people to forget work for a period of time and stretch some muscles that were aching from sitting all day. We will also offer our mobile yoga services to churches, preschools, assisted living facilities, residential care

facilities, synagogues, dance studios, library conference rooms and martial arts studios. These are all places that often have large spaces and may donate or rent that space to us on an hourly basis or engage in a revenue sharing arrangement.
Source:
www.yogaeducationinstitute.com/Yoga-Business-Success.pdf

Staged Yoga/Craft Beer Events

We will approach microbreweries about holding yoga events, because millennials have embraced exercise as a social venue. Starting in California, Oregon and New England, microbreweries and beer bars have begun offering regular yoga classes. This is proof positive that millennial women have embraced craft beer, and men who love millennial women are willing to do anything, including wearing spandex, in order to be near them. Attendees are usually asked to bring their own mats and towels.
Source:
http://www.tampabay.com/things-to-do/food/dining/beer-plus-yoga-local-breweries-say-yes-with-classes/2284193
http://www.bloomberg.com/news/articles/2016-07-05/no-pain-no-gain

Specialty Focused Yoga Classes

We will create specialty classes around a common bond, objective or interest. We will offer specialty classes for a particular demographic, such as:

A.	Men only	B.	Skiers
C.	Post-natal mothers	D.	Cyclists
E.	Seniors	F.	Golfers
G.	Rock Climbers	H.	Teens
I.	Business Executives	J.	Gymnasts
K.	Overweight/Obese Persons		

Example:

We will develop a class called 'Fat Person Yoga', and the class will be a welcome center for all genders, body shapes, sizes and levels of fitness. We will help each student to find a variation that best suits his or her body type. We will place yoga props, such as chairs, partitions, blocks, blankets, bolsters and straps around the room so that if a student finds he or she needs extra support during a pose, it's available and within reach. We will create and foster an atmosphere of acceptance, rather than harsh judgment, which should keep students coming back to class. We will help students to feel comfortable about their body image and how to maintain a positive outlook.
Source:
http://styleblueprint.com/birmingham/everyday/fat-girl-yoga/

Expand Yoga Personal Impact

Our innovative yoga program will expand upon the idea of helping people learn more about themselves and how to pursue better overall wellness, personal growth and spiritual development, through the practice of yoga. Our business will not just be about yoga. It will be about a building a sense of community, promoting the concepts of health and wellness, and the power of messaging. We will basically combine a yoga studio with a health and wellness center. We will appeal to people who just want to learn how they can

live their lives based more in the things that really matter to them.
Source:
www.democratandchronicle.com/story/lifestyle/2016/07/25/woman-watch-erica-denman/
87525018/

Space Time-sharing Arrangements

The basic idea is to share a space on a long-term, committed basis, with a complementary business or businesses and pay only for the times that we utilize. We will seek to team up with people who are in complementary businesses, such as massage therapists, Pilates teachers, dance teachers, martial arts teachers, kid's activity studio, and rent space that we can each use at certain times. In this scenario, we will only pay for the time we use; we will not have to worry about maintenance, high, fixed rent, utilities, space-utilization, repairs, long-term leases, big-deposits and seasonal changes in business.

Destination Yoga Weekends and Week-Long Retreats

We will look for hotels or resorts with large garden areas and the amenities we need to conduct both indoor and outdoor yoga classes. We will seek to earn a sales commission on the negotiation of an all-inclusive group package deal and a separate fee for the yoga sessions. We will also charter a bus to generate a secondary revenue stream. For a full weekend, we will hand out a schedule of the activities and a map of the grounds, so people know where they are going and at what time. We will also include a description of extra services that are available during down times, such as massages, facials, etc, where to go for those services, the fees and a short bio on each practitioner. We will also allow time for more optional health services and for excursions into the surrounding area. We will also approach cruise lines about booking yoga themed cruises, and the offering of healthy meal options and informative seminars and workshops.

Virtual On-demand Yoga Classes

We plan to develop and offer live real-time class streaming or virtual on-demand subscription based group fitness or yoga classes, that can be easily access via the internet or a kiosk. This will expand our target market to include the world. We will also offer higher priced teacher channels.

Resources:
Namastream   https://namastream.com/
Provides the software to build a course where the content is scheduled or "dripped" to students over time, creates a membership and generates recurring revenue. Users are able to bundle a number of videos (or audios or docs) together and sell them as a product.

Examples:
https://www.fitnessondemand247.com/
https://www.drishtiqyoga.com/virtual-yoga/on-demand-videos/
https://www.myjoyyoga.com/
http://www.yogaworks.com/classes/online/
http://www.lesmills.com/virtual/

4.0 Market Analysis Summary

Our Market Analysis will serve to accomplish the following goals:
1. Define the characteristics, and needs and wants of the target market.
2. Serve as a basis for developing sales, marketing and promotional strategies.
3. Influence the e-commerce website design.

The market for Yoga continues to grow for the following reasons:
1. Need for more socialization opportunities and experiences.
2. Pursuit of a healthier lifestyle and enjoyable exercise programs.
3. After-school enrichment programs for latch-key kids.
4. The desire of corporations to build team spirit and reduce employee stress.
5. The obesity challenge facing people.
6. The pursuit of affordable escapism from mental anxiety.
7. The desire to find pain relief without harmful side effects.

The goal of _____ (studio name) is to help people of all ages to achieve their goal of becoming more confident in their actions and more at peace with themselves. . Our marketplace mission is to enrich our clients' lifestyle through movement and body awareness, uniting mind, body and spirit in a positive, holistic environment.

Our demographic research has shown that an opportunity exists in our local marketplace of _____(city). There are no other affiliated Yoga Studios in the _____ area. A sizable opportunity for growth exists in this market, and _____ (company name) believes that our position as the potential leader in our marketplace is an achievable objective.

_____ (city) is emerging from the recent recession to regain it economic growth position. The growth has been fueled by the increased employment in the city's _____ (financial/high tech?) companies. Currently, _____ (#) professionals work in ___ (city). We believe that a yoga studio can be very attractive to our customers if we create a program that fits the time constraints of their jobs. Our location is within easy walking distance from most office buildings in the _____ area. We plan to offer our members a program that will allow them to use their lunch hours to attend workshops.

The Owner, _____, has a solid reputation in the Yoga field, and will be a positive draw for those who have some experience with yoga instruction. The key to the success of _____ (company name) will be attracting new people to yoga instruction.

4.1 Secondary Market Research

We will research demographic information for the following reasons:
1. To determine which segments of the population, such as Hispanics and the elderly, have been growing and may now be underserved.
2. To determine if there is a sufficient population base in the designated service area

to realize the company's business objectives.
3. To consider what products and services to add in the future, given the changing demographic profile and needs of our service area.

We will pay special attention to the following general demographic trends:
1. Population growth has reached a plateau and market share will most likely be increased through innovation and excellent customer service.
2. Because incomes are not growing and unemployment is high, process efficiencies and sourcing advantages must be developed to keep prices competitive.
3. The rise of non-traditional households, such as single working mothers, means developing more innovative and personalized programs.
4. As the population shifts toward more young to middle aged adults, ages 30 to 44, and the elderly, aged 65 and older, there will be a greater need for child-rearing and geriatric mobile support services.
5. Because of the aging population, increasing pollution levels and high unemployment, new 'green' ways of dealing with the resulting challenges will need to be developed.

We will collect the demographic statistics for the following zip code(s):

_____

We will use the following sources: www.census.gov, www.zipskinny.com, www.city-data.com, www.demographicsnow.com, www.freedemographics.com, www.ffiec.gov/geocode, www.esri.com/data/esri_data/tapestry and www.claritas.com/claritas/demographics.jsp. This information will be used to decide upon which targeted programs to offer and to make business growth projections. **Resource:** www.sbdcnet.org/index.php/demographics.html

Snapshots of consumer data by zip code are also available online:
http://factfinder.census.gov/home/saff/main.html?_lang=en
http://www.esri.com/data/esri_data/tapestry.html
http://www.claritas.com/MyBestSegments/Default.jsp?ID=20

1.	**Total Population**	_____
2.	**Number of Households**	_____
3.	**Population by Race:**	White ____% Black ___%
		Asian Pacific Islander ___% Other ____%
4.	**Population by Gender**	Male ____% Female ____%
5.	**Income Figures:**	Median Household Income $_____
		Household Income Under $50K ____%
		Household Income $50K-$100K ____%
		Household Income Over $100K ____%
6.	**Housing Figures**	Average Home Value - $_____
		Average Rent $_____
7.	**Homeownership:**	Homeowners % _____
		Renters % _____

8.	**Education Achievement**	High studio Diploma	% _____
		College Degree	% _____
		Graduate Degree	% _____
9.	**Stability/Newcomers**	Longer than 5 years	% _____
10.	**Marital Status**	___% Married ___% Divorced ___% Single	
		___% Never Married __% Widowed __% Separated	
11.	**Occupations**	___%Service ___% Sales ___% Management	
		___% Construction ___% Production	
		___% Unemployed ___% Below Poverty Level	
12.	**Age Distribution**	___% 20-29 ___% 30-39 ___% 40-49 __% 50-59	
		___% 60-69 ___% 70-79 ___% 80+ years	
13.	**Prior Growth Rate**	_____ % from _____ (year)	
14.	**Projected Population Growth Rate**	_____ %	
15.	**Employment Trend**	_____	
16.	**Unemployment Rate**	_____ %	

Demographic Conclusions:

This area will be demographically favorable for our business for the following reasons:

_____

_____

Resources:

www.allbusiness.com/marketing/segmentation-targeting/848-1.html

http://www.sbdcnet.org/industry-links/demographics-links

http://factfinder2.census.gov/faces/nav/jsf/pages/index.xhtml

4.1.1   Primary Market Research

We plan to develop a survey for primary research purposes and mail it to a list of local home and arts magazine subscribers, purchased from the publishers by zip code. We will also post a copy of the survey on our website and encourage visitors to take the survey. We will use the following survey questions to develop an Ideal Customer Profile of our potential client base, so that we can better target our marketing communications. To improve the response rate, we will include an attention-grabbing _____ (discount coupon/ dollar?) as a thank you for taking the time to return the questionnaire.

1. What is the primary benefit you will receive from using our Yoga Studio, versus that of a competitor?
2. What is your zip-code?   _____
3. Are you single, divorced, separated, widowed or married? _____
4. Are you male or female?   _____
5. What is your age?   _____
6. What is your approximate household income?   _____
7. What is your educational level?   _____
8. What is your profession?   _____

9.   Do you have children? If Yes, what are their ages?   _____

10.   What are your favorite magazines?   _____

11.   What is your favorite local newspaper?   _____

12.   What is your favorite radio station?   _____

13.   What are your favorite television programs?   _____

14.   What organizations are you a member of?   _____

15.   How frequently do you use the services of a Yoga Studio? _____

16.   For which occasions would you consider using the services of a Yoga Studio?

17.   Describe your experience with other Yoga Studios.

19.   What can we do to improve/differentiate our product and service offerings?

20.   How did you first hear about us?

21.   Please indicate the name of a possible referral candidate.

22.   Please rank (1 to 12) the importance of the following factors when choosing a Yoga Studio:

       ___ Quality of Services   ___ Product Selection
       ___ Customer Service   ___ Instructor Competence
       ___ Instructor Friendliness   ___ Course Selection.
       ___ Scheduling Convenience   ___ Location Convenience
       ___ Value Proposition   ___ Studio Atmosphere
       ___ Price   ___ Referral
       ___ Other _____

23.   In what price range do you typically buy Yoga sessions? _____ to _____

24.   Where are you currently receiving Yoga sessions?

25.   What are their business strengths?

26.   What are their businesses weaknesses or shortcomings?

27.   What would it take for us to earn your Yoga instruction business?

28.   Do you buy private or group sessions?

29.   What are your favorite Yoga courses? _____

30.   What is the best way for us to market our Yoga studio? _____

31.   If you switch to another service provider, please indicate your reasons for doing so. (Select all that apply).

       ___ Better quality instruction   ___ Better Value
       ___ Service easier to use.   ___ Friendlier Service

32.   Have you purchased Yoga sessions within the past year?

33.   How interested are you in purchasing Yoga sessions within a year?

34.   Describe why you are not interested in purchasing Yoga sessions?

35.   What information would you like to see in a company newsletter?

36.   Which online social groups have you joined? Choose the ones you access.

       ___ Facebook   ___ MySpace
       ___ Twitter   ___ LinkedIn
       ___ Ryze   ___ Ning

Instructions: Circle all that apply.

37.   What are your motivations for pursuing Yoga sessions?

Technical Training/Recreational Fun/Weight Loss/Exercise/Competition/Career/
Creative Expression/Self-Confidence Building/Discipline Training/Physical Fitness/

Coordination Training/Social Networking

38. What types of Yoga sessions would most interest you?

_____

39. What types of new programs would most interest you?

_____

40. What types of after-school programs would most interest your children?

_____

41. Is there a scheduled time for a class you would like to become available?
Time: _____ Type of Class: _____ Start Date: _____

42. What has prevented you from experiencing the benefits of Yoga instruction?

43. What are your suggestions for realizing a better Yoga Studio experience?

44. In general, where do you get most of your info about programs for your children?
Direct Mail / Friends & Family / Billboards / Studio Notices / Brochure Displays

45. Are you on our mailing list? Yes/No   If No, can we add you? Yes / No

We very much appreciate your participation in this survey. If you provide your name, address and email address, we will sign you up for our e-newsletter, and enter you into our monthly drawing for a free _____.

Name

Address   Email   Phone

Resource: www.surveymonkey.com

4.1.2   Voice of the Customer

To develop a better understanding of the changing needs and wants of our Yoga Studio customers, we will institute the following ongoing listening practices:

1. Focus Groups
   Small groups of customers will be invited to meet with a facilitator to answer open-ended questions.

2. Individual Interviews
   We will conduct face-to-face personal interviews to understand customer thought processes and preferences.

3. Customer Panels
   A small number of customers will be invited to answer open-ended questions on a regular basis.

4. Customer Tours
   We will invite customers to visit our facilities to discuss how our processes can better serve them.

5. Visit Customers
   We will observe customers as they actually use our products to uncover the pains and problems they are experiencing during usage.

6. Trade Show Meetings
   Our trade show booth will be used to hear the concerns of our customers.

7. Toll-free Numbers
   We will attach our phone number to all products and sales literature to encourage

the customer to call with problems or positive feedback.

8.   Customer Surveys
We will use surveys to obtain opinions on closed-ended questions, and solicit feedback, referrals, testimonials and improvement suggestions.

9.   Mystery Shoppers
We will use mystery shoppers to report on how our employees treat our customers.

10.   Salesperson Debriefing
We will ask our salespeople to report on their customer experiences to obtain insights into what the customer faces, what they want and why they failed to make a sale.

11.   Customer Contact Logs
We will ask our sales personnel to record interesting customer revelations.

12.   Customer Serviceperson's Hotline
We will use this dedicated phone line for service people to report problems.

13.   Discussions with competitors.

14.   Installation of suggestion boxes to encourage constructive feedback. The suggestion card will have several statements customers are asked to rate in terms of a given scale. There are also several open-ended questions that allow the customer to freely offer constructive criticism or praise. We will work hard to implement reasonable suggestions in order to improve our service offerings as well as show our commitment to the customer that their suggestions are valued.

4.2   Market Segmentation

Market segmentation is a technique that recognizes that the potential universe of users may be divided into definable sub-groups with different characteristics. Segmentation enables organizations to target messages to the needs and concerns of these subgroups. We will segment the market based on the needs and wants of select customer groups. We will develop a composite customer profile and a value proposition for each of these segments. The purpose for segmenting the market is to allow our marketing/sales program to focus on the subset of prospects that are "most likely" to purchase our yoga studio products and services. If done properly this will help to insure the highest return for our marketing/sales expenditures.

People who practice Yoga are also consumers of natural and organic products, complementary medicine, personal development, socially responsible investing, alternative transportation, renewable energy, green building, recycling and other sustainable products and services. Many are willing to pay more for products and services that are made to minimize harm to themselves, the environment or society.
Studies issued by researches from the National Health Statistics Report and National Institutes of Health, t found that female adults 18 to 44 years old were most likely to practice yoga. Overall, the study also found that adults in the United States use complementary healthy approaches such as yoga, acupuncture, supplements, chiropractic

care, hypnosis, folk medicine or traditional healers, and other approaches, in tandem with more conventional treatments rather than as a replacement.

_____ (company name) will focus on the following two customer groups:

Middle Income Professionals:
This group is the core segment of potential students of _____ (company name). Their demographic characteristics are the following:
>Ages: 26-40.
>Sex: 30% male, 70% female.
>Family Income: $30,000-$50,000.
>Health/Lifestyle Issues: Active individuals that are focused on healthy food and dieting. Over 70% of this group are members of gyms. Approximately, 40% of potential customers have taken yoga classes before.
>Social Pattern: Will more likely attend as part of group.
>Our selling points: - Located close to work.
>   - Sessions lowers stress.
>   - Can be attended with associates as a group activity.

Upper Income:
The upper income customer will be a secondary target group. Their demographic characteristics are the following:
>Ages: 40-60.
>Sex: 30% male, 70% female.
>Family Income: $60,000+.
>Health/Lifestyle Issues: Active individuals that are focused on healthy food and dieting. Over 90% of this group are members of gyms.
>Social Pattern: Will more likely attend alone.
>Our selling points: - Close to work.
>   - The session lowers stress levels.

Corporations
>Businesses are constantly looking for new ways to build a spirit of teamwork and improve productivity, while reducing stress levels among employees. We will develop workshops to capture this target market.

Composite Customer Profile:

By assembling this composite customer profile, we will know what needs and wants to focus on and how best reach our target market. We will use the information gathered from our customer research survey to assemble the following composite customer profile:

Ideal Customer Profile

Who are they?
- age   _____
- gender   _____
- occupation   _____
  location: zip codes   _____
- income level   _____

marital status   _____

ethnic group   _____

education level   _____

family life cycle   _____

number of household members   _____

household income   _____

association memberships   _____

leisure activities   _____

hobbies/interests   _____

core beliefs   _____

Where are they located (zip codes)?   _____

Most popular product/service model?   _____

Lifestyle Preferences?   Trendsetter/Trend follower/Other _____

How often do they buy?   _____

What are most important purchase factors?   Price/Brand Name/Quality/Financing/Sales Convenience/Packaging/Other_____

What is their key buying motivator?   _____

How do they buy it?   Cash/Credit/Terms/Other_____

Where do they buy it from (locations)?   _____

What problem do they want to solve?   _____

What are the key frustrations/pains that these customers have when buying?   _____

What search methods do they use?   _____

What is preferred problem solution?   _____

Table: Market Analysis

Potential Customers	Growth	Annual Sales Dollars		
		2018	2019	2020
Middle Income Professionals	10%			
Upper Income Singles	10%			
Corporations	10%			
Other	10%			
Totals:	10%			

4.3 Target Market Segment Strategy

Our target marketing strategy will involve identifying a group of customers to which to direct our yoga studio products and services. Our strategy will be the result of intently listening to and understanding customer needs, representing customers' needs to those responsible for product production and service delivery, and giving them what they want. In developing our targeted customer messages, we will strive to understand things like: where they work, worship, party and play, where they shop and go to school, how they spend their leisure time, what magazines they read and organizations they belong to, and where they volunteer their time. We will use research, surveys and observation to uncover this wealth of information to get our product details and brand name in front of our customers when they are most receptive to receiving our messaging.

Target Market Worksheet   (optional)

Note: Use this worksheet to explore potential target markets for your products and services.

Product Benefits: Actual factor (cost effectiveness, design, performance, etc.) or perceived factor (image, popularity, reputation, etc.) that satisfies what a customer needs or wants. An advantage or value that the product will offer its buyer.

Products Features: One of the distinguishing characteristics of a product or service that helps boost its appeal to potential buyers. A characteristic of a product that describes its appearance, its components, and its capabilities. Typical features include size and color.

Product or Service	Product/ Service Benefits	Product/ Service Features	Potential Target Markets

_____ (company name) will tailor its course schedule to work within the time constraints of the target customer. Yoga classes will be no longer than 45 minutes and be scheduled to fit the break and rolling lunch schedules that exist in the local business community.

The focus of the instruction will also have to be tailored to a clientele that will be seeking maximum relief from the pressure of work and then returning to the workplace. ___ (company name) will strive to create a noticeable difference in the customers' sense of well-being. This will make the customer come to depend on our Yoga instruction as a escape during the day. These kinds of positive and relaxing experiences will create a tremendous word of mouth and bring in more first-time students.

Our objective is to present the benefits of Yoga to the local population, and introduce and develop interest in the community for Yoga as a relaxing exercise alternative and a social networking means. Our target market consists of people who want to take responsibility for their well-being, who are thoughtful about their bodies and who have a high level of education.

Target Niches with Specific Needs

Need	Class Title	Target
People suffering from arthritis	Yoga for the Inflexible	Physicians
Athletes training for endurance	Yoga for Endurance Athletes	Sports Teams
Injured Athletes	Yoga for Healing Injuries	Sports Teams

| Accident victims | Yoga for Healing Injuries | Rehab Centers |
| People suffering from depression | Yoga for Treating Depression | Psychiatrists |

Target Physicians
The mental focus and controlled breathing required to perform Yoga correctly helps reduce stress. The exercises also help regulate sleep and improve mood, according to the Mayo Clinic. Yoga may help reduce symptoms such as fatigue associated with a variety of disorders including cancer, depression and chronic pain.

Target Chiropractors
We target Chiropractors because they sometime recommend yoga exercises to their patients.

Target Rehabilitation Patients
We will provide private yoga therapy sessions for patients recovering from injury or surgery. Our Yoga Therapy program will provide a holistic approach to the healing process. Yoga therapy is different from other modalities of healing in that it integrates the healing of the body with the healing of the mind and emotions. We will make presentations to surgeons and hospital outpatient treatment centers.

Target Families
We will target families with children by offering classes for babies, toddlers and pregnant mothers, and in-studio child care during adult classes. We will also provide tea and healthy raisin oatmeal cookies after class.

Target Kids and Teens
We will develop our Grounded Kids & Teens yoga program. We will make demonstration presentations in our local schools and to PTA groups.

Target Parents of Toddlers
We will give free mini-sessions at local pre-schools and daycare centers, and give each toddler a flyer to bring home to their parents. Our toddler program will be about learning relaxation techniques, balance, coordination and developing functional motor skills at an early age.
Source: www.nwcn.com/news/health/a-balancing-act-toddlers-in-yoga/355912916

Target Dance Studios/Dancers/Athletes
Practicing Yoga can help improve flexibility, range of motion, balance and posture. Yoga strengthens and tones muscles without adding bulk, making it an exercise of choice among dancers and other athletes.

Target Apartment Complexes and Homeowner's Associations
We will inquire about teaching our yoga classes at their community centers. If they don't have the space or desire for that, maybe they will allow us to come in and give a seminar about how yoga can help the residents. We will give out coupons and information about our yoga studio at these events.

Target Fitness Clubs

We will partner with budget-priced gyms in our community to offer Yoga classes at discounted prices for members.

Target Hotels

We will seek to form partnerships with hotels and teach yoga to hotel guests. We will also make the hotel concierge aware of our mobile yoga programs.
Source:
http://www.racked.com/2014/6/16/7592393/tara-stiles-strala-yoga

Target Modeling Agencies

We will target modeling agencies because they often seek out models with unusual flexibility.

Target Dance Schools and Ballet Theater Companies

We will pursue dance and ballet students because yoga may be a way to prevent serious injuries, relieve back pains and improve the quality of performances.

Target Team Coaches

We will visit local team coaches and make them aware of the fact that Yoga can help athletes to improve focus.

Target Health Fairs

We will either organize or participate in holistic health fairs in our area. This will help our studio to develop a rapport with other local business owners in the health, fitness and alternative medicine arenas as well as give us a chance to showcase our new yoga studio to prospective yoga clients. We will target our comprehensive system for personal and professional growth to people with no aspirations of ever becoming a yoga teacher, but who just want to learn how they can live their lives based more in the things that really matter to them.

Target Alternative Healthcare Professionals

We will contact and network with groups specializing in alternative medicine, mental health, physical fitness and healthy living. We will give free sample yoga sessions to these professionals to generate referrals.

Target College Students

We plan to work with the local college to offer classes and part-time instructor assignments to their participants for college credit. We will cater to a college schedule and young people working later hours. Our fees will also have to fit into their budget. We would also like to get college participants involved in our studio events through college newsletter announcements. We will produce a flyer with a coupon and contact information that can be distributed easily through college campuses. Every advertisement will feature a link to our studio's website featuring pictures of our studio, course menus, participant discounts and instructor biographies. We will also distribute a postcard that

basically tells students that the best cure for a hangover is a yoga class, because yoga is not designed to get people to stop doing all the bad stuff, it's designed to help balance it out. We will also offer a 'Yoga for Athletes' class to attract college students.
Resource: https://www.yogajournal.com/poses/yoga-for/athletes

Target Millennials
As an emerging breed of studios finds success in catering to the millennial set with hip-hop soundtracks, hang-out zones, etc. The newest teacher training curricula will focus on translating traditional teachings for the next generation of yogis. We will use our social media sites to reach millennials.

Target Teens
We will conduct school demonstrations and seminars at local studios to show the fun, weight management and social aspects of Yoga.

Target Singles
For singles, we offer another way to meet people and socialize.

Target Married Adults
This group is generally looking for new things to learn, try and do together in a social context. They are also interested in stress reduction and lifestyle enrichment.

Target Retired People and Seniors
We will market Yoga as a recreational hobby with low impact exercise and social meeting benefits. Yoga helps seniors to meditate and safely manage their aches and pains. We plan to offer our services to local nursing homes, social clubs and community centers. Our target group will be active, older men. We will teach a style of yoga that is inclusive, welcoming those with chronic back pain, anxiety, depression or any number of other seeming limitations to a more active and happy lifestyle. We will actively encourage men we know, and think might enjoy participating to maintain a healthy blood pressure level, and healthy levels of blood sugar and cholesterol. We will also focus on the stress-busting and calming aspects of the program, which will come through emphasis on deep breathing and short meditation sessions held at the end of each weekly class.

Target Corporations
We will approach large businesses in our area to ask if we can do yoga classes during lunch break. Many big companies are focusing on having healthy, productive employees, and we may be able to help them with this by teaching relaxation yoga classes to the employees a couple times a week. We will target corporations because we will be saving our corporate clientele from the exorbitant costs associated with stress, workers' compensation claims, and turnover. Since corporate Yoga is a stress management tool, corporations can easily justify spending money on such programs. We will also market to corporations wanting to build team spirit. To market to corporations, we will visit business managers in the areas we plan to work in and ask to speak with the human resources manager. We will leave a sales packet for future reference. Our sales packet will include a business card, sales cover letter, full-color sales brochure, a list of

companies, we have worked for in the past, workshop agenda and a price guidance sheet. We also plan to become a member of the local Chamber of Commerce. We will work to teach corporations, via seminars and article reprints, how our program can build a spirit of teamwork within the company. We will also conduct external demos at local office buildings, and offer limited time sessions on-site to pique their interest. We will also offer special on-site lunchtime yoga classes for companies, because companies are investing in staff bonding and retention, as well as activities which improve productivity and wellbeing.

Source:

http://bookible.com/blog/2017/09/28/5-effective-yoga-marketing-ideas-yoga-teachers-studios/

Target Rehab Centers and Physical Therapy Clinics

We will set-up a mutual referral relationship with rehab centers and physical therapy clinics that do not offer Yoga training. This will help our company to stabilize cash flow, and establish a cash-based Yoga niche. We will target these niches because many patients who use Yoga in rehabilitation see the benefits of this form of exercise. They also enjoy it, so they're willing and even eager to pay out-of-pocket for these services, even after their insurance benefits run out. We will provide post-rehabilitation Yoga services.

Target Local Businesses

We will give local businesses free vouchers to give to their employees for yoga sessions. When they come in for their free sessions, we will work to turn them into lifelong customers.

Target Microbreweries

We will ask these businesses if they want to form a partnership alliance, whereby we will conduct yoga classes, on a weekly or monthly basis, on their premises. These sessions will end with a beer tasting program.

Target Sports Teams

We will provide a uniquely personalized yoga experience geared to injury prevention and rehabilitation healthcare. Our personalized approach will start with a free posture and joint-mobility evaluation, that will form the basis for a student's chart on file, for teachers to consult before class.

Target Local Ethnic Groups

We will accurately translate our marketing materials into other languages. We will enlist the support of our bilingual employees to assist in reaching the ethnic people in our surrounding area through a referral program, and newspaper and radio ads. We will join the nearest _____ (predominate ethnic group) Chamber of Commerce and partner with _____ (Hispanic/Chinese/Other?) Advocacy Agencies. We will also develop dance programs centered around cultural influences.

Helpful Resources:
U.S. census Bureau Statistics   www.census.gov
U.S. Dept. of Labor/Bureau of Labor Statistics   www.bls.gov/data/home.htm

4.3.1   Market Needs

The market needs for Yoga Studio services are strongly shaped by the participant's desire to build their self-esteem and improve upon their social networking skills and healthier lifestyle opportunities.

Yoga is also seen as a way to achieve a healthier lifestyle by aging Baby Boomers, who are always searching for ways to look and feel better. Parents are also looking for pre-school social and mental development opportunities for their children and constructive after-studio programs for their teenagers.

4.4 Buying Patterns

A Buying Pattern is the typical manner in which /buyers consumers purchase goods or services or firms place their purchase orders in terms of amount, frequency, timing, etc. In determining buying patterns, we will need to understand the following:
        - Why consumers make the purchases that they make?
        - What factors influence consumer purchases?
        - The changing factors in our society.

Yoga experts agree that economic factors will continue to play a role in the future.
In this recessionary economy, we may see more Yoga in health clubs and fewer smaller studios. We just aren't going to see the growth rate we had for a while, with new studios opening just blocks from each other.

But, overall, Yoga has held its own in a challenging economy.

Some of the mat classes have gotten bigger because it's an economical way to experience Pilates. There has been some drop-in income in our area, but most people don't want to let go of what makes them feel good. The recession has driven the growth of less expensive group classes and training sessions.

To thrive in this economy, Yoga Studios must offer more group mat classes, group reformer classes, exercise classes and other programs. Group programs are bringing a huge influx of clients. We must also be receptive to renting out space to physical therapists, who refer patients to us.

More specialization of skills is also anticipated, as Yoga plays more of a role in hospitals; physical therapy clinics; spas; football, rugby and tennis clubs; and many golf clubs.

Yoga will become much more specialized.

The blockbuster trend in Yoga is the move toward applications in rehabilitation, physical therapy and other medical areas. Yoga is being prescribed by doctors, and reformers are showing up in physical therapists' offices. For physical therapists who invest in training, Yoga can present an alternative income stream with far less paperwork. For Yoga instructors, the medical community is a growing source of referrals.

The major reasons for the participants to return to a Yoga Studio are quality of instruction, attractive atmosphere, socializing opportunities, pain management, stress reduction and value pricing. _____ (company name) will gear its class offerings, marketing, and pricing policies to establish a loyal client base. Our affordable pricing, attractive facility, social events and quality of instruction will be welcomed in _____ (city) and contribute to our success.

4.5 Market Growth

We will assess the following general factors that affect market growth:

Current Assessment

1. Interest Rates _____
2. Government Regulations _____
3. Perceived Environment Impact _____
4. Consumer Confidence Level _____
5. Population Growth Rate _____
6. Unemployment Rate _____
7. Political Stability _____
8. Currency Exchange Rate _____
9. Innovation Rate _____
10. Home Sales _____
11. Gasoline Prices _____
12. Overall Economic Health _____

Yoga enjoyed skyrocketing mainstream acceptance in the early and mid-2000s. The SGMA reported Yoga participation jumped 31 percent to 9.1 million in 2001, with the trend expected to continue. Meanwhile, Yoga participation leapt 41 percent to 2.4 million. Yoga classes are increasingly being offered as part of overall fitness programs at health clubs, greatly accelerating participation.

Yoga has become so popular because it's very versatile—there's something in it for everyone—and because it makes people feel better. Yoga has grown in popularity likely because people have realized the benefit of low-impact activities and the need to keep an active lifestyle.

The popularity of Yoga may also have to do with its long-term appeal and the fact that participants can keep learning. An increasing focus on integrative exercise, mind-body fitness and functional fitness has brought the universes of fitness and Yoga together. Now the two worlds are coming together, especially at the more advanced level, such as in personal training. There is now more fitness training in Yoga Studios and more Yoga sessions in fitness clubs.

Additionally, the _____ area is expected to grow _____ % annually. The _____ zip code area is expected to grow ____% annually. These estimates are based on the most recent census data and projected growth rate for the _____ area. In summary, the general industry analysis shows that _____ (city) is expected to experience substantial population, housing and commercial business growth, which makes it a prime location for a Yoga Studio business.

4.6   Service Business Analysis

Typically, yoga centers are located away from the city's commercial/business center. _____ (company name) will focus less on serving a large number of beginners and will be more focused on obtaining long term students. Students are attracted to a specific type of yoga and the reputation and skills of the studio leader.

The Yoga Studio market is highly fragmented, with the overwhelming majority of the small studios offering only a limited line of services. Customer satisfaction is highly dependent upon quality of instruction, customer service and value pricing. In the _____ metro area, there are _____ (#) businesses that fall into the general category of Yoga Studio. _____ (company name) seeks to provide it customers with affordable, quality instruction in a fun, convenient, comfortable and supportive environment.

Regardless of the absolute numbers, which may be affected by the methodology of each survey, the growth numbers are a clear confirmation that wellness activities are taking hold in North America. Along those lines, is the thinking that someone who will discover Yoga classes via their gym pass is now more likely to eventually go for the full experience in a specialized facility. Additionally, there is a growing body of research on the benefits of meditation, which are the basis for Yoga exercises. Driving the demand is also the fact that Yoga has been scientifically proven beneficial in the treatment of stress disorders.

The Yoga industry has experienced substantial growth in the past decade. The following factors have caused a rise in demand for Yoga instruction:
1.   Yoga has come to be seen as a part of a trend toward the pursuit of a healthier lifestyle.
2.   There has been an increase in the range of career opportunities in the field of Yoga in recent years, fed by the increased demand for Yoga activity in a variety of settings.
3.   Overall, there has been a increase in demand for sport and physical activity by women. For women, Yoga courses are an appealing alternative to fitness centers,

aerobics and other sports.

4. More men are attending Yoga classes to meet interesting women, and, at the same time, appear interesting to them.

5. Learning to do Yoga translates into the development of a skill, which serves to increase self-esteem and self-confidence.

6. Studies reveal that Yoga has the ability to alleviate everyday stress, and provides an excellent form of relaxation. In fact, Yoga is seen as a fun activity, because a person is able to discover the possibilities of movement.

7. More fitness minded people, see Yoga as an enjoyable way to achieve weight management and body toning.

4.7   Barriers to Entry

_____ (company name) will benefit from the following combination of barriers to entry, which cumulatively present a moderate degree of entry difficulty.

1.	Industry Experience.	2.	Business Software Implementation
3.	Vendor Research	4.	Community Network Connections
5.	Referral Program Set-up	5.	People Skills
6.	Marketing Skills	7.	Facility Artistic Design Capabilities
8.	Operations/Cash Flow Management	9.	Website Design
10.	Yoga Instructor Credentials		

4.7.1   Porter's Five Forces Analysis

We will use Porter's five forces analysis as a framework for the industry analysis and business strategy development. It will be used to derive the five forces which determine the competitive intensity and therefore attractiveness of our market. Attractiveness in this context refers to the overall industry profitability.

Competitors   The degree of rivalry is high in this segment, but less when compared to the overall category. There are _____ (#) major competitors in the _____ area and they include: _____

Threat of Substitutes
Substitutes are high for this industry. These include other yoga studios, health and fitness clubs, health and wellness centers, community colleges, community centers, mobile yoga studios, etc.

Bargaining Power of Buyers
Buyer power is moderate in the business. Buyers are sensitive to quality and pricing as the segment attempts to capitalize on the pricing and quality advantage.

Bargaining Power of Suppliers
Supplier power is moderate in the industry. Inventory can be obtained from a number of distributors. A high level of operational efficiency for managing supplies can be achieved.

Threat of New Entrants

           Relatively high in this segment. The business model can be easily copied.
Conclusions: _____ (company name) is in a competitive field and has to move fast to retain its competitive advantage. The key success factors are to develop operational efficiencies, innovative programs, cost-effective marketing and customer service excellence.

4.8   Competitive Analysis

Competitor analysis in marketing and strategic management is an assessment of the strengths and weaknesses of current and potential competitors. This analysis will provide both an offensive and defensive strategic context through which to identify our business opportunities and threats. We will carry out continual competitive analysis to ensure our market is not being eroded by developments in other firms. This analysis will be matched with the target segment needs to ensure that our products and services continue to provide better value than the competitors. The competitive analysis will show very clearly why our products and services are preferred in some market segments to other offerings and to be able to offer reasonable proof of that assertion.

We will conduct good market intelligence for the following reasons:
1.   To forecast competitors' strategies.
2.   To predict competitor likely reactions to our own strategies.
3.   To consider how competitors' behavior can be influenced in our own favor.

Overall competition in the area is _____ (weak/moderate/strong).

Competitive analysis conducted by the company owners has shown that there are _____ (# or no other?) companies currently offering some kind of Yoga Studio services in the _____ (city) area. However, the existing competitors offer only a limited line of Yoga Studio products and services. In fact, of these _____ (#) competitors only _____ (#) offered a range of Yoga studio services comparable with what _____ (company name) plans to offer to its customers.

There are a few independent Yoga Instructors, who teach classes at _____ (local community college/community center?) or rent floor space. There is also a local group, called _____, that holds Yoga sessions on ____(Friday) nights at the local _____. This group does not have a studio and its main purpose is to find places for people to do Yoga.

This leaves the independent contractors as a major source of competition. _____ (company name) plans to work in conjunction with these instructors and will offer them a place to rent Yoga floor space to continue teaching on their own.

The key to competition within the yoga business is the quality of the instructor. There are a number of instructors around ____ area who are well respected, and _____ (company name) will strive to attract these teachers to its facility. The location, quality and ambiance of the facility will be a real competitive advantage for our studio. Because it is the most attractive facility in town, teachers will want to teach here and clients will want to "get away" here. _____ (company name) will focus of presenting our studio as the perfect place to learn yoga skills that will improve the student physically and reduce the daily stress of the work world.

Other "schools" in the area will be able to match the quality of instruction, but are often held in church halls, community centers, fitness centers, etc. and do not have the relaxing ambiance that is so important to the discipline.

The following is the list of the major competitors with a brief description of their Yoga Studio services:

1. _____
2. _____
3. _____

Competitor	What You Can Do and They Can't	What They Can Do and You Can't

Self-assessment

Competitive Rating Assessment: **1 = Weak ....5 = Strong**

	Our Company	Prime Competitor	Compare
Our Location			
Our Facilities			
Our Products			
Our Services and Amenities			
Our Management Skills			
Our Training Programs			
Our Research & Development			
Our Company Culture			
Our Business Model			
Our Distribution System			
Overall Rating			

Rationale: _____

The following establishments are considered direct competitors in _____ (city):

Competitor	Address	Market Share	Primary Focus	Secondary Prod/Svcs	Strengths	Weaknesses

Indirect Competitors include the following:

Alternative Competitive Matrix

Competitor Name: <u>Us</u> _____ _____ _____

Comparison Items:

Location
Location Assessment
Facilities Assessment
Primary Target Market
Secondary Market
No. of Instructors
Certifications
Number of participants
Class schedules
Operating hours
Services provided
Amenities
Equipment
Fitness programs
Additional Services
Pro Shop Products
Age Group Serviced
Yoga Levels Offered
Pricing Strategy
Member Rates
Yrs in Business
Reputation
Marketing Strategy
Sales Brochure/Catalog
Website URL
Website Assessment
Sales Revenues
Years in Business
Guarantees
Competitive Advantage
Comments

Competitor Profile Matrix

Critical Success Factors	Our Score	Competitor 1 Rating	Score	Competitor 2 Rating	Score	Competitor 3 Rating	Score
Advertising							
Product Quality							
Service Quality							
Price Competition							
Management							
Financial Position							
Customer Loyalty							
Brand Identity							

Market Share _____
Total _____

Sources of competition analysis information include:

1. Competitor company websites.
2. Mystery shopper visits.
3. Annual Reports   (www.annual reports.com)
4. Thomas Net   (www.thomasnet.com)
5. Trade Journals
6. Trade Associations
7. Sales representative interviews
8. Research & Development may come across new patents.
9. Market research can give feedback on the customer's perspective
10. Monitoring services will track a company or industry you select for news.
    Resources: www.portfolionews.com   www.Office.com
11. Hoover's   www.hoovers.com
12. www.zapdata.com   (Dun and Bradstreet) You can buy one-off lists here.
13. www.infousa.com   (The largest, and they resell to many other vendors)
14. www.onesource.com (By subscription, they pull information from many sources)
15. www.capitaliq.com   (Standard and Poors).
16. Obtain industry specific information from First Research
    (www.firstresearch.com) or IBISWorld, although both are by subscription only,
    although you may be able to buy just one report.
17. Get industry financial ratios and industry norms from RMA (www.rmahq.com) or
    by using ProfitCents.com software.
18. Company newsletters
19. Industry Consultants
20. Suppliers
21. Customer interviews regarding competitors.
22. Analyze competitors' ads for their target audience, market position, product
    features, benefits, prices, etc.
23. Attend speeches or presentations made by representatives of your competitors.
24. View competitor's trade show display from a potential customer's point of view.
25. Search computer databases (available at many public libraries).
26. Review competitor Yellow Book Ads.
27. www.bls.gov/cex/ (site provides information on consumer expenditures
    nationally, regionally, and by selected metropolitan areas).
28. www.sizeup.com
29. Business Statistics and Financial Ratios   www.bizstats.com

4.9 Market Revenue Projection

For each of our chosen target markets, we will estimate our market share in number of
customers, and based on consumer behavior, how often do they buy per year? What is the

average dollar amount of each purchase? We will then multiply these three numbers to project sales volume for each target market.

Target Market	Number of Customers	No. of Purchases per Year	Average Dollar Amount per Purchase	Total Sales Volume
	A x	B	x C	= D

Using the target market number identified in this section, and the local demographics, we have made the following assessments regarding market opportunity and revenue potential in our area:

Potential Revenue Opportunity =

	_____	Local Adult Population
(x)	_____	Expected ___% Market Share
(=)	_____	Number of likely local clients
(x)	$ _____	Average class transaction dollar amount
(x)	_____	Average number of classes taken per year
(=)	$ _____	Annual Individual Revenue Opportunity.
(+)		
	_____	Number of Local Businesses
(x)	_____	Expected Market Share
(=)	_____	Number of likely local business clients
(x)	$ _____	Average transaction dollar amount
(x)	_____	Average number of workshops ordered per year
(=)	$ _____	Annual Corporate Revenue Opportunity.
(=)	$ _____	Total Annual Revenue Opportunity

Or

	Fees	Avg. Class Size	Classes per Month	Revenue
Per session (drop-in)				
Multi-session package				
Monthly membership				
Total:				
Times:				x12
Annual Fee Revenue:				
Product Sales				
Total:				

Cycle Note: Generally lower attendance in December and during the summer, with higher attendance during early fall and January/February.

Recap:

Month	Jan Feb Mar Apr May Jun Jul Aug Sep Oct Nov Dec	Total
Products		

Services

Gross Sales: _____

(-) Returns _____

Net Sales _____

Revenue Assumptions:

1. The sources of information for our revenue projection are:

    _____

2. If the total market demand for our product/service = 100%, our projected sales volume represents _____% of this total market.

3. The following factors might lower our revenue projections:

    _____

5.0   Industry Analysis

SIC Code 799949, Yoga Instruction
NAICS Code 611699, Miscellaneous Schools & Instruction

Day spas (which included yoga studios) provide the US economy with over $12 billion dollars a year of revenue. Revenues directly from yoga instruction are estimated to generate $2 billion dollars per year. Nationwide, there are over 33,000 businesses that focus on providing massage and non-medically oriented spa services. Additionally, the industry employs more than 378,000 people and provides average annual payrolls of $2.8 billion dollars per year. This industry has exploded as the economic tastes of Americans have changed significantly over the last five years as the overall wealth of the country has grown. As Americans now have more access to capital and an increased borrowing capacity, their ability to spend money on brand name and luxury items/services has also increased. In the last five years, gross annual receipts from yoga studios have increased 40% with the number of studios increasing by 20% during the same period. This trend is expected to continue as the economy remains strong.

5.1   Key Industry Statistics

These 2008 statistics are from YIAS (Yoga in America Study).
7.5% of U.S. adults of 16.5 million people now practice yoga
the fastest growing segment is the 18-24 age group, which increased by 46% in one year
77.1% of yoga practitioners are women and 22.9% are men.
Gender of US yoga practitioners: 72.2% Female   27.8% Male
44% - Percentage of U.S. yoga practitioners with household income of more than $75,000; 24% earn more than $100,000.
Age of U.S. yoga practitioners: 40.6%: 18 - 34 years of age, 41.0%: 35 - 54 years of age, 18.4%: Over 55 years of age
Age of U.S. yoga practitioners: Median age: 36-45

Where U.S. yoga practitioners live (2003):

West Coast: 20%	Northeast: 30%
Central (inc. OH): 30%	Other parts: 20%

About 15 million Americans practiced yoga in 2004, and more than 12 percent of United States residents are "very interested" or "extremely interested" in yoga, according to Yoga Journal.

The National Center for Complementary and Integrative Health says as of 2012, 9.5% of American adults do yoga.

Americans spend about $27 billion on yoga products annually, according to NAMASTA, the North American Studio Alliance.

5.2   Yoga Industry Trends

We will determine the trends that are impacting our consumers and indicate ways in which our customers' needs are changing and any relevant social, technical or other changes that will impact our target market. Keeping up with trends and reports will help management to carve a niche for our business, stay ahead of the competition and deliver products that our customers need and want.

1.   The Yoga Studio now has a stylish club feel, complete with comfy couches, which makes it perfect for Friday and Saturday night Yoga parties.
2.   Yoga Studios are diversifying into health and fitness training.
3.   With baby boomers having more discretionary income with which to spoil their grandchildren, tweens have also become markets.
4.   With a whopping 64% of Americans considered obese or overweight, businesses that offer products and services to help people manage the problem and develop more healthy habits are growing in popularity.
5.   Dual income working families have a need for after-studio enrichment programs for their teens.
6.   In response to yoga's increasing availability and the wide variety of yoga options, consolidation and specialization is occurring, with big players getting bigger and solo practitioners cultivating specialized niches.
7.   Yoga will continue to make headway in the health-care establishment as it becomes more and more widely accepted as a complementary alternative medicine
8.   To compete with popular Yoga Studios, gyms are expanding their group exercise offerings to include more than the standard Yoga classes.
9.   Gyms and studios are finally recognizing the importance of properly certified trainers and instructors.
10.   More studios are rolling out programs for older adults and children.
11.   More personal trainers are looking at the baby boom generation and creating age-appropriate fitness programs.
12.   Trainers and personal fitness instructors are getting accredited in nutrition to round out their skills to gain the most clients for a long term professional relationship.
13.   Bootcamps are growing in popularity as they roll core, strength and age-appropriate training into one program that centers around cardiovascular and endurance work outs in outdoor and indoor settings.
14.   Employers are pushing worksite health promotion because they realize that healthier employees equal fewer sick days and a lower bottom line for health care costs.
15.   More people are signing up for group personal training to save money and socialize.
16.   Sport-specific training to gain muscles to aid in agility for specific sports.
17.   A new focus on preventing injury through the inclusion of physicians or accredited personal trainers in training programs.
18.   Wellness coaching is growing in popularity as a motivational tool.

19. Citing laws that govern vocational schools, like those for hairdressers and truck drivers, regulators have begun to require licenses for yoga schools that train instructors, with all the fees, inspections and paperwork that entails.

20. The increasing population of fitness enthusiasts is the primary factor in the demand for more yoga instructors.

21. Health clubs are also showing a continuing trend towards more personalized service, resulting in a greater number of fitness classes.

22. Yoga and other forms of low-impact exercise are becoming especially popular among the elderly population.

23. The pay-what-you-can studio business model concept is trying to make yoga accessible to as many people as possible, opening to the studio to all students, regardless of experience level or financial means.

24. Fitness clubs are experimenting with a combination Spinning/Yoga class, which follows 45 minutes of high-intensity spinning with 45 minutes of elementary yoga to relax the body after the intense workout.

25. More studios are signing up with the ClassPass Network.
Note: ClassPass teams up with over 1,000 classes at boutique studios to offer everything from cycling to yoga to dance to martial arts for its members. For a $79-$99 (varies by city) monthly fee, members enjoy unlimited classes to studios in the ClassPass.com network and can attend the same studio up to three times every month. To deter people from skipping class, members are charged a cancellation fee when they don't show up for a reservation.

26. Some yoga studios are offering more intense physical workouts as a way to attract more men to the discipline of yoga.

27. An increasing number of people are looking to yoga techniques as a path to healing and wellness, and to aid with weight loss, depression, insomnia, arthritis, and other mood disorders.

28. The newest teacher training curriculums from studios like Sky Ting in New York City and Y7 in Los Angeles and NYC are going beyond the basic requirements, injecting extra lessons on everything from playlist crafting to Chinese medicine and Taoist theory.

29. The only community-based yoga studios that seem to be thriving are those that have diversified their offerings to include fitness classes.

30. Local yoga studios are giving way to the corporate studio revolution, with its turnkey operations and cookie-cutter approach to yoga.

5.3   Industry Leaders

We plan to study the best practices of industry leaders and adapt certain selected practices to our business model concept. Best practices are those methods or techniques resulting in increased customer satisfaction when incorporated into the operation.

Golden Bridge Yoga   **www.goldenbridgeyoga.com/**
Billing itself as a "spiritual village," this Hollywood mega-hot spot is known as the

epicenter of Kundalini yoga and for its celebrity yoga guru, Gurmukh. By opening a new larger location, Golden Bridge took Los Angeles yoga to another level, offering 18,000 square feet of enlightenment, including five studios, an organic café, bookstore, wellness center and more than 100 classes, ranging from pre-natal and kids' yoga to Kundalini, Hatha, Sadhana and Jivamukti. The studio provides an entire yoga community and caters to those looking for a more spiritual experience. It expanded to a second location in New York City in 2007.

The Stress Reduction Clinic   **www.stressreductionclinic.org/**
The oldest and largest hospital-based mind/body center of its kind in the United States, treating more than 10,000 patients since opening in 1979. The clinic delivers meditation and yoga-based classes to clients ranging from judges and correctional staff to the Chicago Bulls, and offers a five-day retreat for CEOs in the Arizona desert. A majority of the clinic's patients report lasting decreases in both physical and psychological symptoms of stress. They also experience an increased ability to relax, greater energy and enthusiasm for life, improved self-esteem, and increased ability to cope more effectively with stressful situations. Recently, the clinic's parent institute, The Center for Mindfulness in Medicine, Health Care, and Society, launched an eight-week mindfulness-based stress reduction program for corporations. Its goal is to teach participants how to manage stress, enhance clarity and creative thinking, improve communication skills, cultivate leadership and teamwork, and increase overall effectiveness in the workplace.

Yoga Studio Franchises:
www.yogafitstudios.com/yoga-franchise-opportunities
http://yogapodcommunity.com/yogapreneur/
https://www.franchisehelp.com/franchises/corepower-yoga/

Snap Fitness Inc.
Parent company Lift Brands has announced the details of its deal with yoga-instructor training school YogaFit Inc. to launch a new line of fitness studios. The new YogaFit Studios will offer live and virtual yoga classes, featuring videos of instructors on a 120-inch, high-definition screen. The clubs will be 1,500 to 2,000 square feet, compared to a range of 3,500 to 5,000 square feet for Snap Fitness locations. Members will pay $49 to $79 per month for unlimited access. The studios also will offer a 10-visit punch card for $145 or a 20-visit punch card for $225.

Yoga Tree   **https://www.yogatreesf.com/**
A chain of successful San Francisco yoga studios, is still eliciting new clients in every almost every class, mostly through word of mouth. The company has seven locations and a retreat center. It sees competitors and the mainstream popularity of yoga as a boon for their business. As people discover yoga at their gym or neighborhood yoga studios, they become hooked and eventually look to branch out to different styles or studios. The owner also credits his effort to build community among clientele as a foundation of his success. Many classes at his studio begin with students introducing themselves to the people next to them to build a sense of community.

Breathe Yoga   www.breatheyoga.com

They have a café that offers a catering service, and they offer meditation classes and massage sessions.

Example:

www.breatheyoga.com/wp-content/uploads/2017/11/Breathe_CateringMenuList_Nov2017-WEB.pdf

Release Studio   www.releasestudio.us/

Located in the Art District on Santa Fe in Denver CO. They offer everything from introductory and advanced levels of yoga to Dope Yoga (dopamine) accompanied by DJs. Even sexy workout time is on the roster, which includes pole dancing and burlesque classes. They also host Naked Yoga Classes for women as a way to explore self-acceptance. The goal is to hold a safe space for women to learn to fully love and accept their bodies and themselves. The hour-long class starts in a softly lit room, clothing on, focusing on breath and movement. Then the instructor guides patrons through disrobing while she gradually turns up the lights. The class finishes with the lights fully on, ending in a final savasana in the nude, and patrons learning to relax.

5.4 Industry Terms

We will use the following term definitions to help our company to understand and speak the common language of our industry, and aid efficient communication.

Ashtanga

Means 8 limbs. Is the name given to the system of yoga taught by Sri K. Pattabhi Jois. It involves synchronizing breathing with progressive and continuous series of postures producing intense internal heat and a profuse, purifying sweat that detoxifies muscles and organs.

Bandhas

Energy locks in the body. They direct the energy flow (prana) inside the body so that blockages and repressed energy are alleviated. There are three bandhas; Mula, our root lock located at the base of the spine; Uddiyana, which moves energy upward from the earth and is located in the lower abdomen, and finally the Jalandhara, our throat lock, which continues to move the energy upward to connect the head with the rest of the body.

Differentiated Instruction

Occurs when a yoga instructor's teaching is student-centered--adapted for each student's needs, interests, abilities, and learning styles.

Drishti

A point of focus where the gaze rests while doing yoga postures or meditation practice. Focusing on a drishti aids concentration, since it is easier to become distracted when the eyes are wandering all over the room.

Hatha Raja Yoga

The practice primarily taught in the United States. Focuses on yoga poses and controlled breathing as well as ethical principles, such as truthfulness and non-harming.

Karma Yoga

It's about using one's energies for benevolent causes and reaching out to one's classmates and neighbors. It's a way to inject inner healing into the collective consciousness.

Mindfulness

Mindfulness is about paying attention on purpose, choosing to focus and be fully aware of the present moment. Due to the increasingly fast-paced and reactive culture in which we live, it has become a skill less and less available to modern human beings. Feeling scattered, distracted and overwhelmed has become a way of life and many of us can relate to feeling more like a "human doing" than a human being. Mindfulness is about connecting with one's inherent, internal resources, in order to rediscover, remember and experience the depth of our being. These practices strengthen and deepen the human capacity in order to live more meaningful and peaceful lives.

Meditation

The intentional, conscious cultivation of attention and awareness, often called mindfulness. The basic idea associated with why people meditate is that during our day we are constantly subjected to sensory input and our minds are always active in the process of thinking. Typically, as we do our normal activities we engage in a constant mental commentary, sort of an inner "The Drama of Me." Usually people aren't fully aware of all the mental thought activity that we are constantly engaged in. In many cases these recurring thoughts cause us a great deal of anxiety and stress. Meditation allows all this activity to settle down, and often results in the mind becoming more peaceful, calm and focused.

Namaste

A common spoken greeting originating from India. It is commonly accompanied by a slight bow made with hands pressed together, palms touching and fingers pointed upwards, in front of the chest. Its meaning is "The Divinity within me perceives and adores the Divinity within you." We end our yoga practice with Namaste.

Professional Malpractice (or Negligence)

The failure to follow professional standards of care (or "due care;" "reasonable care under the circumstances"), thereby injuring the patient. Yoga teachers are legally, as well as ethically and professionally, obligated to take due care in their teaching and any adjustments.

Stress

The reaction of a body to adjust or adapt in light of change. Since change is an element of being alive, we can't really expect to be stress free. We can explore ways to identify and reduce the stressors in our lives and learn new ways to manage and respond to stress which can't be avoided.

Sun Salutation

Also known as Salute to the Sun and Surya Namaskar, is a flowing series of poses which help warm up the body and also improve strength and flexibility of the muscles and spinal column.

Ujjayi Pranayama

Ujjayi means rising victoriously. This form of breath is done by inhaling and exhaling through the nose. It is a diaphragmatic breath, which first fills the lower belly, rises to the lower rib cage, and finally moves into the upper chest and throat. This breathe helps oxygenate the blood supply and create a sound that helps focus the mind and thus relax the body. This form of breathing is used in most of our yoga practice and your teacher will guide you through the technique.

Vinyasa
Yoga poses will flow from one to another in conjunction with the breath.

Yoga
Derived from the Sanskrit word for "yoke" or "join together." Essentially, it means union. It is the science of uniting the individual soul with the cosmic spirit through physical disciplines (postures) and mental disciplines (meditation). Patanjali offers the best definition: "Yoga is the cessation of mind." An ancient discipline that uses physical exercises, proper breathing, mental focus and conscious awareness to bring about a harmonious body and mind. Practiced properly, yoga can help develop strength and flexibility, release stress, alleviate structural pain (such as knees, back, neck), feel more calm and centered, regain vitality and interest in life.

Yogi
Someone who practices yoga. (A female yoga is called a yogini.)

5.5   New Yoga Studio Concepts

Tantris Center   **https://www.tantris.com/studio/**
Located in West Hollywood, this concept was developed by Russell Simmons and focuses on the teaching of Yogic Science. They offer a Karma class every week, and other events throughout the year to fulfill their Karmic Duty. The 8,000-square-foot, two-story space offers a juice bar, a blow-dry bar stocked with Jessica Alba's Honest Beauty products (for sprucing up after sweating it out), and a retail area carrying the Tantris apparel line and other yoga essentials. Step into their new eco-friendly space with natural lighting, hardwood floors, infrared heat, a featured Starke sound system, renowned teachers and luxury amenities to create ultimate yoga experience. They offer infrared heated and restorative non-heated classes designed for everybody. Classes, which will be offered all day, include asana, vinyasa, regular restorative yoga and various heated flow sessions for all-levels. Meditation sessions are scheduled separately. It is designed to be a spiritual center, a devotional yoga school, and not a gym.
Source:
www.hollywoodreporter.com/news/russell-simmons-opens-tantris-yoga-studio-947842

6.0 Strategy and Implementation Summary

____ (company name) will market through the several fitness clubs, beauty salons, tanning salons and boutiques. We will offer the free open workshop for beginners. In addition, ____ (company name) will initiate a program that will give a ___% session discount to members who successfully recruit new members to our Yoga studio.

We intend to develop and offer our customers a wide range of Yoga packages in an attempt to make Yoga affordable and accessible to any budget at any interest level. Instructors will be highly skilled and certified to meet our high-performance standards. They will participate in consultative sales training and receive regular sales coaching.

Our sales strategy is based on serving our niche markets better than the competition and leveraging our competitive advantages. These advantages include superior attention to understanding and satisfying participant needs and wants, an elegant facility design, and value pricing.

The objectives of our marketing strategy will be to recruit new participants, retain existing customers, get good customers to spend more and return more frequently. Establishing a loyal customer base is very important because such core customers will not only generate the most lifetime sales, but also provide valuable referrals.

We will generate word-of-mouth buzz through direct-mail campaigns, exceeding customer expectations, developing a Web site and getting involved in community events and with local businesses, and donating our services at charity functions in exchange for press release coverage. Our sales strategy will seek to convert potential and first-time participants into long-term relationships and referral agents.

The combination of our competitive advantages, targeted marketing campaign and networking activities, will enable __(company name) to continue increasing our market share.

6.1 Promotion Strategy

Promotion strategies will be focused to the target market segment. Given the importance of word-of-mouth/referrals among the area residents, we shall strive to efficiently service all our customers to gain their business regularly, which is the recipe for our long-term success. We shall focus on direct resident marketing, publicity, coupon sampling, and advertising as proposed. Our promotion strategy will focus on generating referrals from existing clients and professionals, community involvement and direct mail campaigns. We will run promotional programs, such as free first classes, to get people interested in our yoga studio.

- **Advertising**

- o Grand Opening Event celebration with invitations to local businesses.
- o Yearly anniversary parties to celebrate the success of each year.
- o Multiple Yellow Pages ads in the book and online directories.
- o Flyers promoting new Yoga Studio service and product introductions.
- 0 Doorknob hangers, if not prohibited by neighborhood associations.

- **Local Marketing / Public Relations**
  - o Customer raffle for gift certificates or discount coupons
  - 0 Participation in local civic groups.
  - 0 Press release coverage of complimentary sessions to nonprofit organizations and studio contests.
  - 0 Article submissions to magazines describing the health benefit of Pilates.

- **Local Media**
  - o Direct Mail - Containing our prices and an explanation of our Yoga Studio program benefits to rehab centers, school administrators and corporate human resource directors.
  - o Radio Campaign - We will make "live on the air" presentations of our discount coupons to the disk jockeys, hoping to get the promotions broadcasted to the listening audience.
  - o Newspaper Campaign - Placing several ads for special holiday promotions. We will include a discount coupon in the ad to track the return on investment.
  - o Webpage – This will give the internet users access to our Yoga Studio product catalog and provide class selection advice. We will also collect email addresses for a monthly newsletter.

6.1.1   Grand Opening

Our Grand Opening celebration will be a very important promotion opportunity to create word-of-mouth advertising results. We will advertise the date of our grand opening in local newspapers and on local radio. We will provide the community with a reason to visit our Yoga Studio, such as offering adults a free wine and cheese sampling.

We will do the following things to make the open house a successful event:
1.   Enlist local business support to contribute a large number of door prizes.
2.   Use a sign-in sheet to create an email/mailing list.
3.   Sponsor a fitness contest.
4.   Schedule appearance by local celebrities.
5.   Create a festive atmosphere with balloons, beverages and music.
6.   Get the local radio station to broadcast live from the event and handout fun gifts.
7.   Offer an application fee waiver.
8.   Giveaway our logo imprinted T-shirts as a contest prize.
9.   Allow potential customers to view your facility and ask questions.
10.   Print promotional flyers and pay a few kids to distribute them locally.
11.   Arrange for face painting, storytelling, clowns, and snacks for everyone.
12.   Arrange for local politician to do the official opening ceremony so all the local

newspapers came to take pictures and do a feature story.

13.   Arrange that people can tour our facility on the open day in order to see our facilities, collect sales brochures and find out more about our services.

14.   Allocate staff members to perform specific duties, handout business cards and sales brochures and instruct them to deal with any questions or queries.

16.   Organize a drawing with everyone writing their name and phone numbers on the back of business cards and give a voucher as a prize to start a marketing list.

17.   Hand out free samples of products and coupons.

Sample Grand Opening Announcement

_____ **(owner name)** is introducing his/her new yoga studio, _____ (studio name), in the _____ shopping center, _____ (address), with an open house from ___ a.m. to ___ p.m. on _____ (date). All ages are invited to walk in to see the space, meet the instructors and participate in a short demonstration — street clothes are fine. Nia Technique, a non-impact, barefoot dance that incorporates yoga, martial arts, dance moves and healing arts, will be demonstrated in the morning, and yoga will be offered in the afternoon during the open house. _____ (owner name) and her ____ (#) instructors will offer Nia and Hatha yoga at the studio during various sessions throughout the week. Classes begin during the week following the open house. _____ (owner name) has taught yoga at _____, in ____ (city) and other venues in the metro area for more than ____ (#) years. See more at _____ (website), call ____ or email _____.

6.1.2   Unique Value Proposition

Our value proposition will summarize why a consumer should use our services and the unique set of benefits our customers will get from choosing to participate in our Yoga classes over those of our competitors. We will enable quick access to our broad line of quality Yoga products and innovative services, out of our conveniently located and clean studio in the _____ (city) area. Our value proposition will convince prospects that our services will add more value and better solve their need for a welcoming, one-stop Yoga Studio. We will use this value proposition statement to target customers who will benefit most from using our services. These baby boomers looking to socialize, tone their bodies and engage in pain management and prevention with no harmful side effects. Our value proposition will be concise and appeal to the customer's strongest decision-making drivers, which are schedule convenience, product quality, program selection, personalized instruction, and quality of personal relationships with instructors.

___ (company name) will position itself as a provider of quality Yoga studio services and products, that can be easily personalized to meet the needs of wants of participants. Our website will enable customers to save time with our efficient online registration process and receive good value for their money. We will also guarantee that the customer receive first class service or a full refund in the event the customer is not completely satisfied.

Recap of Our Value Proposition:

Trust – We are known as a trusted business partner with strong customer and vendor endorsements. We have earned a reputation for quality, integrity, and delivery of successful _____ solutions.

Quality – We offer _____ experience and extensive professional backgrounds in _____ at competitive salary rates.

Experience – Our ability to bring people with ____ (#) years of _____ experience with deep technical knowledge of _____ is at the core of our success.

True Vendor Partnerships – Our true vendor partnerships with _____ and _____ enable us to offer the resources of much larger organizations with greater flexibility.

Customer Satisfaction and Commitment to Success – Through partnering with our customers and delivering quality solutions, we have been able to achieve an impressive degree of repeat and referral business. Since _____ (year), more than _____% of our business activity is generated by existing customers. Our philosophy is that "our customer's satisfaction is our success." Our success will be measured in terms of our customer's satisfaction survey scores and testimonials.

Examples of unique value propositions include:

1. Adding extra services like Tai Chi or Meditation Classes or martial arts.
2. Having a licensed physical therapist or dietitian on staff.
3. Creating a superior ambiance with the interior design of the studio.
4. Offering special class hours for groups like Moms, kids, nudists, business people, or students.
5. Offering chair-based classes for the elderly.
6. Teaming up with local brew-pubs or wineries for Yoga with beer or wine classes.
7. Creating specialty classes for golfers, runners, swimmers, etc.

6.1.3   Positioning Statement

We will create a positioning statement for our company that describes what distinguishes our Yoga Studio business from the competition. We will keep it simple, memorable and snappy. We will test our positioning statement to make certain that it appeals to our target audience. We will continue to refine it until it speaks directly to our targeted customer wants, needs and aspirations. We will use our positioning statement in every written communication to customers. This will ensure that our message is consistent and comes across loud and clear. We will create quality image marketing materials that communicate our positioning.

Our positioning strategy will be the result of conducting in-depth consumer market research to find out what benefits consumers want and how our Yoga Studio products and services can meet those needs. Due to the increase in two-income families, many service-oriented professions are leaning toward positioning themselves on the basis of convenience. This is also what we intend to do. For instance, we plan to have extended, "people" studio hours on various days of the week and offer mobile at-home services.

We also plan to develop specialized services that will enable us to pursue a niche focus on specific interest based programs, such as pain and weight management sessions. These objectives and value-added services will position us at the _____ (high-end) of the market and will allow the company to realize a healthy profit margin in relation to its low-end, discount rivals and achieve long-term growth.

Market Positioning Recap

Price: The strategy is to offer competitive prices that are lower that the market leader, yet set to indicate value and worth.

Quality: The _____ quality will have to be very good as the finished service results will be showcased in highly visible situations.

Service: Highly individualized and customized service will be the key to success in this type of business. Personal attention to the customers will result in higher sales and word of mouth advertising.

6.1.4   Unique Selling Proposition (USP)

Our unique selling proposition will answer the question why a customer should choose to do business with our Yoga Studio versus any and every other option available to them in the marketplace. Our USP will be a description of a unique important benefit that our Yoga Studio offers to customers, so that price is no longer the key to our sales.

Our USP will include the following:
Who our target audience is: _____
What we will do for them: _____
What qualities, skills, talents, traits do we possess that others do not: _____
What are the benefits we provide that no one else offers: _____
Why that is different from what others are offering: _____
Why that solution matters to our target audience: _____

6.1.5   Distribution Strategy

Customers can contact the _____ (company name) by telephone, fax, internet and by dropping in. Our nearest competitors are ____ (#) miles away in either direction. The studio will also stock special request items for members.

Our customers will have the following access points:
1.   Order by Phone
        Customers can contact us 24 hours a day, 7days a week at _____.
        Our Customer Service Representatives will be available to assist customers
        Monday through Friday from ____ a.m. to ____ p.m. EST.

2. **Order by Fax**

Customers may fax their orders to _____ anytime.
They must provide: Account number, Billing and shipping address, Purchase order number, if applicable, Name and telephone number, Product number/description, Unit of measure and quantity ordered and Applicable sales promotion source codes.

3. **Order Online**

Customers can order online at www._____.com.Once the account is activated, customers will be able to place orders, browse the catalog, check stock availability and pricing, check order status and view both order and transaction history.

4. **In-person**

All customers can be serviced in person at our facilities Monday through Friday from ____ a.m. to ____ p.m. EST.

.5. **Order by EDI (Electronic Data Interchange)**

Wholesale customers can enter the order once directly into our dealer management system and it is transmitted to us. We will provide customers with electronic notification of expected ship-date, prices, tracking numbers, order status and distribution center from which the order will be shipped. Orders may be reviewed right from the dealer management system.

6. **Sales Consultants/Distributors**

We plan to pursue the following distribution channels for Yoga products and services:

		Number	Reason Chosen	(select) Sales Costs
1.	Our own retail outlets			
2.	Independent retail outlets			
3.	Chain store retail outlets			
4.	Wholesale outlets			
5.	Independent distributors			
6.	Independent commissioned sales reps			
7.	In-house sales reps			
8.	Direct mail using own catalog or flyers			
9.	Catalog broker agreement			
10.	In-house telemarketing			
11.	Contracted telemarketing call center			
12.	Cybermarketing via own website			
13.	Online sales via amazon, eBay, etc.			
14.	TV and Cable Direct Marketing			
15.	TV Home Shopping Channels			
16.	Mobile Units			
17.	Franchised Business Units			
18.	Trade Shows			
19.	High-end Flea Markets			

20. Consignment Shops _____
21. Home Party Sales Plans _____
22. Trunk Sales _____
23. Fundraisers _____
24. Farmer's Markets _____
26. Kiosks _____
27. Sublet Retail Boutique Space _____
28. In-home Boutique _____

6.1.6   Sales Rep Plan

We will use sales reps to sell our stress reduction and productivity improving yoga classes to local corporations.

1.   In-house or Independent _____
2.   Salaried or Commissioned _____
3.   Salary or Commission Rate _____
4.   Salary Plus Commission Rate _____
5.   Special Performance Incentives _____
6.   Negotiating Parameters   Price Breaks/Added Services/
_____
7.   Performance Evaluation Criteria   No. of New Customers/Sales Volume/
_____
8.   Number of Reps _____
9.   Sales Territory Determinants   Geography/Demographics/
_____
10.   Sales Territories Covered _____
11.   Training Program Overview _____
12.   Training Program Cost _____
13.   Sales Kit Contents _____
14.   Primary Target Market _____
15.   Secondary Target Market _____

Rep Name   Compensation Plan   Assigned Territory

_____

_____

6.2   Competitive Advantages

A **competitive advantage** is the thing that differentiates a business from its competitors. It is what separates our business from everyone else. It answers the questions: "Why do customers buy from us versus a competitor?", and "What do we offer customers that is unique?". We will make certain to include our key competitive advantages into our marketing materials. We will use the following competitive advantages to set us apart from our competitors. The distinctive competitive advantages which _____ (company name) brings to the marketplace are as follows: (Note: Select only those you can support)

The distinctive competitive advantages which _____ (company name) brings to marketplace are as follows:
1.   Our instructor experience in the Yoga industry ensures customer satisfaction.
2.   Value Pricing = High Quality/ Low price
        Our rates are below others in the market, while the quality and service exceeds customer expectations.
3.   By keeping overhead low, we will be able to funnel profits back into operations and thus avoid high debt and lost sales opportunities.
4.   We are locally owned and operated, and remain focused on our participant needs.
5.   We will post to YouTube.com a series of instructional Yoga lesson videos that will enable our participants to get additional practice time at home.
6.   Our location and the quality and ambiance of the facility will set us apart.
7.   We will offer our members excellent instruction that fits into their busy day, providing them a sanctuary from daily pressure.

Outstanding customer service and the making of customer satisfaction a top priority will give our company an additional edge in the competitive local market, and the ability to develop long-term relationships with our participants.

Other important competitive advantages include:
1.   Mobile Yoga sessions at homes and offices.
2.   Commitment to superior customer service.
3.   Educational seminars and workshops related to Yoga health benefits.
4.   Referral program incentives
6.   Facility design creativity.
7.   Club membership benefits.
8.   Detailed customer needs assessment.
9.   Unconditional Satisfaction Guarantee
10.   Online order status checking/ Email order status notifications.
11.   Comprehensive and continuous instructor training program.
12.   Stay abreast of latest Yoga trends.
13.   Fully stocked Pro Shop.
14.   We will practice just-in-time inventory management to reduce carrying costs.
17.   We will offer only the finest quality products.
18.   No long-term contracts required
19.   Programs customized to age groups and ability levels.
20.   Small instructor-to-participant Ratio
21.   A nurturing, welcoming and learning environment.
23.   Free introductory sessions
24.   Easy Payment Plans and Options
25.   Ample Parking
26.   Personalized Yoga assessments; includes a complete health analysis.

22. We offer nutritional counseling for those who are looking for some healthy eating guidance.
23. We only use Certified Yoga instructors.
24. Our highly certified instructors will work safely with participants and offer the best core training and mind-body workout available.

6.2.1   Branding Strategy

Our branding strategy involves what we do to shape what the customer immediately thinks our business offers and stands for. The purpose of our branding strategy is to reduce customer perceived purchase risk and improve our profit margins by allowing use to charge a premium for our Yoga Studio courses.

We will invest $____ every year in maintaining our brand name image, which will differentiate our yoga studio from other companies. The amount of money spent on creating and maintaining a brand name will not convey any specific information about our products, but it will convey, indirectly, that we are in this market for the long haul, that we have a reputation to protect, and that we will interact repeatedly with our customers. In this sense, the amount of money spent on maintaining our brand name will signal to consumers that we will provide products and services of consistent quality.

We will use the following ways to build trust and establish our personal brand:
1. Build a consistently published blog and e-newsletter with informational content.
2. Create comprehensive social media profiles.
3. Contribute articles to related online publications.
4. Earn Career Certifications

Resources:
https://www.abetterlemonadestand.com/branding-guide/

Our key to marketing success will be to effectively manage the building of our brand platform in the marketplace, which will consist of the following elements:

Brand Vision - our envisioned future of the brand is to be the local source for _____ solutions to manage the complications of stress management.

Brand Attributes - Partners, problem solvers, responsive, comprehensive, reliable, flexible, yoga experts, stress relief, and easy to work with.

Brand Essence - the shared soul of the brand, the spark of which is present in every experience a customer has with our products, will be "Problem Solving" and "Responsive" This will be the core of our organization, driving the type of people we hire and the type of behavior we expect.

Brand Image - the outside world's overall perception of our organization will be that we are the 'Yoga' pros who are alleviating the complications of selecting the right beverage for the right occasion.

Brand Promise - our concise statement of what we do, why we do it, and why customers should do business with us will be, "To realize solid instructional values with the help of our knowledgeable staff"

We will use the following methodologies to implement our branding strategy:

1. Develop processes, systems and quality assurance procedures to assure the consistent adherence to our quality standards and mission statement objectives.
2. Develop business processes to consistently deliver upon our value proposition.
3. Develop training programs to assure the consistent professionalism and responsiveness of our service personnel.
4. Develop marketing communications with consistent, reinforcing message content.
5. Incorporate testimonials into our marketing materials that support our promises.
6. Develop marketing communications with a consistent presentation style. (Logo design, company colors, slogan, labels, packaging, stationery, etc.)
7. Exceed our brand promises to achieve consistent customer loyalty.
8. Use surveys, focus groups and interviews to consistently monitor what our brand means to our customers.
9. Consistently match our brand values or performance benchmarks to our customer requirements.
10. Focus on the maintenance of a consistent number of key brand values that are tied to our company strengths.
11. Continuously research key pet industry trends in our markets to stay relevant to our customer needs and wants.
12. Attach a logo-imprinted product label and business card to all products, marketing communications and invoices.
13. Develop a memorable and meaningful tagline that captures the essence of our brand. (Ex: Yoga is not only our business, its our Passion)
14. Prepare a one-page company overview and make it a key component of our logo embossed sales presentation folder.
15. Hire and train sales associate to put the interests of customers first.
16. Develop a professional website that is updated with fresh content on a regular basis.
17. Use our blog to circulate content that establishes our niche expertise and opens a two-way dialogue with our customers.
18. Attractive and tasteful uniforms will also help our staff's morale. The branding will become complete with the addition of our corporate logo, or other trim or accessories which echo the style and theme of our establishment.
19. Create an effective slogan with the following attributes:
    a. Appeals to customers' emotions.
    b. Shows off how our service benefits customers by highlighting our customer service or care.
    c. Has 8 words or less and is memorable
    d. Can be grasped quickly by our audience.
    e. Reflects our business' personality and character.
    f. Shows sign of originality.
20. Create a Proof Book that contains before and after photos, testimonial letters, our mission statement, copies of industry certifications and our code of ethics.

21.   Make effective use of trade show exhibitions and email newsletters to help brand our image.

The communications strategy we will use to build our brand platform will include the following items:

   Website - featuring product line information, research, testimonials, cost benefit analysis, frequently asked questions, and policy information. This website will be used as a tool for both our sales team and our customers.

   Presentations, brochures and mailers geared to the consumer, explaining the benefits of our product line as part of a comprehensive good health plan.

   Presentations and brochures geared to the family decision maker explaining the benefits of our club programs in terms of positive outcomes, reduced cost from complications, and reduced risk of lawsuits or negative survey events.

   A presentation and recruiting brochure geared to prospective sales people that emphasizes the benefits of joining our organization.

   Training materials that help every employee deliver our brand message in a consistent manner.

6.2.2   Brand Positioning Statement

We will use the following brand positioning statement to summarize what our brand means to our targeted market:

To _____ (target market)
_____ (company name) is the brand of _____ (product/service frame of reference) that enables the customer to _____ (primary performance benefit) because ____ (company name) _____ (products/services) _____ (are made with/offer/provide) the best _____ (key attributes)

6.3   Business SWOT Analysis

Definition: SWOT Analysis is a powerful technique for understanding your Strengths and Weaknesses, and for looking at the Opportunities and Threats faced.

Strategy: We will use this SWOT Analysis to uncover exploitable opportunities and carve a sustainable niche in our market. And by understanding the weaknesses of our business, we can manage and eliminate threats that would otherwise catch us by surprise. By using the SWOT framework, we will be able to craft a strategy that distinguishes our business from our competitors, so that we can compete successfully in the market.

   Strengths
   What Yoga Studio products and services are we best at providing?
   What unique resources can we draw upon?

1. Experienced management team from Yoga industry.
2. Strong networking relationships with many different organizations.
3. Excellent instructor staff who are experienced, highly trained and very participant attentive.
4. Wide diversity of service offerings.
5. High customer loyalty.
6. Remarkable introduction of creativity into the teaching process.
7. Developed several survey mechanisms to collect valuable feedback from participants.
8. _____

Weaknesses

In what areas could we improve?

Where do we have fewer resources than others?
1. New comer to the area.
2. Lack of marketing experience.
3. The struggle to build brand equity.
4. A limited marketing budget to develop brand awareness.
5. Finding dependable and people oriented staff.
6. Need to develop a structured formal referral program.
7. Need to exploit opportunities for Press Releases
8. Management expertise gaps.
9. Inadequate monitoring of competitor strategies and reviews.
10. _____

Opportunities

What opportunities are there for new and/or improved services?

What trends could we take advantage of?
1. Could take market share away from existing competitors.
2. Greater need for home services by time starved dual income families.
3. Growing market with a significant percentage of the target market still not aware that _____ (company name) exists.
4. The ability to develop many long-term customer relationships.
5. Expanding the range of Yoga packaged offerings.
6. Greater use of direct advertising to promote our services.
7. Establish referral relationships with local businesses serving the same target market segment.
8. Networking with non-profit organizations.
9. Cross-selling of other products and services to client database.
10. Offer Martial Arts training classes
11. _____

Threats

What trends or competitor actions could hurt us?

What threats do our weaknesses expose us to?
1. Another Yoga Studio could move into this area.

2. Further declines in the economic forecast.
3. Inflation affecting operations for gas, labor, and other operating costs.
4. Keeping trained efficient staff and key personnel from moving on or starting their own business venture.
5. Imitation competition from similar indirect service providers.
6. Price differentiation is a significant competition factor.
7. We need to do a better job of assessing the strengths and weaknesses of all of our competitors.
8. Vulnerability to changes in the popularity of after-school enrichment programs.
9. Increases in the cost of adequate insurance coverage.
10. _____

SWOT Recap:

We will use the following strengths to capitalize on recognized opportunities:
1. _____
2. _____

We will take the following actions to turn our weaknesses into strengths and prepare to defend against known threats.
1. _____
2. _____

6.4.0 Marketing Strategy

_____ (company name) intends to maintain an extensive marketing campaign that will ensure maximum visibility for the business in its targeted market. Below is an overview of the marketing strategies and objectives of the studio.

Marketing Objectives
1. Establish relationships with physicians, chiropractors, and other allied health professionals that will refer their patients to yoga classes at ___ (company name).
2. Implement a local campaign with the Company's targeted market via the use of flyers, local newspaper advertisements, and word of mouth advertising.
3. Develop an online presence by developing a website and placing the Company's name and contact information with online directories.

Marketing Strategies Overview
_____ (company name) will use a number of marketing strategies that will allow the Yoga Studio to easily target men and women within the target market. These strategies include traditional print advertisements and ads placed on search engines on the Internet. Below is a description of how the business intends to market its services to the general public. _____ (company name) will also use an internet based strategy. This is very important as many people seeking local services, such as Yoga instructors/classes, now

turn to the Internet to conduct their preliminary searches. We will register the Yoga Studio with online portals so that potential customers can easily reach the business. The Company will also develop its own online website showcasing the operations of the business, its services, hours of operation, and preliminary pricing information. The Company will initially maintain a sizable amount of print and traditional advertising methods within local markets to promote our Yoga instruction classes.

In order to penetrate the marketplace, we will offer free instruction and will have refreshment available for lunchtime visitors. The complimentary instruction segments will be ___ (#) minutes and focus on exercises that will produce the maximum release of tension.

Our marketing message will emphasize the following benefits of our services:
1. Opportunity to meet new people.
2. Enhance the quality of leisure time.
3. Realize health benefits.
4. Gain life-long skills.
5. Build self-confidence and self-esteem.

The marketing strategy will revolve around two different types of media, sales brochures and a website. These two tools will be used to make customers aware of our broad range of service and product offerings. The company will also rely heavily on word-of-mouth referrals for business.

One focus of our marketing strategy will be to drive customers to our website for class registration and product order submissions. The website will be especially useful for someone out of town who is in need of a gift for a local resident. The website will also educate corporate executives as to the team building benefits of our corporate training program. Additionally, Yoga product orders placed via the website will be rewarded with a ___ % discount.

A combination of local media and event marketing will be utilized. _____ (company name) will create an identity oriented marketing strategy with executions particularly in the local media. Our marketing strategy will utilize radio spots, print ads, press releases, yellow page ads, flyers, bandit signs and newsletter distribution. We will make effective use of direct response advertising, and include coupons in all print ads. We will place small display ads in local editions of fitness themed magazines.

We will use comment cards, newsletter sign-up forms and surveys to collect customer email addresses and feed our client relationship management (CRM) software system. This system will automatically send out, on a predetermined schedule, follow-up materials, such as article reprints, seminar invitations, email messages, surveys and e-newsletters. We will offset some of our advertising costs by asking our suppliers and other local merchants to place ads in our newsletter.

Current Situation

We will study the current marketing situation on a weekly basis to analyze trends and identify sources of business growth. As onsite owners, we will be on hand daily to insure customer service. Our services include products of the highest quality and a prompt response to feedback from customers. Our extensive and highly detailed financial statements, produced monthly, will enable us to stay competitive and exploit presented opportunities.

Marketing Budget

Our marketing budget will be a flexible $_____ per quarter. The marketing budget can be allocated in any way that best suits the time of year.

Marketing budget per quarter:

Newspaper Ads	$_____	Radio advertisement	$_____
Web Page	$_____	Customer contest	$_____
Direct Mail	$_____	Sales Brochure	$_____
Trade Shows	$_____	Seminars	$_____
Superpages	$_____	Google Adwords	$_____
Giveaways	$_____	Vehicle Signs	$_____
Business Cards	$_____	Flyers	$_____
Labels/Stickers	$_____	Videos/DVDs	$_____
Samples	$_____	Newsletter	$_____
Bandit Signs	$_____	Email Campaigns	$_____
Sales Reps Comm.	$_____	Restaurant Placemats	$_____
Press Releases	$_____	Billboards	$_____
Movie Theater Ads	$_____	Fund Raisers	$_____
Infomercials	$_____	Speeches	$_____
Postcards	$_____	Proof Books	$_____
Social Networking	$_____	Charitable Donations	$_____
Other	$_____		
Total:			$_____

Our objective in setting a marketing budget has been to keep it between _____ (5?) and _____ (7?) percent of our estimated annual gross sales.

The following represent a recap of our marketing programs:
Promotion expenses (free gifts for coming in the studio)
Printed materials (sales brochures, pamphlets, fliers, postcards)
Media advertisements (radio, newspapers, outdoor billboards)
Bartering (exchanging our services for ad placement)
Donations (door prizes, building promotions, charities)
Referral Program Brochure
Website Development

Marketing Mix

Clients will primarily come from word-of-mouth and our referral program. The overall market approach involves creating brand awareness through targeted advertising, public relations, co-marketing efforts with select alliance partners, direct mail, email campaigns (with constant contact.com), seminars and a website.

Advertising

_____ (company name) will rely on the recommendations of satisfied customers and preferred vendors as a means of attracting customers away from the competition. Past experience has also proven that many customers come on the recommendations of others. Although word-of-mouth is an effective way of increasing market share, it is also extremely slow. To accelerate the process of expanding the customer base, the business will maintain an advertising budget of $_____ for the first year. The bulk of this budget will be spent on listings in the _____ (city) yellow pages and online directories, complimentary sample sessions, and direct mailings to ad respondents.

Yoga Sampler Program

We will create a sampler Yoga lesson as part of our marketing plan. Complimentary sample Yoga sessions will work well as donations to groups as a door prize.

'Bring A Buddy to Class' Program

The "bring a buddy to class" strategy will be a marketing tool that allows prospective customers to participate and experience what it's like to be a participant at our studio. If Yoga proves to be their thing, they will either want to sign up right away or take information with them so they can sign up later. We will use this technique at least once a quarter.

Video Marketing Clips

We will link to our website a series of YouTube.com based video clips that talk about our range of Yoga services, and demonstrate our expertise with certain Yoga routines. We will create business marketing videos that are both entertaining and informational to raise our search engine rankings.

The video will include:

Student Testimonials - We will let our best customers become our instant sales force because people will believe what others say about you more readily than what you say about yourself

Live Class Demonstrations - We will train and pre-sell our potential clients on our most popular Yoga sessions by talking about and showing them. Often, our potential clients don't know the full range and depth of our services because we haven't taken the time to show and tell them for future reference. Include a free 20-minute yoga routine.

Include Business Website Address

Video Articles: We will take some of our best articles about yoga, and create some slides in PowerPoint, and record them using screen capture software such as Camtasia.

Owner Interview: Explanation of mission statement and unique selling proposition.

Frequently Asked Questions - We will answer questions that we often get, and anticipate rejections we might get and give great reasons to convince potential clients that we are the best Yoga Studio in the area.

Include a Call to Action - We have the experience and the know-how to make Yoga an enjoyable family event. So call us, right now, and let's get started.

Seminar - Include a portion of a seminar on the health benefits of Yoga.

Comment on industry trends and product news - We will appear more in-tune and knowledgeable in our market if we can talk about what's happening in our industry and marketplace.

Resources: www.businessvideomarketing.tv

www.hotpluto.com

www.hubspot.com/video-marketing-kit

www.youtube.com/user/mybusinessstory

Analytics Report

http://support.google.com/youtube/bin/static.py?hl=en&topic=1728599&guide=1 714169&page=guide.cs

Examples:

http://www.videodancestudio.com

http://www.youtube.com/watch?v=G7j4nQqcpq8

http://www.youtube.com/watch?v=3MTL0RLEkPM

Top 11 places where we will share our videos online:

YouTube   **www.youtube.com**

This very popular website allows you to log-in and leave comments and ratings on the videos. You can also save your favorite videos and allows you to tag posted videos. This makes it easier for your videos to come up in search engines.

Google Video   **http://video.google.com/**

A video hosting site. Google Video is not just focused on sharing videos online, but this is also a market place where you can buy the videos you find on this site using Google search engine.

Yahoo! Video   **http://video.yahoo.com/**

Uploading and sharing videos is possible with Yahoo Video!. You can find several types of videos on their site and you can also post comments and ratings for the videos.

Revver   **http://www.revver.com/**

This website lets you earn money through ads on your videos and you will have a 50/50 profit split with the website. Another great deal with Revver is that your fans who posted your videos on their site can also earn money.

Blip.tv   **http://blip.tv/**

Allows viewers to stream and download the videos posted on their website. You can also use Creative Commons licenses on your videos posted on the website. This allows you to decide if your videos should be attributed, restricted for commercial use and be used under specific terms.

Vimeo   **http://www.vimeo.com/**

This website is family safe and focuses on sharing private videos. The interface of the website is similar to some social networking sites that allow you to customize your profile page with photos from Flickr and embeddable player. This site allows users to socialize through their videos.

Metacafe   **http://www.metacafe.com/**

This video sharing site is community based. You can upload short-form videos and share it to the other users of the website. Metacafe has its own system called VideoRank that ranks videos according to the viewer reactions and features the most popular among the viewers.

ClipShack   **http://www.clipshack.com/**

Like most video sharing websites, you can post comments on the videos and even tag some as your favorite. You can also share the videos on other websites through the html code from ClipShack and even sending it through your email.

Veoh   **http://www.veoh.com/**

You can rent or sell your videos and keep the 70% of the sales price. You can upload a range of different video formats on Veoh and there is no limit on the size and length of the file. However, when your video is over 45 minutes it has to be downloaded before the viewer can watch it.

Jumpcut   **http://download.cnet.com/JumpCut/3000-18515_4-10546353.html**

Jumpcut allows its users to upload videos using their mobile phones. You will have to attach the video captured from your mobile phone to an email. It has its own movie making wizard that helps you familiarize with the interface of the site.

DailyMotion   **www.dailymotion.com**

As one of the leading sites for sharing videos, Dailymotion attracts over 114 million unique monthly visitors (source: comScore, May 2013) 1.2 billion videos views worldwide (source: internal). Offers the best content from users, independent content creators and premium partners. Using the most advanced technology for both users and content creators, provides high-quality and HD video in a fast, easy-to-use online service that also automatically filters infringing material as notified by content owners.

Offering 32 localized versions, their mission is to provide the best possible entertainment experience for users and the best marketing opportunities for advertisers, while respecting content protection.

Community Outreach Programs

We will conduct community outreach programs to accomplish the following:

1.   Raise the profile of the studio in the community.
2.   Provides participants with real world experiences.
3.   Help build self-esteem in youth.
4.   Create lasting partnerships in the community with organizations such as Boys and Girls Clubs, Community Centers, and other youth development organizations.

Networking

Networking will be a key to success, because referrals and alliances formed can help keep our business growing. We will strive to build long-term mutually beneficial relationships with our networking contacts and join the following types of organizations:

1.   We will form a LeTip Chapter to exchange business leads.
2.   We will join the local BNI.com referral exchange group.
3.   We will join the Chamber of Commerce to further corporate relationships.
4.   We will join the Rotary Club, Kiwanis Club, Church Groups, etc.
5.   We will become an active member of the local Yoga instructor association.
6.   We will join the local Parent Teachers Association (PTA).
7.   We will join the he Yoga & Pilates Network™, which is a hand-picked assembly

of grass-roots, independent Yoga studios nationwide, prescreened for sample acceptability.

Source: http://samplingstore.com/custom-sampling/yoga-pilates-network/

8. We will join the World Yoga Network and participate in upcoming Yoga Events.

Source: http://www.worldyoganetwork.com/

We will use our metropolitan _____ (city) Chamber of Commerce to target prospective corporate contacts. We will mail letters to each prospect describing our products and team building benefits. We will follow-up with phone calls and offer to give an educational seminar presentation on improving productivity through better team spirit. Our studio will use online networking platforms such as Ning.com or KickApps.com to create and customize their own interface, branding it and making it blend into an existing website. We will also use YogaTag.com, a free site designed to allow teachers to post a profile, schedule, and media while creating a community of colleagues and students.

Newsletter

We will produce a member newsletter titled 'The Yoga Press'. We will include information on class dates, times and prices, along with more in-depth articles on how Yoga exercises could enhance sport and fitness performance and improve one's daily functions. We will also feature the comments of members currently involved in the program. Our events bulletin board will be used to present testimonials and pictures showcasing our Yoga "stars" performing their favorite mat or reformer exercise.

We will develop a monthly e-newsletter to stay in touch with participants, concerning regular class and holiday schedules, and new class offerings. The newsletter can be created on our computer and printed out at a copy shop. A version can also reside online for our computer-literate participants. We will also open the door for dialogue with letters to and from the Instructors, or a participant message board.

We will include the following types of information:

1.	Success case studies	2.	New Product/Service Introductions
3.	Instructor/participant of the month	4.	Yoga trends.
5.	Client endorsements/testimonials.	6.	Classified ads: sponsors/suppliers.
7.	Upcoming events/class schedules.	8.	Yoga health benefits.
9.	Participant Message Board	10.	Instructor Letters

Resources: Microsoft Publisher   www.aweber.com

We will adhere to the following newsletter writing guidelines:
1. We will provide content that is of real value to our subscribers.
2. We will provide solutions to our subscriber's problems or questions.
3. We will communicate regularly on a weekly basis.
4. We will create HTML Messages that look professional and allow us to track how many people click on our links and/or open our emails.
5. We will not pitch our business opportunity in our Ezine very often.
6. We will focus our marketing dollars on building our Ezine subscriber list.
7. We will focus on relationship building and not the conveying of a sales message.

8. We will vary our message format with videos, articles, checklists, quotes, pictures and charts.
9. We will recommend occasionally affiliate products in some of our messages to help cover our marketing costs.
10. We will include eye-catching photos, graphics and/or videos.
11. We will consistently follow the above steps to build a database of qualified prospects and customers that have given their permission to receive the newsletter.

Resources:

wwwconstantcontact.com

www.mailchimp.com

http://lmssuccess.com/10-reasons-online-business-send-regular-newsletter-customers/

www.smallbusinessmiracles.com/how/newsletters/

www.fuelingnewbusiness.com/2010/06/01/combine-email-marketing-and-social-media-
for-ad-agency-new-business/

www.yogajournal.com/article/teach/send-the-right-message/

Examples:

http://www.thematyogastudio.com/resources/newsletters

http://thegivingtreeyogastudio.com/TGTYS_newsletters.html

Trade Shows

We will exhibit at as many local trade shows per year as possible. These include Home and Garden Shows, County Fairs, Business Expos, open exhibits in shopping malls, business spot-lights with our local Chamber of Commerce, and more. The objective is to get our company name and service out to as many people as possible. We will do our homework and ask other stores where they exhibit their products and services. When exhibiting at a trade show, we will put our best foot forward and represent ourselves as professionals. We will be open, enthusiastic, informative and courteous. We will exhibit our services with sales brochures, logo-imprinted giveaways, sample products, a photo book for people to browse through and a computer to run our video presentation through. We will use a 'free drawing' for a gift basket prize and a sign-in sheet to collect names and email addresses. We will also develop a questionnaire or survey that helps us to assemble an ideal customer profile and qualify the leads we receive. We will train our booth attendants to answer all type of questions and to handle objections. We will also seek to present educational seminars at the show to gain increased publicity, and name and expertise recognition. Most importantly, we will develop and implement a follow-up program to stay-in-touch with prospects.

Resources: www.tsnn.com   www.expocentral.com
              www.acshomeshow.com/   www.EventsInAmerica.com
              www.Biztradeshows.com   www.commerce.gov
              www.newpa.com   www.sba.gov/international
              www.expoworld.net   www.biztradeshows.gov
              www.eventseye.com   www.trade-show-advisor.com
              www.fita.org   www.tscentral.com

New Homeowners / Movers

We will reach out to new movers in our immediate neighborhood. Marketing to new movers will help bring in more long-term customers. And, because new movers are five times more likely to become loyal, this marketing program, will generate new, fresh customers who are likely to turn in to the regular customers. The value of a new loyal customer will be significant, as a new loyal customer who comes in ___ (#) times a month can be worth up to $_____ a year for standard services. Furthermore, many studies suggest that new movers typically stay in their new homes for an average of 5.6 years. We will also participate in local Welcome Wagon activities for new residents, and assemble a mailing list to distribute sales literature from county courthouse records and Realtor supplied information. We will use a postcard mailing to promote a special get-acquainted offer to new residents.

We will adhere the following routine when marketing to new local homeowners:
1. Send out a friendly welcome letter / flyer / brochure welcoming each new family to the community along with information on our pest control services.
2. Include a gift certificate or a new client discount coupon / certificate to entice the new family to try our service, risk free with no obligation.
3. Send out a new client discount or offer an initial free evaluation.
4. Send out a postcard with a discount or coupon.

Resources:
Welcome Wagon   www.WelcomeWagon.com
Welcome Mat Services   www.WelcomeMatServices.com
Welcomemat Services uses specialized, patent-pending technology to store and log customer demographics for use by the local companies it supports.

Vehicle Signs
We will place magnetic and vinyl signs on our vehicles and include our company name, phone number, company slogan and website address, if possible. We will create a cost-effective moving billboard with high-quality, high-resolution vehicle wraps. We will wrap a portion of the vehicle or van to deliver excellent marketing exposure.
Resource: http://www.fastsigns.com/

Design Tips:
1. Avoid mixing letter styles and too many different letter sizes.
2. Use the easiest to recognize form of your logo.
3. The standard background is white.
4. Do not use a background color that is the same as or close to your vehicle color.
5. Choose colors that complement your logo colors.
6. Avoid the use too many colors.
7. Use dark letter colors on a light background or the reverse.
8. Use easy to read block letters in caps and lower case.
9. Limit content to your business name, slogan, logo, phone number and website-address.
10. Include your license number if required by law.
11. Magnetic signs are ideal for door panels (material comes on 24" wide rolls).

12.   Graphic vehicle window wraps allow the driver to still see out.
13.   Keep your message short so people driving by can read it at a glance.
14.   Do not use all capital letters.
15.   Be sure to include your business name, phone number, slogan and web address.

Vehicle Wraps

Vehicle wrapping will be one of our preferred marketing methods. According to company research, wrapped vehicles have more impact than billboards, create a positive image for the company and prompt the public to remember the words and images featured in the company's branding. Vehicle wrapping is also an inexpensive marketing strategy. A typical truck wrap costs about $2,500, and is a one-time payment for an ad that spans the life of a truck's lease.

DVD Presentation

We plan to create a DVD with samples of our Yoga sessions and participant testimonials. We will include this DVD in our sales presentation folder and direct mail package.

Up-selling and Reselling

We plan to develop a broad range of Yoga products and services in various price categories, so that we up-sell to current customers and re-sell to inactive accounts.

Advertising Wearables

We will give all preferred club members an eye-catching T-shirt or sweatshirt with our company name and logo printed across the garment to wear about town, as a thank you for their referral activities. We will wear our logo-imprinted shirts during off-site demonstrations and open house events.

Charitable Donations

We will use these coupon donation opportunities to demonstrate our newly acquired mind-body workout skills, meet and greet many new potential clients and distribute lots of sales brochures and business cards to event sponsors and attendees.

Corporate Promotional Kit

Our promotional sales presentation kit will contain the following items:

- Resume	- Client List
- Press Clippings	- Article Reprints
- DVD Presentation	- Sales Brochures
- FAQs	- Business Cards
- Press Releases	- Community Service Awards
- Testimonials	- Instructor Credentials

Stage Events

We will stage external events to become known in our community. This is essential to attracting referrals. We will schedule regular external events, such as seminar talks, festival appearances and fundraiser demonstrations. We will use event registration forms, our website and an event sign-in sheet to collect the names and email addresses of all attendees. This database will be used to feed our automatic customer relationship follow-up program and newsletter service.

Resource: www.eventbrite.com

Ex: Open House Event Press Release

The _____ Studio, located at _____, invites the ____ (city) community to attend a week of its full schedule of Yoga Classes entirely for free, from Sunday, ____ (date) through Friday, ____ (date), as part of an open house to welcome all students, new and seasoned.

Special Event Examples:
Restorative Chakra Yoga and Sound Healing
        http://www.exhalepittsburgh.com./special-events/

Demonstrations

To attract new participants, we will showcase our Yoga routines at demonstration performances. We will sign up our studio to perform at local fairs, malls, festivals and trade shows. This will be a way to let people in our community see who we are and what you do. We will make sure to have flyers and business cards to pass out.

Sales Brochures

Our sales brochure will include the following contents and become a key part of our direct mail package:

- Contact Information   - Company Description
- Customer Testimonials   - List of Services/Benefits
- Competitive Advantages   - Owner Resume/Credentials
- Coupon   - Vendor Testimonials

Resources:
https://www.pinterest.com/ojarnold/yoga-brochures/
https://creativemarket.com/themesflow/53689-Yoga-Studio-Brochure

Sales Brochure Design
1.   Speak in Terms of Our Prospects Wants and Interests.
2.   Focus on all the Benefits, not Just Features.
3.   Put the company logo and Unique Selling Proposition together to reinforce the fact that your company is different and better than the competition.
4.   Include a special offer, such as a discount, a free report, a sample, or a free trial to increase the chances that the brochure will generate sales.

We will incorporate the following Brochure Design Guidelines:
1.   Design the brochure to achieve a focused set of objectives (marketing of programs) with a target market segment (residential vs. commercial).

2.   Tie the brochure design to our other marketing materials with colors, logo, fonts and formatting.
3.   List capabilities and how they benefit clients.
4.   Demonstrate what we do and how we do it differently.
5.   Define the value proposition of our engineering installing services
6.   Use a design template that reflects your market positioning strategy.
7.   Identify your key message (unique selling proposition)
8.   List our competitive advantages.
9.   Express our understanding of client needs and wants.
10.   Use easy to read (scan) headlines, subheadings, bullet points, pictures, etc.
11.   Use a logo to create a visual branded identity.
12.   The most common and accepted format for a brochure is a folded A3 (= 2 x A4), which gives 4 pages of information.
13.   Use a quality of paper that reflects the image we want to project.
14.   Consistently stick to the colors of our corporate style.
15.   Consider that colors have associations, such as green colors are associated with the environment and enhance an environmental image.
16.   Illustrations will be appropriate and of top quality and directly visualize the product assortment, product application and production facility.
17.   The front page will contain the company name, logo, the main application of your product or service and positioning message or Unique Selling Proposition.
18.   The back page will be used for testimonials or references, and contact details.

Sales Presentation Folder Contents

1.	Resumes	2.	Before and After Photos
3.	Contract/Application	4.	Frequently Asked Questions
5.	Sales Brochure	6.	Business Cards
7.	Testimonials/References	8.	Program Descriptions
9.	Informative Articles	10.	Referral Program
11.	Company Overview	12.	Operating Policies
13.	Order Forms		

Coupons

We will use coupons with limited time expirations to get prospects to try our Yoga class programs. We will also accept the coupons of our competitors to help establish new client relationships. We will run ads directing people to our Web site for a $____ gift certificate. This will help to draw in new business and collect e-mail addresses for the distribution of a monthly newsletter. We will distribute free class coupons at staged events.

Research indicates that we can use our coupons to spark online searches of our website and drive sales. This will help to draw in new clients and collect e-mail addresses for the distribution of a monthly newsletter. We will include a coupon with each sale, or send them by mail to our mailing list.

We will use coupons selectively to accomplish the following:
1.   To introduce a new product or service.
2.   To attract loyal customers away from the competition

3. To prevent customer defection to a new competitor.
4. To help celebrate a special event.
5. To thank customers for a large order and ensure a repeat order within a certain limited time frame.

Examples:
http://www.retailmenot.com/coupons/yogastudio

Types of Coupons:
1.	Courtesy Coupons	Rewards for repeat business
2.	Cross-Marketing Coupons	Incentive to try other products/services.
3.	Companion Coupon	Bring a friend incentive.

Resources:
www.valpack.com

Websites like Groupon.com, LivingSocial.com, Eversave.com, SignPost.com and BuyWithMe.com sell discount vouchers for services ranging from custom _____ to _____ consultations. Best known is Chicago-based Groupon. To consumers, discount vouchers promise substantial savings — often 50% or more. To merchants, discount vouchers offer possible opportunities for price discrimination, exposure to new customers, online marketing, and "buzz." Vouchers are more likely to be profitable for merchants with low marginal costs, who can better accommodate a large discount and for patient merchants, who place higher value on consumers' possible future return visits through a well-developed retention plan.

Resource:
https://zenplanner.com/groupon-tips-for-yoga-studios/
Examples:
https://www.groupon.com/local/yoga

Yipit.com
Gathers over 30,000 offers per month from 809 daily deal sites like Groupon, LivingSocial, Gilt City, Google Offers and filters them based on where subscribers are located and what types of deals they want to be notified of. Yipit is a simple way to access them all - via web, a personalized email or iPhone - in 118 cities in North America.
Examples:
http://yipit.com/business/the-yoga-studio-2/

Cross-Promotions
We will contact local businesses with customer profiles similar to ours, and ask them to hand out discount coupons to each of their customers. This will get us access to that business's customer base, as well as a personal recommendation from that business to try our Yoga Studio services.

Premium Giveaways
We will distribute logo-imprinted promotional products at events, also known as giveaway premiums, to foster top-of-mind awareness (www.promoideas.org). These

items include logo-imprinted T-shirts, business cards with magnetic backs, mugs with contact phone number and calendars that feature important date reminders.

Newspaper Ads

We will use these ads to announce the opening of our store and get our name established. We will adhere to the rule that frequency and consistency of message are essential. We will include a list of our top brand names and specialty services. We will include a coupon to track the response in zoned editions of 'Shopper' Papers, Theater Bills, and Community Newsletters and Newspapers. We will use the ad to announce any weekly or monthly price specials.

Our newspaper ads will utilize the following design tips:

1. We will start by getting a media kit from the publisher to analyze their demographic information as well as their reach and distribution.
2. Don't let the newspaper people have total control of our ad design, as we know how we want our company portrayed to the market.
3. Make sure to have 1st class graphics since this will be the only visual distinction we can provide the reader about our business.
4. Buy the biggest ad we can afford, with full-page ads being the best.
5. Go with color if affordable, because consumers pick color ads over black 82% of the time.
6. Ask the paper if they have specific days that more of our type of buyer reads their paper.
7. If we have a hit ad on our hands, we will make it into a circular or door-hanger to extend the life of the offer.
8. Don't change an ad because we are getting tired of looking at it.
9. We will start our headline by telling our story to pull the reader into the ad.
10. We will use "Act Now" to convey a sense of urgency to the reader.
11. We will use our headline to tell the reader what to do.
12. The headline is a great place to announce a free offer.
13. We will write our headline as if we were speaking to one person, and make it personal.
14. We will use our headline to either relay a benefit or intrigue the reader into wanting more information.
15. Use coupons giving a dollar amount off, not a percentage, as people hate doing the math.

Business Journal Display Ads

We will consider placing display ads in business journals read by professionals and possibly renting a list of their local subscribers for a planned direct mailing. The mailing will describe our corporate team building and stress reduction programs and past success stories.

Doorhangers

Our doorhangers will feature a calendar of 'Free Stress Reduction Seminars'. The doorhanger will include a list of all our product categories and info about our Yoga program options. We will also attach our business card to the doorhanger and distribute the doorhangers multiple times to the same subdivision.

Resources:

https://www.psprint.com/resources/yoga-studios-marketing-materials/

Article Submissions

We will pitch articles to consumer magazines, local newspapers, business magazines and internet articles directories to help establish our specialized expertise and improve our visibility. Hyperlinks will be placed within written articles and can be clicked on to take the customer to another webpage within our website or to a totally different website. These clickable links or hyperlinks will be keywords or relevant words that have meaning to our Yoga Studio. In fact, we will create a position whose primary function is to link our Yoga Studio with opportunities to be published in local publications.

Publishing requires an understanding of the following publisher needs:

1.	Review of good work.	2.	Editor story needs.
3.	Article submission process rules	4.	Quality photo portfolio
5.	Exclusivity requirements.	6.	Target market interests

Our Article Submission Package will include the following:

1.	Well-written materials	2.	Good Drawings
3.	High-quality Photographs	4.	Well-organized outline.

Examples of General Publishing Opportunities:

1.	Document a new solution to old problem	2.	Publish a research study
3.	Mistake prevention advice	4.	Present a different viewpoint
5.	Introduce a local angle on a hot topic.	6.	Reveal a new trend.
7.	Share specialty niche expertise.	8.	Share health benefits

Examples of Specific Article Titles:

1. "Everything You Ever Wanted to Know About the Health Benefits of Yoga"
2. "How to Evaluate and Compare Yoga Studios"
3. "New Trends in Yoga Courses"
4. "The Top Ten Reasons to Take Yoga Classes"
5. "How Yoga Can Improve Vital Mind-Body Outlook"
6. "How Yoga Improves A Person's Mental Outlook"
7. "Using Yoga as a Means to Achieve Stress Reduction".
8. "Yoga versus Pilates".
9. "How Yoga Can Help You to Run a Successful Business"
   Ex: http://collectivehub.com/2016/04/4-ways-yoga-can-help-you-run-a-successful-business/

Write Articles with a Closing Author Resource Box or Byline

1.	Author Name with credential titles.	2.	Explanation of area of expertise.
3.	Mention of a special offer.	4.	A specific call to action
5.	A Call to Action Motivator	6.	All possible contact information

7.   Helpful Links   8.   Link to Company Website.

Article Objectives:

Article Topic	Target Audience	Target Date

Article Tracking Form

SubjectPublication	Target Audience	Business Development	Resources Needed	Target Date

Possible Magazines to submit articles include:

1.   Men's Health Magazine   2.   Cosmopolitan Magazine
Resources: Writer's Market   www.writersmarket.com
                Directory of Trade Magazines   www.techexpo.com/tech_mag.html

Internet article directories include:

http://ezinearticles.com/
http://www.wahm-articles.com
http://www.articlecity.com
http://www.articledashboard.com
http://www.webarticles.com
http://www.article-buzz.com
www.articletogo.com
http://article-niche.com
www.internethomebusinessarticles.com
http://www.articlenexus.com
http://www.articlefinders.com
http://www.articlewarehouse.com
http://www.easyarticles.com
http://ideamarketers.com/
http://clearviewpublications.com/
http://www.goarticles.com/
http://www.webmasterslibrary.com/
http://www.connectionteam.com
http://www.MarketingArticleLibrary.com
http://www.dime-co.com
http://www.allwomencentral.com
http://www.reprintarticles.com
http://www.articlestreet.com
http://www.articlepeak.com
http://www.simplysearch4it.com
http://www.zongoo.com
http://www.mainstreetmom.com
http://www.valuablecontent.com
http://www.article99.com

http://www.mommyshelpercommunity.com
http://www.ladypens.com/
http://www.amazines.com
http://www.submityourarticle.com/articles
http://www.articlecube.com
http://www.free-articles-zone.com
http://www.content-articles.com
http://superpublisher.com
http://www.site-reference.com
www.articlebin.com
www.articlesfactory.com
www.buzzle.com
www.isnare.com
//groups.yahoo.com/group/article_announce
www.ebusiness-articles.com
www.authorconnection.com/
www.businesstoolchest.com
www.digital-women.com/submitarticle.htm
www.searchwarp.com
www.articleshaven.com
www.marketing-seek.com
www.articles411.com
www.articleshelf.com
www.articlesbase.com
www.articlealley.com
www.selfgrowth.com
www.LinkGeneral.com
www.articleavenue.com
www.virtual-professionals.com

Celebrity Endorsements/Testimonials

Please refer to the copies of testimonial and 'thank you' letters contained in the appendix section of this plan.

Online Classified Ad Placements

The following free classified ad sites, will enable our Yoga Studio to thoroughly describe the benefits of our products and services:

1.	**Craigslist.org**	2.	Ebay Classifieds
3.	Classifieds.myspace.com	4.	KIJIJI.com
5.	//Lycos.oodle.com	6.	Webclassifieds.us
7.	USFreeAds.com	8.	www.oodle.com
9.	Backpage.com	10.	stumblehere.com
11.	Classifiedads.com	12.	gumtree.com
13.	Inetgiant.com	14.	www.sell.com
15.	Freeadvertisingforum.com	16.	Classifiedsforfree.com
17.	www.olx.com	18.	www.isell.com
19.	Base.google.com	20.	www.epage.com
21.	Chooseyouritem.com	22.	www.adpost.com
23.	Adjingo.com	24.	Kugli.com

Sample CraigsList.org Classified Ad#1

Turn Your Next Family Celebration into a Yoga Party.
We strive to provide our Customers with the best Yoga party planning in ____ Area!
Free estimates, affordable prices, quality catered food and dependable service.
We are the Yoga Party Caterers to hire for a very special birthday celebration!
Call _____. or e-mail _____ for further info or to schedule an estimate.
References are available upon request. Visit our website _____ for our Customers' reviews and to see photos of our catered Yoga party celebrations.

Two-Step Direct Response Classified Advertising

We will use 'two-step direct response advertising' to motivate readers to take a step or action that signals that we have their permission to begin marketing to them in step two. Our objective is to build a trusting relationship with our prospects by offering a free unbiased, educational report in exchange for permission to continue the marketing process. This method of advertising has the following benefits:

1.	Shorter sales cycle.	2.	Eliminates need for cold calling.
3.	Establishes expert reputation.	4.	Better qualifies prospects
5.	Process is very trackable.	6.	Able to run smaller ads.

Sample Two-Step Lead Generating Classified Ad:

FREE Report Reveals "The Secrets to Hiring the Best Yoga Instructor"
Or… "Learn the Health Benefits of a Yoga".
Or… "How to Choose a Yoga Studio that Meets Your Personal Goals".

Call 24 hour recorded message and leave your name and address or visit our website at
_____ and enter your contact information. Your report will be sent out immediately.

Note: The respondent has shown they have an interest in our Yoga service benefits. We will send this lead the report with excellent and impartial advice. We will also include a section in the report on our complete range of our Yoga products and services, and contact information, along with a coupon for a free Yoga lesson sampling, initial consultation and a sales brochure.

Yellow Page Ads

Research indicates that the use of the traditional Yellow Page Book is declining, but that new residents or people who don't have many personal acquaintances or internet access will look to the Yellow Pages to establish a list of potential businesses to call upon. Even a small 2" x 2" boxed ad can create awareness and attract the desired target client, above and beyond the ability of a simple listing. We will use the following design concepts:
1.   We will use a headline to sell people on the health benefits of our Yoga Classes.
2.   We will include a service guarantee to improve our credibility.
3.   We will include a coupon offer and a tracking code to monitor the response rate and decide whether to increase or decrease our ad size in subsequent years.
4.   We will choose an ad size equal to that of our competitors, and evaluate the response rate for future insertion commitments.
5.   We will include our hours of operation, motto or slogan and logo.
6.   We will list some of the most popular benefits of using our studio services.
7.   We will include our competitive advantages, specialties and years in business.
Resource: www.superpages.com   www.yellowpages.com
Example: www.yellowpages.com/miami-fl/mip/corpo-yoga-studio-452247687
Ad Information:

Book Title: _____	Coverage Area: _____
Yearly Fee: $_____	Ad Size: _____ page
Renewal date: _____	Contact: _____

Cable Television Advertising

Cable television will offer us more ability to target certain market niches or demographics with specialty programming. We will use our marketing research survey to determine which cable TV channels our customers are watching. It is expected that many watch the Home & Garden TV channel, and that people with surplus money for remodeling projects watch the Golf Channel and the Discovery Channel. Our plan is to choose the audience we want, and to hit them often enough to entice them to take action. We will also take advantage of the fact that we will be able to pick the specific areas we want our commercial to air. Ad pricing will be dependent upon the number of households the network reaches, the ratings the particular show has earned, and the supply and demand for a particular network.
Resources:
Spot Runner   www.spotrunner.com
Television Advertising   http://televisionadvertising.com/faq.htm

Ad Information:

Length of ad "spot": ___ seconds   Development costs: $____ (onetime fee)
Length of campaign: __ (#) mos.   Runs per month: Three times per day
Cost per month.: $_____   Total campaign cost: $_____ .

Radio Advertising

We will use non-event based radio advertising. This style of campaign is best suited for non-sales driven retail businesses, such as our yoga studio. We will utilize a much smaller schedule of ads on a consistent long-range basis (48 to 52 weeks a year) with the objective of continuously maintaining top-of-mind-awareness. This will mean maintaining a sufficient level of awareness to be either the number one or number two choice when a triggering-event, such as a _____ moves the consumer into the market for services and forces "a consumer choice" about which _____ company in the consumer's perception might help them the most. This consistent approach will utilize only one ad each week day (260 days per year) and allow our company to cost-effectively keep our message in front of consumers once every week day. The ad copy for this non-event campaign, called a positioning message, will not be time-sensitive. It will define and differentiate our business' "unique market position", and will be repeated for a year. Note: On the average, listeners spend over 3.5 hours per day with radio.

Radio will give us the ability to target our audience, based on radio formats, such as news-talk, classic rock and the oldies. Radio will also be a good way to get repetition into our message, as listeners tend to be loyal to stations and parts of the day.

1. We will use radio advertising to direct prospects to our Web site, advertise a limited time promotion or call for an informational Yoga brochure.
2. We will try to barter our services for radio ad spots.
3. We will use a limited-time offer to entice first-time customers to use our services.
4. We will explore the use of on-air community bulletin boards to play our public announcements about community sponsored events.
5. We will also make the radio station aware of our expertise in the Yoga training field and our availability for interviews.
6. Our choice of stations will be driven by the market research information we collect via our surveys.
7. We will capitalize on the fact that many stations now stream their programming on the internet and reach additional local and even national audiences, and if online listeners like what they hear in our streaming radio spot, they can click over to our website.
8. Our radio ads will use humor, sounds, compelling music or unusual voices to grab attention.
9. Our spots will tell stories or present situations that our target audience can relate to, such as how to improve mobility and flexibility.
10. We will make our call to action, a website address or vanity phone number, easy to remember and tie it in with our company name or message.
11. We will approach radio stations about buying their unsold advertising space for deep discounts. (Commonly known at radio stations' as "Run of Station")
    On radio, this might mean very early in the morning or late at night. We will talk

to our advertising representatives and see what discounts they can offer when one of those empty spaces comes open.

Resources: Radio Advertising Bureau   www.RAB.com
              Radio Locator   www.radio-locator.com
              Radio Directory   www.radiodirectory.com

Ad Information:

Length of ad "spot": ___ seconds   Development costs: $____ (onetime fee)
Length of campaign: __ (#) mos.   Runs per month: Three times per day
Cost per month.: $_____   Total campaign cost: $_____.

Script Resources:

https://voicebunny.com/blog/5-tips-make-radio-ads-grab-attention-sell/

www.voices.com/documents/secure/voices.com-commercial-scripts-for-radio-and-television-ads.pdf

http://smallbusiness.chron.com/say-30second-radio-advertising-spot-10065.html

https://voicebunny.com/blog/5-tips-make-radio-ads-grab-attention-sell/

Talk Radio

National Public Radio (www.NPR.org) plays host to a radio program called _____. The program features _____ (type of experts) who talk and blog about _____ tips. This will help to establish our yoga instructional expertise and build the trust factor with potential clients. Even if we can't get our own nationally syndicated talk show, we will try to make guest appearances and try our hand with podcasting by using apps like Spreaker or joining podcasting communities like BlogTalkRadio.

Resources:

National Public Radio   www.npr.org
Spreaker   http://www.spreaker.com/
Blog Talk Radio   http://www.blogtalkradio.com/

With BlogTalkRadio, people can either host their own live talk radio show with any phone and a computer or listen to thousands of new shows created daily.

Examples:

http://www.blogtalkradio.com/theyogastudiosandiego

E-mail Marketing

We will use the following email marketing tips to build our email address mailing list database, improve communications, boost customer loyalty and attract new and repeat business.

1.   Define our objectives as the most effective email strategies are those that offer value to our subscribers: either in the form of educational content or promotions. To drive sales, a promotional campaign is the best format. To create brand recognition and reinforce our expertise in our industry we will use educational newsletters.

2.   A quality, permission-based email list will be a vital component of our email marketing campaign. We will ask customers and prospects for permission to add them to our list at every touch-point.

3.   We will listen to our customers by using easy-to-use online surveys to ask

specific questions about customers' preferences, interests and satisfaction.

4. We will send only relevant and targeted communications.
5. We will reinforce our brand to ensure recognition of our brand by using a recognizable name in the "from" line of our emails and including our company name, logo and a consistent design and color scheme in every email.

Resources:
https://cbtnews.com/8-tips-drive-successful-email-marketing-campaign/
https://www.inman.com/2017/06/05/4-tips-for-effective-email-marketing/
https://due.com/blog/ways-take-good-care-email-list/

Every ___ (five?) to ____ (six?) weeks, we will send graphically-rich, permission-based, personalized, email marketing messages to our list of customers who registered on our website, or in our Yoga Studio. The emails will alert customers in a ___ (10)-mile radius to promotions as well as other local events sponsored by our company. This service will be provided by VerticalResponse.com, ExactTarget.com or ConstantContact.com. The email will announce a special promotional event and contain a short sales letter. The message will invite recipients to click on a link to our website to checkout more information about the event, then print out the page and bring it with them to the event. The software offered by these companies will automatically personalize each email with the customer's name. The software also provides detailed click-through behavior reports that will enable us to evaluate the success of each message. The software will also allow us to dramatically scale back its direct mail efforts and associated costs. Our company will send a promotional e-mail about a promotion that the customer indicated was important to them in their preferred membership application. Each identified market segment will get notified of new products, specials and offers based on past buying patterns and what they've clicked on in our previous e-newsletters or indicated on their surveys. The objective is to tap the right customer's need at the right time, with a targeted subject line and targeted content. Our general e-newsletter may appeal to most customers, but targeted mailings that reach out to our various audience segments will build even deeper relationships, and drive higher sales.

Resources:
www.constantcontact.com/pricing/email-marketing.jsp
http://www.verticalresponse.com/blog/10-retail-marketing-ideas-to-boost-sales/

Google Reviews
We will use our email marketing campaign to ask people for reviews. We will ask people what they thought of our yoga studio business or services and encourage them to write a Google Review if they were impressed. We will incorporate a call to action (CTA) on our email auto signature with a link to our Google My Review page.
Source:
https://superb.digital/how-to-ask-your-clients-for-google-reviews/

Resources:
https://support.google.com/business/answer/3474122?hl=en
https://support.google.com/maps/answer/6230175?co=GENIE.Platform
    %3DDesktop&hl=en

www.patientgain.com/how-to-get-positive-google-reviews

Example:
We will tell our customers to:
1.	Go to https://www.google.com/maps
2.	Type in your business name, select the listing
3.	There's a "card" (sidebar) on the left-hand side. At the bottom, they can click 'Be the First to Write a Review' **or** 'Write a Review' if you already have one review.
Source:
https://www.reviewjump.com/blog/how-do-i-get-google-reviews/

Voice Broadcasting

A web-based voice broadcast system will provide a powerful platform to generate thousands of calls to clients and customers or create customizable messages to be delivered to specific individuals. Voice broadcasting and voice mail broadcast will allow our company to instantly send interactive phone calls with ease while managing the entire process right from the Web. We will instantly send alerts, notifications, reminders, GOTV - messages, and interactive surveys with ease right from the Web. The free VoiceShot account will guide us through the process of recording and storing our messages, managing our call lists, scheduling delivery as well as viewing and downloading real-time call and caller key press results. The voice broadcasting interface will guide us through the entire process with a Campaign Checklist as well as tips from the Campaign Expert. Other advanced features include recipient targeting, call monitoring, scheduling, controlling the rate of call delivery and customized text to speech (TTS).
Resource:
http://www.voiceshot.com/public/outboundcalls.asp

Facebook.com

We will use Facebook to move our businesses forward and stay connected to our customers in this fast-paced world. Content will be the key to staying in touch with our customers and keeping them informed. The content will be a rich mix of information, before and after photos, interactive questions, current trends and events, industry facts, education, promotions and specials, humor and fun. We will use the following step system to get customers from Facebook.com:
1.	We will open a free Facebook account at Facebook.com.
2.	We will begin by adding Facebook friends. The fastest way to do this is to allow Facebook to import our email addresses and send an invite out to all our customers.
3.	We will post a video to get our customers involved with our Facebook page. We will post a video called "How to Maximize the Benefits from a Yoga Class." The video will be first uploaded to YouTube.com and then simply be linked to our Facebook page. Video will be a great way to get people active and involved with our Facebook page.
4.	We will send an email to our customers base that encourages them to check out

the new video and to post their feedback about it on our Facebook page. Then we will provide a link driving customers to our Facebook page.

5. We will respond quickly to feedback, engage in the dialogue and add links to our response that direct the author to a structured mini-survey.

6. We will optimize our Facebook profile with our business keyword to make it an invaluable marketing tool and become the "go-to" expert in our industry

7. On a monthly basis, we will send out a message to all Facebook fans with a special offer, as Fan pages are the best way to interact with customers and potential customers on Facebook,

8. We will use Facebook as a tool for sharing success stories and relate the ways in which we have helped our customers.

9. We will use Facebook Connect to integrate our Facebook efforts with our regular website to share our Facebook Page activity. This will also give us statistics about our website visitors, and add social interaction to our site.

Resource: www.youtube.com/watch?v=NfYcXflT7XQ
Facebook Ad Power http://www.fbadpower.com/

Examples:
www.facebook.com/pages/Inhale-Yoga-Studio/34780809389

Resources:
http://www.facebook.com/advertising/
http://www.socialmediaexaminer.com/how-to-set-up-a-facebook-page-for-business/
http://smallbizsurvival.com/2009/11/6-big-facebook-tips-for-small-business.html

Facebook Profiles represent individual users and are held under a person's name. Each profile should only be controlled by that person. Each user has a wall, information tab, likes, interests, photos, videos and each individual can create events.

Facebook Groups are pretty similar to Fan Pages but are usually created for a group of people with a similar interest and they are wanting to keep their discussions private. The members are not usually looking to find out more about a business - they want to discuss a certain topic.

Facebook Fan Pages are the most viral of your three options. When someone becomes a fan of your page or comments on one of your posts, photos or videos, that is spread to all of their personal friends. This can be a great way to get your information out to lots of people...and quickly! In addition, one of the most valuable features of a business page is that you can send "updates" about new products and content to fans and your home building brand becomes more visible.

Facebook Live lets people, public figures and Pages share live video with their followers and friends on Facebook.
Source:
https://live.fb.com/about/
Resource:

http://smartphones.wonderhowto.com/news/facebook-is-going-all-live-video-streaming-your-phone-0170132/

Facebook Business Page
Resources:
https://www.facebook.com/business/learn/set-up-facebook-page
https://www.pcworld.com/article/240258/how_to_make_a_facebook_page_for_your_small_business.html
https://blog.hubspot.com/blog/tabid/6307/bid/5492/how-to-create-a-facebook-business-page-in-5-simple-steps-with-video.aspx

Small Business Promotions
This group allows members to post about their products and services and is a public group designated as a Buy and Sell Facebook group.
Source: https://www.facebook.com/groups/smallbusinesspronotions/
Resource:
https://www.facebook.com/business/a/local-business-promotion-ads
https://www.facebook.com/business/learn/facebook-create-ad-local-awareness
www.socialmediaexaminer.com/how-to-use-facebook-local-awareness-ads-to-target-customers/

Facebook Ad Builder
https://waymark.com/signup/db869ac4-7202-4e3b-93c3-80acc5988df9/?partner=fitsmallbusiness

Facebook Lead Ads   www.facebook.com/business/a/lead-ads
A type of sponsored ad that appears in your audience's timeline just like other Facebook ads. However, the goal with lead ads is literally to capture the lead's info without them leaving Facebook. These ads don't link to a website landing page, creating an additional step.

Best social media marketing practices:
1.   Assign daily responsibility for Facebook to a single person on your staff with an affinity for dialoguing.
2.   Set expectations for how often they should post new content and how quickly they should respond to comments – usually within a couple hours.
3.   Follow and like your followers when they seem to have a genuine interest in your area of health and wellness expertise.
4.   Post on the walls of not only your own Facebook site, but also on your most active, influential posters with the largest networks.
5.   Periodically post a request for your followers to "like" your page.
6.   Monitor Facebook posts to your wall and respond every two hours throughout your business day.

We will use Facebook in the following ways to market our Yoga Studio:
1.   Promote our blog posts on our Facebook page

2. Post a video of our service people in action.
3. Make time-sensitive offers during slow periods
4. Create a special landing page for coupons or promotional giveaways
5. Create a Welcome tab to display a video message from our owner.
   Resource: Pagemodo.
6. Support a local charity by posting a link to their website.
7. Thank our customers while promoting their businesses at the same time.
8. Describe milestone accomplishments and thank customers for their role.
9. Give thanks to corporate accounts.
10. Ask customers to contribute stories about _____ occurrences.
11. Use the built-in Facebook polling application to solicit feedback.
12. Use the Facebook reviews page to feature positive comments from customers, and to respond to negative reviews.
13. Introduce customers to our staff with resume and video profiles.
14. Create a photo gallery of unusual ____ (requests/jobs?) to showcase our expertise.

We will also explore location-based platforms like the following:
- FourSquare   - GoWalla
- Facebook Places   - Google Latitude

As a yoga studio serving a local community, we will appreciate the potential for hyper-local platforms like these. Location-based applications are increasingly attracting young, urban influencers with disposable income, which is precisely the audience we are trying to attract. People connect to geo-location apps primarily to "get informed" about local happenings.

Foursquare.com
A web and mobile application that allows registered users to post their location at a venue ("check-in") and connect with friends. Check-in requires active user selection and points are awarded at check-in. Users can choose to have their check-ins posted on their accounts on Twitter, Facebook, or both. In version 1.3 of their iPhone application, foursquare enabled push-notification of friend updates, which they call "Pings". Users can also earn badges by checking in at locations with certain tags, for check-in frequency, or for other patterns such as time of check-in.]
Resource:
https://foursquare.com/business/
Examples:
https://foursquare.com/v/east-gore-liquor-store/4e90dd9677c89cb921eb3b88

Instagram
Instagram.com is an online photo-sharing, video-sharing and social networking service that enables its users to take pictures and videos, apply digital filters to them, and share them on a variety of social networking services, such as
Facebook, Twitter, Tumblr and Flickr. A distinctive feature is that it confines photos to a square shape, similar to Kodak Instamatic and Polaroid images, in contrast to the

16:9 aspect ratio now typically used by mobile device cameras. Users are also able to record and share short videos lasting for up to 15 seconds.

Resources:
http://www.wordstream.com/blog/ws/2015/01/06/instagram-marketing

We will use Instagram in the following ways to help amplify the story of our brand, get people to engage with our content when not at our store, and get people to visit our store or site:
1. Let our customers and fans know about specific product availability.
2. Tie into trends, events or holidays to drive awareness.
3. Let people know we are open and our ambiance is spectacular.
4. Run a monthly contest and pick the winning hash-tagged photograph to activate our customer base and increase our exposure.
5. Encourage the posting and collection of happy onsite or offsite customer photos.

Examples:
https://www.instagram.com/yogatreestudios/?hl=en
https://www.instagram.com/indabayoga/

Note: Commonly found in tweets, a hashtag is a word or connected phrase (no spaces) that begins with a hash symbol (#). They're so popular that other social media platforms including Facebook, Instagram and Google+ now support them. Using a hashtag turns a word or phrase into a clickable link that displays a feed (list) of other posts with that same hashtag. For example, if you click on #_____ in a tweet, or enter #_____ in the search box, you'll see a list of tweets all about _____.

MySpace Advertising

MySpace.com offers a self-service, graphical "display" advertising platform that will enable our company to target our marketing message to our audience by demographic characteristics. With the new MySpace service, we will be able to upload our own ads or make them quickly with an online tool, and set a budget of $25 to $10,000 for the campaigns. We can choose to target a specific gender, age group and geographic area. We will then pay MySpace each time someone clicks on our ad. Ads can link to other MySpace pages, or external websites. MyAds will let us target our ads to specific groups of people using the public data on MySpace users' profiles, blogs and comments. MySpace will enable our company to target potential customers with similar interests to our existing customer base, as revealed via our marketing research surveys. Also, the bulletin function on MySpace will allow us to update customers on our Yoga Studio milestone achievements and coming events. We will also post a short video to our home page and encourage the sharing of the video with other MySpace users.
Ex: www.myspace.com/yogaempowered/photos/
              19220943#%7B%22ImageId%22%3A19220943%7D

LinkedIn.com

Linkedin provides options that will allow our detailed profile to be indexed by search engines, like Google. We will make use of these options so our Yoga Studio business will achieve greater visibility on the Web. We will use <u>widgets</u> to integrate other tools, such as importing our blog entries or Twitter stream into our profile, and go market research and gain knowledge with Polls. We will answer questions in <u>Questions and Answers</u> to show our dance expertise, and ask questions in Questions and Answers to get a feel for what customers and prospects want or think. We will publish our LinkedIn URL on all our marketing collateral, including business cards, email signature, newsletters, and web site. We will grow our network by joining Yogaindustry and alumni groups related to our business. We will update our status examples of recent work, and link our status updates with our other social media accounts. We will start and manage a group or fan page for our product, brand or business. We will share useful articles that will be of interest to customers, and request LinkedIn recommendations from customers willing to provide testimonials. We will post our presentations on our profile using a presentation application. We will ask our first-level contacts for introductions to their contacts and interact with LinkedIn on a regular basis to reach those who may not see us on other social media sites. We will link to articles posted elsewhere, with a summary of why it's valuable to add to our credibility and list our newsletter subscription information and archives. We will post discounts and package deals. We will buy a LinkedIn <u>direct ad</u> that our target market will see. We will find vendors and contractors through <u>connections.</u>
Examples:
http://www.linkedin.com/company/solace-yoga-studio

Twitter

We will use 'Twitter.com' as a way to produce new business from existing clients and generate prospective clients online. Twitter is a free social networking and micro-blogging service that allows its users to send and read other users' updates (otherwise known as tweets), which are text-based posts of up to 140 characters in length. Updates are displayed on the user's profile page and delivered to other users who have signed up to receive them. The sender can restrict delivery to those in his or her circle of friends, with delivery to everyone being the default. Users can receive updates via the Twitter website, SMS text messaging, RSS feeds, or email. We will use our Twitter account to respond directly to questions, distribute news, solve problems, post updates, and offer special discounts on our Yoga Studio products and services.
We will provide the following instructions to register as a 'Follower' of _____ (company name) on Twitter:

1.   In your Twitter account, click on 'Find People' in the top right navigation bar, which will redirect to a new page.
2.   Click on 'Find on Twitter' which will open a search box that says 'Who are you looking for?'
3.   Type '_____ (company name) / _____ (owner name)' and click 'search'. This will bring up the results page.
4.   Click the blue '_____' name to read the bio or select the 'Follow' button.
Example:
http://twitter.com/#!/karmayogastudio

Podcasting

Our podcasts will provide both information and advertising. Our podcasts will allow us to pull in a lot of customers. Our monthly podcasts will be heard by ___ (#) eventual subscribers. Podcasts can now be downloaded for mobile devices, such as an iPod. Podcasts will give our company a new way to provide information and an additional way to advertise. Podcasting will give our business another connection point with customers. We will use this medium to communicate on important issues, what is going on with a planned event, and other things of interest to our health-conscious customers. The programs will last about 10 minutes and can be downloaded for free on iTunes. The purpose is not to be a mass medium. It is directed at a niche market with an above-average educational background and very special interests. It will provide a very direct and a reasonably inexpensive way of reaching our targeted audience with relevant information about our organic ice cream products and services.

Resources:

iTunes (http://www.apple.com/itunes/)

www.apple.com/itunes/download/.

www.cbc.ca/podcasting/gettingstarted.html

www.bizjournals.com/southflorida/blog/2014/11/south-florida-entrepreneurs-how-
    podcasting-helped.html

http://www.smarttimeonline.com/category/podcast/

Example

Yogapeeps (at http://yogapeeps.com/)

http://itunes.apple.com/us/podcast/yoga-classes-live-love-teach/id195484050

Press Release Overview:

We will use market research surveys to determine the media outlets that our demographic customers read and then target them with press releases. We will draft a cover letter for our media kit that explains that we would like to have the newspaper print a story about the start-up of our new local business or a milestone that we have accomplished. And, because news releases may be delivered by feeds or on news services and various websites, we will create links from our news releases to content on our website. These links which will point to more information or a special offer, will drive our clients into the sales process. They will also increase search engine ranking on our site. We will follow-up each faxed package to the media outlet with a phone call to the lifestyle section editor.

Media Kit

We will compile a media kit with the following items:

1.   A pitch letter introducing our Yoga Studio business.
2.   A press release with news story facts about our impact on real people diets.
3.   Biographical fact sheet or sketches of key personnel.
4.   Listing of product and service features and benefits to customers.
5.   Photos of satisfied customers.
6.   Endorsements and Testimonials.

Public Relations

The following represents a partial list of some of the reasons we will issue a free press release on a regular basis:

1. Announce Grand Opening Event and the availability of services.
2. Planned Open House Event
3. Addition of new products or service line.
4. Support for a Non-profit Cause or other local event.
5. Presentation of a free seminar or workshop on Yoga health benefits.
6. Report Survey Results
7. Publication of an article on Yoga trends.
8. Addition of a new staff member.
9. Notable Successes/Case Studies
10. Other Milestone Accomplishments such as an anniversary celebration.
11. Special occasion package introductions, such as wedding first Yoga sessions.
12. Additional training/certifications/licensing received.

Examples:
http://www.zenzenyogaarts.com/press-releases/

We will use the following techniques to get our press releases into print:

1. Find the right contact editor at a publication, that is, the editor who specializes in health, beauty and wellness issues.
2. Understand the target publication's format, flavor and style and learn to think like its readers to better tailor our pitch.
3. Ask up front if the journalist is on deadline.
4. Request a copy of the editorial calendar--a listing of targeted articles or subjects broken down by month or issue date, to determine the issue best suited for the content of our news release or article.
5. Make certain the press release appeals to a large audience by reading a couple of back issues of the publication we are targeting to familiarize ourselves with its various sections and departments.
6. Customize the PR story to meet the magazine's particular style.
7. Avoid creating releases that look like advertising or self-promotion.
8. Make certain the release contains all the pertinent and accurate information the journalist will need to write the article and accurately answer the questions "who, what, when, why and where".
9. Include a contact name and telephone number for the reporter to call for more information.

PR Distribution Checklist

We will send copies of our press releases to the following entities:

1. Send it to clients to show accomplishments.
2. Send to prospects to help prospects better know who you are and what you do.
3. Send it to vendors to strengthen the relationship and to influence referrals.
4. Send it to strategic partners to strengthen and enhance the commitment and support to our firm.

5.	Send it to employees to keep them in the loop.
6.	Send it to Employees' contacts to increase the firm's visibility exponentially.
7.	Send it to elected officials who often provide direction for their constituents.
8.	Send it to trade associations for maximum exposure.
9.	Put copies in the lobby and waiting areas.
10.	Put it on our Web site, to enable visitors to find out who we are and what our firm is doing, with the appropriate links to more detailed information.
11.	Register the Web page with search engines to increase search engine optimization.
12.	Put it in our press kit to provide members of the media background information about our firm.
13.	Include it in our newsletter to enable easy access to details about company activities.
14.	Include it in our brochure to provide information that compels the reader to contact our firm when in need of legal counsel.
15.	Hand-it out at trade shows and job fairs to share news with attendees and establish credibility.

Media List

Journalist	Interests	Organization	Contact Info

Distribution:	www.1888PressRelease.com	www.ecomwire.com	
	www.prweb.com	www.WiredPRnews.com	
	www.PR.com	www.eReleases.com	
	www.24-7PressRelease.com	www.NewsWireToday.com	
	www.PRnewswire.com	www.onlinePRnews.com	
	www.PRLog.org		
	www.businesswire.com	www.marketwire.com	
	www.primezone.com	www.primewswire.com	
	www.xpresspress.com/	www.ereleases.com/index.html	
	www.Mediapost.com		
Journalist Lists:	www.mastheads.org	www.easymedialist.com	
	www.helpareporter.com		

Media Directories

Bacon's – www.bacons.com/		AScribe – www.ascribe.org/
Newspapers – www.newspapers.com/		Gebbie Press – www.gebbieinc.com/

Support Services

PR Web -		http://www.prweb.com
Yahoo News –		http://news.yahoo.com/
Google News –		http://news.google.com/

Resource:

**HARO ("Help A Reporter Out")		www.helpareporter.com/**
An online platform that provides journalists with a robust database of sources for upcoming stories. It also provides business owners and marketers with opportunities to serve as sources and secure valuable media coverage.

School Booster Program

We can boost the local studio's fundraising efforts by offering community members one month of Yoga or fitness sessions. The community will recognize the studio as a force for promoting health and wellness, while the studio can easily raise funds for after-school programs. Participants can offer these special coupons for one month of classes for $____ each to family, friends and anyone else in the community who wants to get fit, while learning new Yoga movement skills. The studio then gets to keep 50% of all the sales revenues collected for studio related activities.

Postcards

1. We will use personalized postcards to stay-in-touch with prior customers.
2. Postcards offer cheaper mailing rates, staying power and attention grabbing graphics, but require repetition, like most other advertising methods.
3. We will develop an in-house list of potential clients for routine communications from open house events, seminar registrations, direct response ads, etc.
4. We will use postcards to encourage users to visit our website, take advantage of a special offer or attend a demonstration event.
5. We will grab attention and communicate a single-focus message in just a few words.
6. The visual elements of our postcard (color, picture, symbol) will be strong to help get attention and be directly supportive of the message.
7. We will facilitate a call to immediate action by prominently displaying our phone number and website address.
8. We will include a clear deadline, expiration date, limited quantity, or consequence of inaction that is connected to the offer to communicate immediacy and increase response.

Resources:
www.Postcardmania.com
www.vistaprint.com/gallery/IAMAFwIBAAAAAAA=/postcards/yoga-pilates.aspx?GP=4%2f14%2f2016+4%3a22%3a16+PM&GPS=3909946042&GNF=1
www.psprint.com/resources/yoga-studios-marketing-copywriting/
www.psprint.com/resources/yoga-studio-marketing-ideas-and-resources/

Flyers

We will post flyers to the bulletin boards in studios, medical practices, college campuses, barber shops, spas and beauty salons, churches, laundromats, and coffee bars. We will also spend time outside a neighborhood grocery store passing out flyers as shoppers come out of the store.

1. We will also seek permission to post flyers on the bulletin boards in local businesses, community centers, hotels, tourism offices, cafés, health food stores and college centers.
2. We will also insert flyers into our direct mailings.
3. We will use our flyers as part of a handout package at open house events.
4. The flyers will feature discount coupons and customer testimonials.

Resources:
www.classifiedflyerads.com/
www.metropilates.com/samples.htm
http://georgewatts.org/2012/05/03/how-to-design-a-yoga-flyer/
http://www.zazzle.com/yoga+flyers

Referral Program

We understand the importance of setting up a formal referral program with the following characteristics:

1. Give a premium reward based simply on people giving referral names.
2. Send an endorsed testimonial letter from a loyal customer to the referred prospect.
3. Include a separate referral form as a direct response device.
4. Provide a space on the response form for leaving positive comments that can be used to build a testimonial letter, that will be sent to each referral.
5. We will clearly state our incentive rewards, and terms and conditions.
6. We will distribute a newsletter to stay in touch with our clients and include articles about our referral program success stories.

Examples:
http://inspirityogastudio.com/inspirit-yoga-referral-program/

Sources:

1. Referrals from other retailers, particularly those of other niche specialties.
2. Give speeches on a complicated niche area that other practitioners may feel is too narrow for them to handle, thus triggering referrals.
3. Structured Client Referral Program.
4. Newsletter Coupons.

Methods:

1. Always have ready a 30-second elevator speech that describes what you do and who you do it for.
2. Use a newsletter to keep our name in front of referrals sources.
3. Repeatedly demonstrate to referral sources that we are also thinking about their practice or business.
4. Regularly send referrals sources articles on unique yet important topics that might affect their businesses.
5. Use Microsoft Outlook to flag our contacts to remind us it is time to give them some form of personal attention.
6. Ask referral sources for referrals.
7. Get more work from a referral source by sending them work.
8. Immediately thank a referral source, even for the mere act of giving his name to a third party for consideration.
9. Remember referral sources with generous gift baskets and gift certificates.
10. Schedule regular lunches with former school classmates and new contacts.

Resources:

http://brightsmack.com/marketing-strategies/37-referral-ideas-to-grow-your-business/
http://www.nisacards.com/Business-Referral-Marketing-Cards.aspx
https://www.referralsaasquatch.com/resources/
https://www.referralcandy.com/blog/47-referral-programs/
www.consultingsuccess.com/10-referral-strategies-to-grow-your-consulting-business

Resources:

Referral Program Software Packages
      www.invitebox.com
      www.referralsaasquatch.com/
      www.referralcandy.com/
      www.getambassador.com/

Statistics that support referral programs include:

92% of consumers trust peer recommendations, 40% trust advertising in search results, 36% trust online video ads, 36% trust sponsored ads on social networking sites and 33% trust online banner ads.

The average value of a referred customer is at least 16% higher than that of a non-referred customer with similar demographics and time of acquisition.

We will offer an additional donation of $ _____ to any organization whose member use a referral coupon to become a client. The coupon will be paid for and printed in the organization's newsletter.

Referral Tracking Form

Referral Source Name	Presently Referring Yes/No	No. of Clients Referred	Anticipated Revenue	Actions to be Taken	Target Date

Sample Referral Program

We want to show our appreciation to established customers and business network partners for their kind referrals to our business. _____ (company name) wants to reward our valued and loyal customers who support our _____ Programs by implementing a new referral program. Ask any of our team members for referral cards to share with your family and friends to begin saving towards your next _____ (product/service) purchase. We will credit your account $___ (?) for each new customer you refer to us as well as give them 10% off their first visit. When they come for their first visit, they should present the card upon arrival. We will automatically set you up a referral account.

Example:

We offer a referral program that encourages our students to invite their friends, family and associates to join them at Ray of Light. In return, our students get the best pricing possible for yoga classes. For every new student that you refer who purchases a class pack or membership option*, you will receive $10 worth of Yoga Bucks to be used towards your next class package or monthly membership. If you are on a monthly auto-debited membership, your Yoga Bucks will be applied to the next month's payment. There is no limit to how many students you may refer nor how many Yoga Bucks you can rack up! Ten new students equals $100 credit towards your next class package. Source: http://www.rayoflightyoga.net/yoga-bucks-referral-program.html

The Referral Details are as Follows:
1.   You will receive a $__ (?) credit for every customer that you refer for _____ (products/services). Credit will be applied to your referral account on their initial visit.
2.   We will keep track of your accumulated reward dollars and at any time we can let you know the amount you have available for use in your reward account.
3.   Each time you visit ____ (company name), you can use your referral dollars to pay up to 50% of your total charge that day
4.   Referral dollars are not applicable towards the purchase of _____ products.
5.   All referral rewards are for __products and cannot be used towards ___ services.

Referral Coupon Template
Company Name: _____
Address: _____
Phone: _____ Website: _____
Print and present this coupon with your first order and the existing customer who referred you will receive a credit for $_____ .

Current customer	**Referred customer**
Name: _____	Name: _____
Address: _____	Address: _____
Phone: _____	Phone: _____
Email: _____	Email: _____
Date referred:	

Office use only
Credit memo number:_____
Credit issued date: _____   Credit applied by: _____

Invite-A-Friend
We will setup an aggressive invite-a-friend referral program. We will encourage new members or newsletter subscribers, during their initial registration process, to upload and send an invitation to multiple contacts in their email address books. We will encourage them by providing an added incentive, such as a free _____ .

Circular Inserts
The Company plans to advertise through circulars which will be inserted in newspapers or mailed directly to consumers' residences.

Bandit Signs

We plan to use sign holders or bandit signs placed strategically along key roads close to our business to promote special events.

Portable Sales Tents
We will set-up temporary sales tents and tables at local festivals and fairs to handout our business cards and sales brochures.

Guest Instructor @ Local Yoga Club
We will offer to provide free introductory Yoga sessions to the local sports teams. This will give us the opportunity to meet potential new participants, demonstrate our expertise, improve the visibility of our Yoga Studio and collect email addresses for our newsletter. We will readily handout of business card to all lesson attendees.

Online Directory Listings
The following directory listings use proprietary technology to match customers with industry professionals in their geographical area. The local search capabilities for specific niche markets offer an invaluable tool for the customer. These directories help member businesses connect with purchase-ready buyers, convert leads to sales, and maximize the value of customer relationships. Their online and offline communities provide a quick and easy low or no-cost solution for customers to find a Yoga specialist quickly. We intend to sign-up with all no cost directories and evaluate the ones that charge a fee.

1. Yoga City   www.yogacitynyc.com/yogacity_directory.php
2. Gym Ticket   www.gymticket.com/
3. Yoga Finder   www.yogafinder.com
4. Yoga Alliance   www.yogaalliance.org

Other General Directories Include:

Listings.local.yahoo.com	Switchboard Super Pages
YellowPages.com	MerchantCircle.com
Bing.com/businessportal	Local.com
Yelp.com	BrownBook.com
InfoUSA.com	iBegin.com
Localeze.com	Bestoftheweb.com
YellowBot.com	HotFrog.com
InsiderPages.com	MatchPoint.com
CitySearch.com	YellowUSA.com
Profiles.google.com/me	Manta.com
Jigsaw.com	LinkedIn.com
Whitepages.com	PowerProfiles.com
Judysbook.com	Company.com
Google.com	Bing.com
Yahoo.com	

Get Listed   http://getlisted.org/enhanced-business-listings.aspx
Universal Business Listing   https://www.ubl.org/index.aspx
                www.UniversalBusinessListing.org

Universal Business Listing (UBL) is a local search industry service dedicated to acting as a central collection and distribution point for business information online. UBL provides business owners and their marketing representatives with a one-stop location for broad distribution of complete, accurate, and detailed listing information.

Customer Reward / Loyalty Program

As a means of building business by word-of-mouth, customers will be encouraged and rewarded as repeat customers. This will be accomplished by offering a discount coupon to those participants who sign-up for our frequent buyer card and purchase $____ of Yoga products and services within a ____ (#) month period.
Example:
http://www.yogaconnection.org/rewards-program.html

Resources:
http://www.refinery29.com/best-store-loyalty-programs
https://thrivehive.com/customer-retention-and-loyalty-programs/
http://blog.fivestars.com/5-companies-loyalty-programs/
www.americanexpress.com/us/small-business/openforum/articles/10-cool-mobile-apps-
      that-increase-customer-loyalty/
https://squareup.com/loyalty
www.consumerreports.org/cro/news/2013/10/retailer-loyalty-rewards-
      programs/index.htm

Frequent Buyer Program Types:

1.	Punch Cards	Receive something for free after? Purchases.
2.	Dollar-for-point Systems	Accrue points toward a free product.
3.	Percentage of Purchase	Accrue points toward future purchases.

Sample: Loyalty Program
_____ (company name) LOYALTY PROGRAM
ACCRUE YOUR POINTS WITH THE FOLLOWING:
    Sign-up Bonus receive 1,000 points
    Pre-book your next visit receive 1,000 points
    Refer a Friend receive 2,500 points
    Retail Purchase receive 1 point/dollar spent
    Service Purchase receive 1 point/dollar spent
REDEEMING POINT VALUE 100 POINTS = $1
Ex: For a $100 purchase, you will redeem 10,000 points

Direct Mail Campaign

A direct mail package consisting of a tri-fold brochure, letter of introduction, and reply card will be sent to a list of new businesses in _____ County. This list can be obtained from International Business Lists, Inc. (Chicago, IL) and is compiled from Secretary of

State incorporation registrations, business license applications, announcements from newspaper clippings, and tax records. The letter will introduce _____ (company name), and describe our employee get-fit and stress reduction programs. The package will also include a promotional offer—the opportunity to sample our Yoga health benefits for free. Approximately ten days after the mailing, a telephone follow-up will be conducted to make sure the brochure was received, whether the prospect has any questions, or would like to schedule an appointment.

We will send out sales letters to local spas, massage therapists, physiotherapy clinics, chiropractors, and family doctors introducing our studio and the type of yoga we teach. It will be a letter of introduction from a service provider who is relevant to the above referenced professionals. The hope is that they will keep this letter for future reference, when the service is needed or is an appropriate referral.

Our direct mail program will feature the following key components:
1. A call to action.
2. Test marketing using a limited 100-piece mailing.
3. A defined set of target markets.
4. A follow up phone call.
5. A special offer, such as an employee physical condition assessment.
6. A personalized cover letter.
7. A free trial offer with an expiration date.

Blogging
We will use our blog to keep customers and prospects informed about products, events and services that relate to our Yoga Studio business, new releases, contests, and specials. Our blog will show readers that we are a good source of expert Yoga and health and wellness information that they can count on. With our blog, we can quickly update our customers anytime our company releases a new product, the holding of a contest or are placing items on special pricing. We will use our blog to share customer testimonials, success stories and meaningful product usage stories. Our visitors will be able to subscribe to our RSS feeds and be instantly updated without any spam filters interfering. We will also use the blog to solicit product usage recommendations and future Yoga program addition suggestions. Additionally, blogs are free and allow for constant ease of updating.

We will also write comments on the yoga blogs of other local yoga teachers as well as yoga blogs in general. We will look for yoga blogs that have "do follow" links so when we place a link we get a link to our website. We will determine if a website has "do follow" comment links by using the Firefox web browser and installing the NoDoFollow add on for Firefox. We will make certain to write great comments and contribute to the dialogue.

Our blog will give our company the following benefits:
1. A cost-effective marketing tool.
2. An expanded network.
3. A promotional platform for new _____ services.

4.	An introduction to people with similar interests.
5.	Builds credibility and expertise recognition.

We will use our blog for the following purposes:
1.	To share customer testimonials, experiences and meaningful success stories.
2.	Update our clients anytime our company releases a new service.
3.	Supply advice on _____ options.
4.	Discuss research findings.
5.	To publish helpful content.
6,	To welcome feedback in multiple formats.
7.	Link together other social networking sites, including Twitter.
8.	To improve Google rankings.
9.	Make use of automatic RSS feeds.

We will adhere to the following blog writing guidelines:
1.	We will blog at least 2 or 3 times per week to maintain interest.
2.	We will integrate our blog into the design of our website.
3.	We will use our blog to convey useful information and not our advertisements.
4.	We will make the content easy to understand.
5.	We will focus our content on the needs of our targeted audience.

Our blog will feature the following on a regular basis:
1.	Useful articles and assessment coupons.
2.	Give away of a helpful free report in exchange for email addresses
3.	Helpful information for our professional referral sources, as well as clients, and online and offline community members.
5.	Use of a few social media outposts to educate, inform, engage and drive people back to our blog for more information and our free report.

To get visitors to our blog to take the next action step and contact our firm we will do the following:
1.	Put a contact form on the upper-left hand corner of our blog, right below the header.
2.	Put our complete contact information in the header itself.
3.	Add a page to our blog and title it, "Become My participant.", giving the reader somewhere to go for the next sign-up steps.
4.	At the end of each blog post, we will clearly tell the reader what to do next; such as subscribe to our RSS feed, or to sign up for our newsletter mailing list.
Resources:	www.blogger.com	www.blogspot.com	www.wordpress.org
http://www.bloggersideas.com/tips-for-small-business-blogging-success/
http://www.blogwritersbootcamp.com/

Example:
www.openmindbody.com

Testimonial Marketing

We will either always ask for testimonials immediately after a completed project or contact our clients once a quarter for them. We will also have something prepared that we would like the client to say that is specific to a service we offer, or anything relevant to advertising claims that we have put together. For the convenience of the client we will assemble a testimonial letter that they can either modify or just sign off on. Additionally, testimonials can also be in the form of audio or video and put on our website or mailed to potential clients in the form of a DVD or Audio CD. A picture with a testimonial is also excellent. We will put testimonials directly on a magazine ad, slick sheet, brochure, or website, or assemble a complete page of testimonials for our sales presentation folder.

Examples:
http://www.pranayogamiami.com/yogi-testimonials/
http://hotyogacville.com/testimonials/
http://inspirityogastudio.com/testimonials/

We will collect customer testimonials in the following ways:
1.   Our website – A page dedicated to testimonials (written and/or video).
2.   Social media accounts – Facebook fan pages offer a review tab, which makes it easy to receive and display customer testimonials.
3.   Google+ also offers a similar feature with Google+ Local.
4.   Local search directories – Ask customers to post more reviews on Yelp and Yahoo Local.
5.   Customer Satisfaction Survey Forms

We will pose the following questions to our customers to help them frame their testimonials:
1.   What was the obstacle that would have prevented you from buying this product?
2.   "What was your main concern about buying this product?"
3.   What did you find as a result of buying this product?
4.   What specific feature did you like most about this product?
5.   What would be three other benefits about this product?
6.   Would you recommend this product? If so, why?
7.   Is there anything you'd like to add?

Business Logo

Our logo will graphically represent who we are and what we do, and it will serve to help brand our image. It will also convey a sense of uniqueness and professionalism. The logo will represent our company image and the message we are trying to convey. Our business logo will reflect the philosophy and objectives of our Yoga Studio business. We will develop a logo and an image that are consistent throughout our promotional materials to begin to build recognition throughout our local community. Our logo will incorporate the following design guidelines:
1.   It will relate to our industry, our name, a defining characteristic of our company

or a competitive advantage we offer.
2. It will be a simple logo that can be recognized faster.
3. It will contain strong lines and letters which show up better than thin ones.
4. It will feature something unexpected or unique without being overdrawn.
5. It will work well in black and white (one-color printing).
6. It will be scalable and look pleasing in both small and large sizes.
7. It will be artistically balanced and make effective use of color, line density and shape.
8. It will be unique when compared to competitors.
9. It will use original, professionally rendered artwork.
10. It can be replicated across any media mix without losing quality.
11. It appeals to our target audience.
12. It will be easily recognizable from a distance if utilized in outdoor advertising.

Resources: www.freelogoservices.com/   www.hatchwise.com
              www.logosnap.com   www.99designs.com
              www.fiverr.com   www.freelancer.com

Logo Design Guide:
www.bestfreewebresources.com/logo-design-professional-guide
www.creativebloq.com/graphic-design/pro-guide-logo-design-21221

Resource:
www.shutterstock.com/pic-405193312/stock-vector-logo-for-the-yoga-studio-fitness-
        flower-symbol-logo-design-template-yoga-vector-logotype.html
www.designhill.com/design-blog/top-10-yoga-logos-that-never-fail-to-inspire/

Fundraisers

Community outreach programs involving charitable fundraising and showing a strong interest in the local studio system will serve to elevate our status in the community as a "good corporate citizen" while simultaneously increasing Yoga Studio interest. We will execute a successful fundraising program for our Yoga Studio and build goodwill in the community, by adhering to the following guidelines:
1. Keep It Local
    When looking for a worthy cause, we will make sure it is local so the whole neighborhood will support it.
2. Plan It
    We will make sure that we are organized and outline everything we want to accomplish before planning the fundraiser.
3. Contact Local Media
    We will contact the suburban newspapers to do stories on the event and send out press releases to the local TV and radio stations.
4. Contact Area Businesses
    We will contact other businesses and have them put up posters in their stores and pass out flyers to promote the event.

5. Get Recipient Support
We will make sure the recipients of the fundraiser are really willing to participate and get out in the neighborhood to invite everyone into our store for the event, plus help pass out flyers and getting other businesses to put up the posters.

6. Give Out Bounce Backs
We will give a "bounce-back" coupon that allows for both a discount and an additional donation in exchange for customer next purchase. (It will have an expiration date of two weeks to give a sense of urgency.)

7. Be Ready with plenty of product and labor on hand for the event.

Fundraiser Action Plan Checklist:
1. Choose a good local cause for your fundraiser.
2. Calculate donations as a percentage for normal sales.
3. Require the group to promote and support the event.
4. Contact local media to get exposure before and after the event.
5. Ask area businesses to put up flyers and donate printing of materials.
6. Use a bounce-back coupon to get new customers back.
7. Be prepared with sufficient labor and product.

Resources:
http://www.yogajournal.com/uncategorized/passionate-cause-hold-yoga-fundraiser/
http://www.yogaactivist.org/for-teachers/fundraising-for-individuals/
http://www.examiner.com/article/giving-back-how-to-plan-a-yoga-fundraiser-1

Billboards

We will use billboard advertising to create brand awareness and strong name recognition. We will design Billboards that are eye-catching and informative. We will include our business name, location, a graphic, and no more than eight words. In designing the billboard, we will consider the fact that the eye typically moves from the upper left corner to the lower right corner of a billboard. We will use colors and pictures to contrast with the sky and other surroundings. We will keep the layout uncluttered and the message simple, and include a direct call to action. Depending on the billboards size and location, the cost will range from $1,000 to $5,000 per month. We will try to negotiate a discount on a long-term contract.

Example: Yoga Your Way to a Healthier Lifestyle!
Resources:
Outdoor Advertising Association of America   www.oaaa.org
EMC Outdoor, Inc.   www.emcoutdoor.com

Theater Advertising

Theater advertising is the method of promoting our business through in-theatre promotions. The objective of theater advertising is to expose the movie patron to our advertising message in various ways throughout the theater. Benefits include; an engaged audience that can't change the channel, an audience that is in a quiet environment, an audience that is in a good mood and receptive, advertising that is targeted to our local

geographic area, full color video advertising on a 40 foot screen, and a moving and interactive ad with music and voiceover.
Resources:
Velocity Cinema Advertising   www.movieadvertising.com/index.html
NCM   www.nationalcinemedia.com/intheatreadvertising/

Mobile Marketing

In a texting component, customers will be able to text "_____" to _____ (#) and receive mobile coupons. The second part of the message asks customers if they would like to register their e-mail addresses to receive weekly communications from _____ (company name). The first mobile coupon will reward customers with $___ off any combination dace products and sessions. Customers will continue to receive additional offers, including special offers on holiday and recital gift items. This will purely an opt in campaign, and will let us create an ongoing conversation with our customers.
Resources:
Mobile Marketing Association   www.mmaglobal.com
BxP Marketing visit   www.bxpmarketing.com.

Google Maps

We will first make certain that our business is listed in Google Maps. We will do a search for our business in Google Maps. If we don't see our business listed, then we will add our business to Google Maps. Even if our business is listed in Google Maps, we will create a Local Business Center account and take control of our listing, by adding more relevant information. Consumers generally go to Google Maps for two reasons: Driving Directions and to Find a Business.
Resource:
http://maps.google.com/

Bing Maps   www.bingplaces.com/
This will make it easy for customers to find our business.

Apple Maps

A web mapping service developed by Apple Inc. It is the default map system of iOS, macOS, and watchOS. It provides directions and estimated times of arrival for automobile, pedestrian, and public transportation navigation.
Resources:
ttps://mapsconnect.apple.com
 http://www.stallcupgroup.com/2012/09/19/three-ways-to-make-your-pawn-business-
      more-profitable-and-sellable/
http://www.apple.com/ios/maps/
https://en.wikipedia.org/wiki/Apple_Maps

Google Places

Google Places helps people make more informed decisions about where to go for a Yoga Studio. Place Pages connect people to information from the best sources across the web, displaying photos, reviews and essential facts, as well as real-time updates and offers from business owners. We will make sure that our Google Places listing is up to date to increase our online visibility. Google Places is linked to our Google Maps listing, and will help to get on the first page of Google search page results when people search for a Yoga Studio in our area.

Resource: www.google/com/places

Yelp.com

We will use Yelp.com to help people find our Yoga Studio. Visitors to Yelp write local reviews, over 85% of them rating a business 3 stars or higher In addition to reviews, visitors can use Yelp to find events, special offers, lists and to talk with other Yelpers. As business owners, we will setup a free account to post offers, photos and message our customers. We will also buy ads on Yelp, which will be clearly labeled "Sponsored Results". We will also use the Weekly Yelp, which is available in 42 city editions to bring news about the latest business openings and other happenings.

Example:

www.yelp.com/biz/yoga-to-the-people-new-york

Manta.com

Manta is the largest free source of information on small companies, with profiles of more than 64 million businesses and organizations. Business owners and sales professionals use Manta's vast database and custom search capabilities to quickly find companies, easily connect with prospective customers and promote their own services. Manta.com, founded in 2005, is based in Columbus, Ohio.

Example:

www.manta.com/c/mmszslb/namaste-yoga-studio

Pay-Per-Click Advertising

Google AdWords, Yahoo! Search Marketing, and Microsoft adCenter are the three largest network operators, and all three operate under a bid-based model. Cost per click (CPC) varies depending on the search engine and the level of competition for a particular keyword. Google AdWords are small text ads that appear next to the search results on Google. In addition, these ads appear on many partner web sites, including NYTimes.com (The New York Times), Business.com, Weather.com, About.com, and many more. Google's text advertisements are short, consisting of one title line and two content text lines. Image ads can be one of several different Interactive Advertising Bureau (IAB) standard sizes.

Through Google AdWords, we plan to buy placements (ads) for specific search terms through this "Pay-Per-Click" advertising program. This PPC advertising campaign will allow our ad to appear when someone searches for a keyword related to our business, organization, or subject matter. More importantly, we will only pay when a potential customer clicks on our ad to visit our website. For instance, since we operate an Yoga

Studio in ____ (city), _____ (state), we will target people using search terms such as "Yoga Studio, Yoga Studio, or Yoga Classes or Stress Relaxation in _____ (city), _____ (state)". With an effective PPC campaign our ads will only be displayed when a user searches for one of these keywords. In short, PPC advertising will be the most cost-effective and measurable form of advertising for our Yoga Studio.
Resources:
http://adwords.google.com/support/aw/?hl=en
www.wordtracker.com

Yahoo Local Listings
We will create our own local listing on Yahoo. To create our free listing, we will use our web browser and navigate to http://local.yahoo.com. We will first register for free with Yahoo, and create a member ID and password to list our business. Once we have accessed http://local.yahoo.com, we will scroll down to the bottom and click on "Add/Edit a Business" to get onto the Yahoo Search Marketing Local Listings page. In the lower right of the screen we will see "Local Basic Listings FREE". We will click on the Get Started button and log in again with our new Yahoo ID and password. The form for our local business listing will now be displayed. When filling it out, we will be sure to include our full web address (http://www.companyname.com). We will include a description of our Yoga Studio products and services in the description section, but avoid hype or blatant advertising, to get the listing to pass Yahoo's editorial review. We will also be sure to select the appropriate business category and sub categories.
Examples:
https://local.yahoo.com/info-61370941

Affiliate Marketing
We will create an affiliate marketing program to broaden our reach. We will first devise a commission structure, so affiliates have a reason to promote our Yoga Studio. We will give them ____ (10) % of whatever sales they generate. We will go after event planner bloggers or webmasters who get a lot of web traffic for our keywords. These companies would then promote our Yoga products and services, and they would earn commissions for the sales they generated. We will work with the following services to handle the technical aspects of our program.

ConnectCommerce	www.connectcommerce.com/
Commission Junction	www.cj.com
ShareASale	www.shareasale.com/
Share Results	
LinkShare	www.linkshare.com
Clickbank	www.clickbank.com
Affiliate Scout	http://affiliatescout.com/
Affiliate Seeking	www.affiliateseeking.com/
Clix Galore	www.clixgalore.com/

Point-of-Purchase Displays (POP)

The term point-of-purchase, or POP, typically refers to the promotional graphics focused on influencing consumer behavior at the moment of the purchasing decision. These graphics serve to impact a buying decision in favor of a specific brand or product in-studio where the purchase is imminent. POP is increasingly becoming one of the more important aspects of advertising and promotion, because of its efficiency in targeting the consumer in the actual buying environment, the decline of network television viewership and newspaper readership, and the stark reality of recession-sized ad budgets. Because of its impact, we will work with our distributor to secure the following types of cooperative advertising funds and items from Yoga product manufacturers, along with permission to use their logos in our advertising materials:

1. Banners
2. Ceiling danglers
3. Themed wall coverings
4. Directional posters
5. Floor Decals
6. Props
7. Flyers

Advertorials

An advertorial is an advertisement written in the form of an objective article, and presented in a printed publication—usually designed to look like a legitimate and independent news story. We will use quotes as testimonials to back up certain claims throughout our copy and break-up copy with subheadings to make the material more reader-friendly. We will include the "call to action" and contact information with a 24/7 voicemail number and a discount coupon. The advertorial will have a short intro about a client's experience with our Yoga Studio and include quotes, facts, and statistics. We will present helpful information about Yoga training methods.

Gift with Purchase (GWP)

A GWP is an item that is presented to our client when he or she spends above a specified amount on products or services. The Gift with purchase or free item could be anything from smoothie energy drink recipes, studio voucher, T-Shirts, product samples, etc. We will attach our marketing logo and business card to the gift and use it as means to thank the customer for their patronage and referrals. We will also explore the dramatic impact of a surprise gift with purchase, because an unexpected bonus item is often very appreciated and remembered.

HotFrog.com

HotFrog is a fast-growing free online business directory listing over 6.6 million US businesses. HotFrog now has local versions in 34 countries worldwide.
Anyone can list their business in HotFrog for free, along with contact details, and products and services. Listing in HotFrog directs sales leads and enquiries to your business. We will be encouraged to add any latest news and information about our Yoga Studio products and services to our listing. HotFrog is indexed by Google and other search engines, meaning that customers can find our HotFrog listing when they use Google, Yahoo! or other search engines.
Resource:

http://www.hotfrog.com/AddYourBusiness.aspx

Local.com

Local.com owns and operates a leading local search site and network in the United States. Its mission is to be the leader at enabling local businesses and consumers to find each other and connect. To do so, the company uses patented and proprietary technologies to provide over 20 million consumers each month with relevant search results for local businesses, products and services on Local.com and more than 1,000 partner sites. Local.com powers more than 100,000 local websites. Tens of thousands of small business customers use Local.com products and services to reach consumers using a variety of subscription, performance and display advertising and website products.
Resource:
http://corporate.local.com/mk/get/advertising-opportunities

Autoresponder

An autoresponder is an online tool that will automatically manage our mailing list and send out emails to our Yoga Studio customers at preset intervals. We will write a short article on warm-up exercises, that is, helpful to potential Yoga Studio participants. We will load this article into our autoresponder. We will let people know of the availability of our article by posting to newsgroups, forums, social networking sites etc. We will list our autoresponder email address at the end of the posting so they can send a blank email to our autoresponder to receive our article and be added to our mailing list. We will then email them at the interval of our choosing with special offers. We will load the messages into our autoresponder and set a time interval for the messages to be mailed out.
Resource: www.aweber.com

Corporate Incentive/Employee Rewards Program

Our Employee Rewards Program will motivate and reward the key resources of local corporations – the people who make their business a success. We will use independent sales reps to market our specialized Yoga programs, such as stress reduction techniques, to local corporations. It will be a versatile program, allowing the corporate client to customize it to best suit the following goals:

1.   Welcome New Hires with a specially designed Yoga orientation program.
2.   Introduce an Employee Discount Program to our Yoga Studio for all staff members.
3.   Reward increases in sales or productivity with an Employee Incentive Program
4.   Thank Retirees for their service to the company with lifetime Yoga Studio membership.
5.   Initiate a Loyalty Rewards Program geared towards the customers of our corporate clients or their employees.

Database Marketing

Database marketing is a form of direct marketing using databases of customers or prospects to generate personalized communications in order to promote a product or service for marketing purposes. The method of communication can be any addressable medium, as in direct marketing. With database marketing tools, we will be able to implement customer nurturing, which is a tactic that attempts to communicate with each customer or prospect at the right time, using the right information to meet that customer's need to progress through the process of identifying a problem, learning options available to resolve it, selecting the right solution, and making the purchasing decision. We will use our databases to learn more about customers, select target markets for specific campaigns, through customer segmentation, compare customers' value to the company, and provide more specialized offerings for customers based on their transaction histories, demographic profile and surveyed needs and wants. This database will gives us the capability to automate regular promotional mailings, to semi-automate the telephone outreach process, and to prioritize prospects as to interests, timing, and other notable delineators. The objective is to arrange for first meetings, which are meant to be informal introductions, and valuable fact-finding and needs-assessment events.

We will use sign-in sheets, coupons, surveys and newsletter subscriptions to collect the following information from our clients:

1.	Name	2.	Telephone Number
3.	Email Address	4.	Home Address
5.	Birth Date	6.	Other Relevant Dates

We will utilize the following types of contact management software to generate leads and stay in touch with customers to produce repeat business and referrals:

1.	Act	www.act.com
2.	Front Range Solutions	www.frontrange.com
3.	The Turning Point	www.turningpoint.com
4.	Acxiom	www.acxiom.com/products_and_services/

We will utilize contact management software, such as ACT and Goldmine, to track the following:
1. Dates for follow-ups.
2. Documentation of prospect concerns, objections or comments.
3. Referral source.
4. Marketing Materials sent.
5. Log of contact dates and methods of contact.
6. Ultimate disposition.

Cause Marketing
Cause marketing or cause-related marketing refers to a type of marketing involving the cooperative efforts of a "for profit" business and a non-profit organization for mutual benefit. The possible benefits of cause marketing for business include positive public relations, improved customer relations, and additional marketing opportunities.
Cause marketing sponsorship by American businesses is rising at a dramatic rate, because customers, employees and stakeholders prefer to be associated with a company that is

considered socially responsible. Our business objective will be to generate highly cost-effective public relations and media coverage for the launch of a marketing campaign focused on _____ (type of cause), with the help of the _____ (non-profit organization name) organization.

Resources:

www.causemarketingforum.com/

www.cancer.org/AboutUs/HowWeHelpYou/acs-cause-marketing

Courtesy Advertising

We will engage in courtesy advertising, which refers to a company or corporation "buying" an advertisement in a nonprofit dinner program, event brochure, and the like. Our company will gain visibility this way while the nonprofit organization may treat the advertisement revenue as a donation. We will specifically advertise in the following non-profit programs, newsletters, bulletins and event brochures: _____

_____

Speaking Engagements

We will consider a "problem/solution" format where we describe a challenge and tell how our expertise achieved an exceptional solution. We will use speaking engagements as an opportunity to expose our areas of expertise to prospective clients. By speaking at conferences and forums put together by professional and industry trade groups, we will increase our firm's visibility, and consequently, its prospects for attracting new business. Public speaking will give us a special status, and make it easier for our speakers to meet prospects. Attendees expect speakers to reach out to the audience, which gives speakers respect and credibility. We will identify speaking opportunities that will let us reach our targeted audience. We will designate a person who is responsible for developing relationships with event and industry associations, submitting proposals and, most importantly, staying in touch with contacts. We will tailor our proposals to the event organizers' preferences.

Speaking Proposal Package:
1.   Speech Topic/Agenda/Synopsis
2.   Target Audience: Community and Civic Groups
3.   Speaker Biography
4.   List of previous speaking engagements
5.   Previous engagement evaluations

Possible Targets:

1.	AARP Groups	2.	Churches
3.	YMCAs	4.	Health Food Stores
5.	Support Groups	6.	Corporations
7.	Concierge Professionals	8.	Community Centers

Possible Speech Topics
1.   Using to Yoga to Stress Down and Shape Up.

2.   How Yoga Can Help You Find Your Way to a Healthier Lifestyle.

Speech Tracking Form

Group/Class	Subject/ Topic	Business Development Potential	Resources Needed	Target Date

We will use the following techniques to leverage the business development impact of our speaking engagements:

1.   Send out press releases to local papers announcing the upcoming speech. We will get great free publicity by sending the topic and highlights of the talk to the newspaper.
2.   Produce a flyer with our picture on it, and distribute it to our network.
3.   Send publicity materials to our prospects inviting them to attend our presentation.
4.   Whenever possible, get a list of attendees before the event. Contact them and introduce yourself before the talk to build rapport with your audience. Arrive early and don't leave immediately after your presentation.
5.   Always give out handouts and a business card. Include marketing materials and something of value to the recipient, so that it will be retained and not just tossed away. You might include tips or secrets you share in your talk.
6.   Give out an evaluation form to all participants. This form should request names and contact information. Offer a free consultation if it's appropriate. Follow up within 72 hours with any members of the audience who could become ideal clients.
7.   Have a place on the form where participants can list other groups that might need speakers, along with the name of the program chairperson or other contact person.
8.   Offer a door prize as incentive for handing in the evaluation. When you have collected all of the evaluations, you can select a winner of the prize.
9.   Meet with audience members, answer their questions and listen to their concerns. Stay after your talk and mingle with the audience. Answer any questions that come up and offer follow-up conversations for additional support.
10.   Request a free ad in the group's newsletter in exchange for your speech.
11.   Send a thank-you note to the person who invited you to speak. Include copies of some of the evaluations to show how useful it was.

Speaking Engagement Package

1.	Video or DVD of prior presentation.	2.	Session Description
3.	Learning Objectives	4.	Takeaway Message
5.	Speaking experience	6.	Letters of recommendation
7.	General Biography	8.	Introduction Biography

Resource:

www.toastmasters.com

www.nationalspeakers.com

Meet-up Group

We will form a meet-up group to encourage people to participate in our introductory Yoga programs.
Resource:
http://www.meetup.com/create/
Example:
http://yoga.meetup.com/

Sampling Program

We will offer a "try before you buy" sample program. We will launch our program with one or more free lunch hour and after work lecture-demos. We will sign people up for an introductory group series or private session, or get their names for follow-up communication.

Signage

_____ (company name) will place prominent signage and banners on the facility to draw a significant amount of foot traffic. We will make sure people can tell what our business is from the outside. This will help us to make the most of passerby traffic. We will also mount an exterior box for our sales brochures.

Marketing Associations/Groups

We will set up a marketing association comprised of complementary businesses. We will market our yoga studio as a member of a group of complementary companies. Our marketing group will include a nutritionist, personal trainer, and a massage therapist. Any business that provides event services will be a likely candidate for being a member of our marketing group. The group will joint advertise, distribute joint promotional materials, exchange mailing lists, and develop a group website. The obvious benefit is that we will increase our marketing effectiveness by extending our reach.

BBB Accreditation

We will apply for BBB Accreditation to improve our perceived trustworthiness. BBB determines that a company meets BBB accreditation standards, which include a commitment to make a good faith effort to resolve any consumer complaints. BBB Accredited Businesses pay a fee for accreditation review/monitoring and for support of BBB services to the public. BBB accreditation does not mean that the business' products or services have been evaluated or endorsed by BBB, or that BBB has made a determination as to the business' product quality or competency in performing services. We will place the BBB Accreditation Logo in all of our ads.
Ex: www.bbb.org/alaska/business-reviews/yoga-instruction/inner-dance-yoga-studio-
            in-anchorage-ak-22576510

Sponsor Events

The sponsoring of events, such as golf tournaments, will allow our company to engage in what is known as experiential marketing, which is the idea that the best way to deepen the emotional bond between a company and its customers is by creating a memorable and interactive experience. We will ask for the opportunity to prominently display our company signage and the set-up of a booth from which to handout sample products and sales literature. We will also seek to capitalize on networking, speech giving and workshop presenting opportunities

Sponsorships

We will sponsor a local team, such as our child's little league baseball team, the local soccer club or a bowling group. We will then place our company name on the uniforms or shirts in exchange for providing the equipment and/or uniforms.

Patch.com

A community-specific news and information platform dedicated to providing comprehensive and trusted local coverage for individual towns and communities. Patch makes it easy to: Keep up with news and events, Look at photos and videos from around town, Learn about local businesses, Participate in discussions and Submit announcements, photos, and reviews.

Examples:

http://bristol-warren.patch.com/listings/bristol-yoga-studio-2

http://petaluma.patch.com/articles/down-to-business-yoga-one-offers-
       personalized-approach-in-a-classroom-setting

Resource:

http://amherst.patch.com/articles/poll-vote-for-the-best-yoga-fitness-studio

MerchantCircle.com

The largest online network of local business owners, combining social networking features with customizable web listings that allow local merchants to attract new customers. A growing company dedicated to connecting neighbors and merchants online to help build real relationships between local business owners and their customers. To date, well over 1,600,000 local businesses have joined MerchantCircle to get their business more exposure on the Internet, simply and inexpensively.

Ex: www.merchantcircle.com/business/Shanti.Yoga.Studio.And.Harmony.Boutique.
       Mccall.ID.208-634-9711

Mobile iPhone Apps

We will use new distribution tools like the iPhone App Store to give us unprecedented direct access to consumers, without the need to necessarily buy actual mobile *ads* to reach people. Thanks to Apple's iPhone and the App Store, we will be able to make cool mobile apps that may generate as much goodwill and purchase intent as a banner ad. We will research Mobile Application Development, which is the process by which application software is developed for small low-power handheld devices, such as personal digital assistants, enterprise digital assistants or mobile phones. These applications are either pre-installed on phones during manufacture, or downloaded by customers from various mobile software distribution platforms. iPhone apps make good marketing tools. The bottom line is iPhones and smartphones sales are continually growing, and people are going to their phones for information. Apps will definitely be a lead generation tool because it gives potential clients easy access to our contact and business information and the ability to call for more information while they are still "hot". Our apps will contain: directory of staffers, publications on relevant issues, office location, videos, etc.

We will especially focus on the development of apps that can accomplish the following:

1. **Mobile Reservations:** Customers can use this app to access mobile reservations linked directly to your in-house calendar. They can browse open slots and book appointments easily, while on the go.

2. **Appointment Reminders:** You can send current customers reminders of regular or special appointments through your mobile app to increase your yearly revenue per customer.

3. **Style Libraries**
   Offer a style library in your app to help customers to pick out a _____ style. Using a simple photo gallery, you can collect photos of various styles, and have customers browse and select specific _____.

4. **Customer Photos**
   Your app can also have a feature that lets customers take photos and email them to you. This is great for creating a database of customer photos for testimonial purposes, advertising, or just easy reference.

5. **Special Offers**
   Push notifications allow you to drive activity on special promotions, deals, events, and offers. If you ever need to generate revenue during a down time, push notifications allow you to generate interest easily and proactively.

6. **Loyalty Programs**
   A mobile app allows you to offer a mobile loyalty program (buy ten ___, get one free, etc.). You won't need to print up cards or track anything manually – it's all done simply through users' mobile devices.

7. **Referrals**
   A mobile app can make referrals easy. With a single click, a user can post to a social media account on Facebook or Twitter about their experience with your business. This allows you to earn new business organically through the networks of existing customers.

8. **Product Sales**
   We can sell yoga products through our mobile app. Customers can browse products, submit orders, and make payments easily, helping you open up a new revenue stream.

Resources:	http://www.apple.com/iphone/apps-for-iphone/
	http://iphoneapplicationlist.com/apps/business/
Software Development:	http://www.mutualmobile.com/
	http://www.avenuesocial.com/mob-app.php#

Example:

http://iphoneappcafe.com/top-5-free-yoga-apps-for-iphone/
https://itunes.apple.com/us/app/yoga-studio/id567767430?mt=8

Resources:
http://yogastudioapp.com/
http://blog.kiip.me/developers/yoga-studio-strikes-the-perfect-pose/
http://yogapanda.co/blog/marketing-yoga-studio-advice/

Flash Buying

Flash Buy will be a group where every local business can play a part. Similar to FLASH MOBBING, where individuals gather secretly to stir up some comedy, this will be an effort for us to plan a visit to a locally-owned business on a particular day, pay for the goods/services, and help the chosen business reach an epic day of profits. For example, we will plan for local business group members to visit our yoga studio on a certain date. Group members will go there, any time that they wish throughout the selected day, receive a modest discount, and this will spark a rise in profits. This will be an opportunity for other businesses to become aware of and experience our yoga studio, and create word-of-mouth advertising.

Transit Ads

According to the Metropolitan Transportation Authority, MTA subways, buses and railroads provide billions of trips each year to residents. Marketing our yoga studio in subway cars and on the walls of subway stations will be a great way to advertise our studio to a large, captive audience.

Tumblr.com

Tumblr will allow us to effortlessly share anything. We will be able to post text, photos, quotes, links, music, and videos, from our browser, phone, desktop, email, or wherever we happen to be. We will be able to customize everything, from colors, to our theme's HTML.
Ex: http://juliahanlonyoga.tumblr.com/post/8600808891/
week-of-8-8-8-14-class-schedule-monday-o

Gift Certificates

We will offer for sale Gift Certificates via our website. This will provide an excellent way to be introduced to new clients and improve our cash flow position. An e-commerce platform for small businesses. BoomTime protects info with 256-bit SSL encryption when transmitting certain kinds of information, such as financial services information or payment information. An icon resembling a padlock is displayed on the bottom of most browser windows during SSL transactions, which you can also verify by looking at the address bar, which will start with "https://" instead of just "http://". The information you provide will be stored securely on BoomTime servers.
Resources:
        Boom Time   https://ps1419.boomtime.com/lgift

Gift Cards   www.giftcards.com
Gift Card Café   www.TheGiftCardCafe.com
Allows companies to create their own special deals and discount services, and send it to just the contacts in their client database.
Examples:
http://ahimsaoakparkyoga.com/gift-certificates/
https://clients.mindbodyonline.com/asp/main_shop.asp?pMode=2&tabID=3

thumbtack.com

A directory for finding and booking trustworthy local services, which is free to consumers.
Resource:
www.thumbtack.com/postservice
Examples:
https://www.thumbtack.com/ny/nanuet/yoga/yoga-studio

Citysearch.com

Citysearch.com is a local guide for living bigger, better and smarter in the selected city. Covering more than 75,000 locations nationwide, Citysearch.com combines in-the-know editorial recommendations, candid user comments and expert advice from local businesses. Citysearch.com keeps users connected to the most popular and undiscovered places wherever they are.
Resource: http://losangeles.citysearch.com/bestof/winners/yoga

Gift Registry

We will add a gift registry service to our website to facilitate the gift giving of our yoga inspired gift baskets.

Publish e-Book

Ebooks are electronic books which can be downloaded from any website or FTP site on the Internet. Ebooks are made using special software and can include a wide variety of media such as HTML, graphics, Flash animation and video. We will publish an e-book to establish our yoga expertise, and reach people who are searching for ebooks on how to make better use our products and/or services. Included in our ebook will be links back to our website, product or affiliate program. Because users will have permanent access to it, they will use our ebook again and again, constantly seeing a link or banner which directs them to our site. The real power behind ebook marketing will be the viral aspect of it and the free traffic it helps to build for our website. ebook directories include:
www.e-booksdirectory.com/
www.ebookfreeway.com/p-ebook-directory-list.html
www.quantumseolabs.com/blog/seolinkbuilding/top-5-free-ebook-directories-
     subscribers/
Resources:
www.free-ebooks.net/
www.designhill.com/design-blog/top-10-marketing-ideas-for-yoga-studios/

e-books are available from the following sites:

Amazon.com   Createspace.com
Lulu.com   Kobobooks.com
BarnesandNoble.com Scribd.com
AuthorHouse.com

Resource:
www.smartpassiveincome.com/ebooks-the-smart-way/
https://georgewatts.org/2014/09/11/12-steps-create-yoga-ebook-day/

Business Card Exchanges

We will join our Chamber of Commerce or local retail merchants' association and volunteer to host a mixer or business card exchange at our store. We will take the opportunity to invite social and business groups to our studio to enjoy wine tastings, and market to local businesses that will be looking for employee and customer holiday gifts cards. We will also build our email database by collecting the business cards of all attendees.

Storefront Banner Advertising

We will use banners as an affordable way to draw attention to our business. We will place one on the side or front of our building, or on a prominent building and have it point to ours. We will use colorful storefront banners with catchy phrases to grab the attention of local foot and vehicle traffic.
Resource: http://www.fastsigns.com/

Hubpages.com

HubPages has easy-to-use publishing tools, a vibrant author community and underlying revenue-maximizing infrastructure. Hubbers (HubPages authors) earn money by publishing their Hubs (content-rich Internet pages) on topics they know and love, and earn recognition among fellow Hubbers through the community-wide HubScore ranking system. The HubPages ecosystem provides a search-friendly infrastructure which drives traffic to Hubs from search engines such as Google and Yahoo, and enables Hubbers to earn revenue from industry-standard advertising vehicles such as Google AdSense and the eBay and Amazon Affiliates program. All of this is provided free to Hubbers in an open online community.
Examples:
http://lillm.hubpages.com/hub/First-Yoga-Class

Pinterest.com

The goal of this website is to connect everyone in the world through the 'things' they find interesting. They think that a favorite yoga book, energy drink recipe or yoga accessories look can reveal a common link between two people. With millions of new pins added every week, Pinterest is connecting people all over the world based on shared tastes and interests. What's special about Pinterest is that the boards are all visual, which is a very important marketing plus. When users enter a URL, they select a picture from the site to pin to their board. People spend hours pinning their own content, and then finding content on other people's boards to "re-pin" to their own boards. We will use Pinterest for remote personal shopping appointments. When we have a customer with specific needs, we will create a board just for them with items we sell that would meet their needs, along with links to other tips and content. We will invite our customer to check out the board on Pinterest, and let them know we created it just for them.

Examples:
http://pinterest.com/erikadevito/yoga-studio-ideas/
Resources:
www.copyblogger.com/pinterest-marketing/
www.shopify.com/infographics/pinterest
www.pinterest.com/entmagazine/retail-business/
www.pinterest.com/brettcarneiro/ecommerce/
www.pinterest.com/denniswortham/infographics-retail-online-shopping/
www.cio.com/article/3018852/e-commerce/how-to-use-pinterest-to-grow-your-
        business.html

Pinterest usage recommendation include:
1.   Conduct market research by showing photos of potential products or test launches, asking the customer base for feedback.
2.   Personalize the brand by showcasing style and what makes the brand different, highlighting new and exciting things through the use of imagery.
3.   Add links from Pinterest photos to the company webstore, putting price banners on each photo and providing a link where users can buy the products directly.
4.   Share high-quality pictures or property images and put links back to our blog/website.
5.   Make Boards interesting with yoga studio décor photos.
6.   Showcase beautiful pictures of homes listed and include a link back to our website or blog.
7.   Focus on educating followers and sharing what they would like to see, like images from a design company.
8.   Ask happy clients to pin pictures of themselves in their new yoga studios.
9.   We will create a video and add a Call to Action in the description or use annotations, such as check my YouTube article, for the viewers to Pin videos or follow our Pins on Pinterest.
10.   Encourage followers' engagement with a call to action, because 'likes', home décor questions, comments and 'repins' will help our pins get more authority and visibility.
11.   Optimize descriptions with keywords that people might be looking for when searching Pinterest, as we can add as many hashtags as we want.
12.   Be consistent by pinning regularly.
13.   Let people know we are on Pinterest by adding "Pin it" and "follow" buttons to our blog and/or website.

Topix.com

Topix is the world's largest community news website. Users can read, talk about and edit the news on over 360,000 of our news pages. Topix is also a place for users to post their own news stories, as well as comment about stories they have seen on the Topix site. Each story and every Topix page comes with the ability to add your voice to the conversation.

Examples:

http://www.topix.com/forum/city/middlesboro-ky/TENRAUROCPBDPUTUU/new-yoga-studio

Survey Marketing

We will conduct a door-to-door survey in our target area to illicit opinions to our proposed business. This will provide valuable feedback, lead to prospective clients and serve to introduce our yoga studio business, before we begin actual operations.

'Green' Marketing

We will target environmentally friendly customers to introduce new customers to our business and help spread the word about going "green". We will use the following 'green' marketing strategies to form an emotional bond with our customers:

1.   We will use clearly labeled 'Recycled Paper' and Sustainable Packaging, such as receipts and storage containers.
2.   We will use "green", non-toxic cleaning supplies.
3.   We will install 'green' lighting and heating systems to be more eco-friendly.
4.   We will use web-based Electronic Mail and Social Media instead of using paper advertisements.
5.   We will find local suppliers to minimize the carbon footprint that it takes for deliveries.
6.   We will use products that are made with organic ingredients and supplies.
7.   We will document our 'Green' Programs in our sales brochure and website.
8.   We will be a Certified Energy Star Partner.
9.   We will install new LED warehouse lighting, exit signs, and emergency signs.
10.   We will install motion detectors in low-traff7ic areas both inside and outside of warehouses.
11.   We will implement new electricity regulators on HVAC units and compressors to lower energy consumption.
12.   We will mount highly supervised and highly respected recycling campaigns.
13.   We will start a program for waste product to be converted into sustainable energy sources.
14.   We will start new company-wide document shredding programs.
15.   We will use of water-based paints during the finishing process to reduce V.O.C.'s to virtually zero.
16.   Use of solar panels for non-critical sections and facilities in the complex.
17.   Use of only hybrid or electric vehicles.

Sticker Marketing

Low-cost sticker, label and decal marketing will provide a cost-effective way to convey information, build identity and promote our company in unique and influential ways. Stickers can be affixed to almost any surface, so they can go and stay affixed where other marketing materials can't; opening a world of avenues through which we can reach our target audience. Our stickers will be simple in design, and convey an impression quickly and clearly, with valuable information or coupon, printed optionally as part of its backcopy. Our stickers will handed-out at trade shows and special events, mailed as a postcard, packaged with product and/or included as part of a mailing package. We will insert the stickers inside our product or hand them out along with other marketing tools such as flyers or brochures. Research has found that the strongest stickers are usually less than 16 square inches, are printed on white vinyl, and are often die cut. Utilizing a strong design, in a versatile size, and with an eye-catching shape, that is, relevant to our business, will add to the perceived value of our promotional stickers.

We will adhere to the following sticker design tips:

1. We will strengthen our brand by placing our logo on the stickers and using company colors and font styles.
2. We will include our phone number, address, and/or website along with our logo to provide customers with a call to action.
3. We will write compelling copy that solicits an emotional reaction.
4. We will use die-cut stickers using unusual and business relevant shapes to help draw attention to our business.
5. We will consider that size matters and that will be determined by where they will be applied and the degree of desired visibility to be realized.
6. We will be aware of using color on our stickers as color can help create contrast in our design, which enables the directing of prospect eyes to images or actionable items on the stickers.
7. We will encourage customers to post our stickers near their phones, on yellow page book covers, on event invitations, on notepads, on book covers, on gift boxes and product packaging, etc.
8. We will place our stickers on all the products we sell.

USPS Every Door Dircct Mail Program

Every Door Direct Mail from the U.S. Postal Service® is designed to reach every home, every address, every time at a very affordable delivery rate. Every business and resident living in the _____ zip code will receive an over-sized post card and coupon announcing the _____ (company name) grand opening 7-days before the grand opening:

Price – USPS Marketing Mail™ Flats up to 3.3 oz
EDDM Retail® USPS Marketing Flats $0.177 per piece
EDDM BMEU USPS Marketing Mail at $0.156 per piece

Resource:
https://www.usps.com/business/every-door-direct-mail.htm
https://eddm.usps.com/eddm/customer/routeSearch.action

Google Calendar   www.google.com/calendar
We will use Google Calendar to organize our mobile Yoga Studio schedule and share events with friends.

ZoomInfo.com
Their vision is to be the sole provider of constantly verified information about companies and their employees, making our data indispensible — available anytime, anywhere and anyplace the customer needs it. Creates just-verified, detailed profiles of 65 million businesspeople and six million businesses. Makes data available through powerful tools for lead generation, prospecting and recruiting.

Zipslocal.com
Provides one of the most comprehensive ZIP Code-based local search services, allowing visitors to access information through our online business directories that cover all ZIP Codes in the United States. Interactive local yellow pages show listings and display relevant advertising through the medium of the Internet, making it easy for everyone to find local business information

Hold Biggest Fan Contest
Do you love _____ (company name)? Do you have a great story about how the team at _____ (company Name) helped you "get there" to achieve your goals? Well, then _____ (company name) wants to hear from you! _____ (company name) has launched the "Biggest Fan Contest" on its Facebook Page at the beginning of _____ (month), inviting current and former customers to share why they are _____'s (company name) "Biggest Fan." Participants are eligible to win a number of prizes including:_____.
To enter, visit www.facebook.com/_____ (company name), "like" the page, and click the "Biggest Fan Contest" tab on the right hand side. Participants are then asked to write a short blurb or upload a photo sharing why they love _____ (company name). If you have a story to tell or photo to share, enter today. Contest ends _____ (date). See contest tab for full details.

BusinessVibes   www.businessvibes.com/about-businessvibes
A growing B2B networking platform for global trade professionals. BusinessVibes uses a social networking model for businesses to find and connect with international partner companies. With a network of over 5000+ trade associations, 20 million companies and 25,000+ business events across 100+ major industries and 175 countries, BusinessVibes is a decisive source to companies looking for international business partners, be they clients, suppliers, JV partners, or any other type of business contact.
Examples:
https://www.businessvibes.com/companyprofile/Lahinch-Yoga-Studio

Yext.com
Lets companies manage their digital presence in online maps, directories and apps. Over 400,000 businesses make millions of monthly updates across 85+ exclusive global

partners, making Yext the global market leader. Digital presence is a fundamental need for all 50 million businesses in the world, and Yext's mission is perfect location information in every hand. Yext is based in the heart of New York City with 350 employees and was named to Forbes Most Promising Companies lists for 2015 and 2016, as well as the Fortune Best Places to Work 2015 list.

Google+

We will pay specific attention to Google+, which is already playing a more important role in Google's organic ranking algorithm. We will create a business page on Google+ to achieve improved local search visibility. Google+ will also be the best way to get access to Google Authorship, which will play a huge role in SEO. Aside from having all the necessary information like hours and contact information, quality photos and visuals will be essential on our Google+ local page. To go above the basics, we will have a local Google photographer visit and create a virtual tour.

Resources:
https://plus.google.com/pages/create
http://www.google.com/+/brands/
https://www.google.com/appserve/fb/forms/plusweekly/
https://plus.google.com/+GoogleBusiness/posts
http://marketingland.com/beyond-social-benefits-google-business-73460
http://searchenginewatch.com/sew/how-to/2124899/seo-for-google-profiles-and-pages
Examples:
https://plus.google.com/+ShreeYogaStudiosSaddleRiver

Inbound Marketing

Inbound marketing is about pulling people in by sharing relevant yoga information, creating useful content, and generally being helpful. It involves writing everything from buyer's guides to blogs and newsletters that deliver useful content. The objective will be to nurture customers through the buying process with unbiased educational materials that turn consumers into informed buyers.
Resource:
www.Hubspot.com

Google My Business Profile   www.google.com/business/befound.html

We will have a complete and active Google My Business profile to give our yoga studio company a tremendous advantage over the competition, and help potential customers easily find our studio and provide relevant information about our business.

Sampling Program

We will give each sample with a mini-survey to enable customers to rate the product or service, and supply constructive feedback.

Reddit.com

An online community where users vote on stories. The hottest stories rise to the top,

while the cooler stories sink. Comments can be posted on every story, including stories about startup yoga studios.
Examples:
https://www.reddit.com/r/yoga/

Exterior Signage
We will make effective use of the following types of signage: (select)
1. **Channel Letter**
   Channel letters can be illuminated by LED or neon and come in a variety of colors and sizes. Front-lit signs are illuminated from the letter face, while reverse-lit signs are lit from behind the sign. Open-face channel letters lit by exposed neon work well to create a night presence.
2. **Monument Signs**
   Monument signs are usually placed at the entrance to a parking lot or a building. This sign can easily be installed on a median or lawn. The size for a monument sign is typically based on city regulations for the specific location. These signs can be illuminated or non-illuminated, single- or double-sided.
3. **Pylon Signs**
   Also known as pole signs, they soar high above a business location to set the business apart from other businesses. They get attention from highway motorists who are still a distance away.
4. **Cabinet Signs**
   Commonly called "wall" or "box" signs, they are a traditional form of signage. They effectively use a large copy area and eye-popping graphics. This type of signage can highlight our business day or night because we have the option to add illumination. The background can be the element that lights up, and the copy can be lit or non-lit.
5. **Sandwich Signs**
   This sign will be placed on the sidewalk in front of our business to attract foot traffic.

6.4.1   Strategic Alliances

We will form strategic alliances to accomplish the following objectives:

1.   To share marketing expenses.
2.   To realize bulk buying power on wholesale purchases.
3.   To engage in barter arrangements.
4.   To collaborate with industry experts.
5.   To set-up mutual referral relationships.

We will partner with similar but non-competing businesses to offer hospitality packages. For example, we will go in with a hotel and/or a masseuse to offer a "Stress Melt Package." Visiting patrons will purchase the package when they get their hotel room, and they will get a discount for purchasing all three services.

We will develop strategic alliances with the following service providers by conducting introductory 'cold calls' to their offices and making them aware of our capabilities by distributing our brochures and business cards:

1.	Event Planners	2.	Hotel Business Offices
3.	Health and Wellness Centers	4.	Bridal Expos
5.	Nutrition Centers	6.	Physical Therapy Clinics
7.	Rehabilitation Centers	8.	Fitness Clubs
9.	Physicians	10.	Chiropractors
11.	Natural Food Stores	12.	Alternative Health Centers
13.	Massage Therapy Clinics	14.	Vitamin Shops
15.	Nutritionists	16.	Breweries
17.	Wineries	18.	Country Clubs
19.	Resorts/Boutique Hotels		

We will assemble a sales presentation package that includes sales brochures, business cards, and a DVD presentation. We will print coupons that offer a discount or other type of introductory deal. We will ask to set-up a take-one display for our sales brochures at the business registration counter. We will give the referring business any one or combination of the following reward options:

1.	Referral fees	2.	Free services
3.	Mutual referral exchanges		

We will monitor referral sources to evaluate the mutual benefits of the alliance and make certain to clearly define and document our referral incentives prior to initiating our referral exchange program.

6.4.2   Monitoring Marketing Results

To monitor how well _____ (company name) is doing, we will measure how well the advertising campaign is working. We will take random customer surveys. What we would like to know is how they heard of us and how they like and dislike about our services. In order to get responses to the surveys, we will be give discounts as thank you rewards.

Response Tracking Methods
  Coupons: ad-specific coupons that easily enable tracking
  Landing Pages: unique web landing pages for each advertisement
  800 Numbers: unique 1-800-# per advertisement
  Email Service Provider: Instantly track email views, opens, and clicks
  Mailing addresses with embedded department codes.

Our financial statements will offer excellent data to track all phases of sales. These are available for review on a daily basis. _____ (company name) will benchmark our objectives for sales promotion and advertising in order to evaluate our return on invested marketing dollars, and determine where to concentrate our limited advertising dollars to realize the best return. We will also strive to stay within our marketing budget.

Key Marketing Metrics
We will use the following two marketing metrics to evaluate the cost-effectiveness of our marketing campaign:
1.   The cost to acquire a new customer: The average dollar amount invested to get one new client. Example: If you invest $3,000 on marketing in a single month and end the month with 10 new customers, your cost of acquisition is $300 per new customer.
2.   The lifetime value of the average active client. The average dollar value of an average customer over the life of their business with you. To calculate this metric for a given period of time, take the total amount of revenue your business generated during the time period and divide it by the total number of customers you had from the beginning of the time period.
3.   We will track the following set of statistics on a weekly basis to keep informed of the progress of our practice:
       A.   Number of total referrals.
       B.   Percentage increase of total referrals (over baseline).
       C.   Number of new referral sources.
       D.   Number of new customers/month.
       E.   Number of Leads

Key Marketing Metrics Table
We've listed some key metrics in the following table. We will need to keep a close eye on these, to see if we meet our own forecasted expectations. If our numbers are off in too many categories, we may, after proper analysis, have to make substantial changes to our marketing efforts.

Key Marketing Metrics	2018	2019	2020
Revenue			
Leads			
Leads Converted			
Avg. Transaction per Customer			
Avg. Dollars per Customer			
Number of Referrals			

Number of PR Appearances   _____
Number of Testimonials   _____
Number of New Club Members   _____
Number of Returns   _____
Number of BBB Complaints   _____
Number of Completed Surveys   _____
Number of Blog readers   _____
Number of Twitter followers   _____
Number of Facebook Fans   _____

Metric Definitions

1. Leads: Individuals who step into the store to consider a purchase.
2. Leads Converted: Percent of individuals who actually make a purchase.
3. Average Transactions Per Customer: Number of purchases per customer per month. Expected to rise significantly as customers return for more and more _____ items per month
4. Average $ Per Customer: Average dollar amount of each transaction. Expected to rise along with average transactions.
5. Referrals: Includes customer and business referrals
6. PR Appearances: Online or print mentions of the business that are not paid advertising. Expected to be high upon opening, then drop off and rise again until achieving a steady level.
7. Testimonials: Will be sought from the best and most loyal customers. Our objective is ___ (#) per month) and they will be added to the website. Some will be sought as video testimonials.
8. New Loyalty Club Members: This number will rise significantly as more customers see the value in repeated visits and the benefits of club membership.
9. Number of Returns/BBB Complaints: Our goal is zero.
10. Number of Completed Surveys: We will provide incentives for customers to complete customer satisfaction surveys.

6.4.3   Word-of-Mouth Marketing

We plan to make use of the following techniques to spur word-of-mouth advertising:
1. Repetitive Image Advertising
2. In-studio activities, such as demonstrations or special events.
3. Make trial easy with a coupon or introductory discount.
4. Web and magazine article submissions
5. Sampling Program
6. Forwarded email.
7. Shared relevant and believable testimonial letters
8. Publish staff bios.
9. Product/service upgrade announcements
10. Reward Programs

11. Contests or sweepstakes
12. Involvement with community events.
13. Suggestion Box rewards
14. Newsletter
15. Shared easy-to-understand information (via an article or seminar).
16. Personalized marketing communications.
17. Referral Programs
18. Sharing of Community Commonalities
19. Invitations to join our community of shared interests.
20. Information Exchange Forums
21. Provide meaningful comparisons with competitors.
22. Clearly state our user benefits.
23. Ironclad guarantees
24. Support in the pre-sale decision making process.
25. Host Free Informational Seminars or Workshops
26. Involvement with local business organizations.
27. Press Release coverage of charitable involvements.
28. Traveling company demonstrations/exhibitions/competitions.
29. Staying in touch with inactive clients.

6.4.4   Customer Satisfaction Survey

We will design a customer satisfaction survey to measure the "satisfaction quotient" of our Yoga Studio customers. By providing a detailed snapshot of our current customer base, we will be able to generate more repeat and referral business and enhance the profitability of our yoga studio.

Our Customer Satisfaction Survey will include the following basics:
1. How do our customers rate our business?
2. How do our customers rate our competition?
3. How well do our customers rate the value of our products or services?
4. What new customer needs and trends are emerging?
5. How loyal are our customers?
6. What can be done to improve customer loyalty and repeat business?
7. How strongly do our customers recommend our business?
8. What is the best way to market our business?
9. What new value-added services would best differentiate our business from that of our competitors?
10. How can we encourage more referral business?
11. How can our pricing strategy be improved?

Our customer satisfaction survey will help to answer these questions and more. From the need for continual new Yoga products and services to improved customer service, our satisfaction surveys will allow our organization to quickly identify problematic and underperforming areas, while enhancing our overall customer satisfaction.

Examples:
https://www.surveymonkey.com/r/?sm=8TGwGsewStKtiFG8mTrC6A%3D%3D
http://www.questionpro.com/a/showSurveyLibrary.do?surveyID=306530
http://survey.constantcontact.com/survey/a07e3ukp1a3gnj07bp4/a007godiadam/
    questions

Resources:
https://www.survata.com/
https://www.google.com/insights/consumersurveys/use_cases
https://www.surveymonkey.com/mp/customer-satisfaction-survey-questions/
http://www.smetoolkit.org/smetoolkit/en/content/en/6708/Customer-Satisfaction-Survey-
    Template-
http://smallbusiness.chron.com/common-questions-customer-service-survey-1121.html

6.4.5　　Marketing Training Program

Our Marketing Training Program will include both an initial orientation and training, as well as ongoing continuing education classes. Initial orientation will be run by the owner until an HR manager is hired. For one week, half of each day will be spent in training, and the other half shadowing the operations manager.

Training will include:
    Learning the entire selection of yoga studio products and services.
    Understanding our Mission Statement, Value Proposition, Position Statement and
        Unique Selling Proposition.
    Appreciating our competitive advantages.
    Understanding our core message and branding approach.
    Learning our store's policies; returns processing, complaint handling, etc.
    Learning our customer services standards of practice.
    Learning our customer and business referral programs.
    Learning our Membership Club procedures, rules and benefits.
    Becoming familiar with our company website, and online ordering options.
    Service procedures specific to the employee's role.

    Ongoing workshops will be based on customer feedback and problem areas identified
        by mystery buyers, which will better train employees to educate customers. These
        ongoing workshops will be held _____ (once?) a month for _____ (three?) hours.

6.5　　Sales Strategy

The development of our sales strategy will start by developing a better understanding of our customer needs. To accomplish this task, we will pursue the following research methods:

1. Join the associations that our target customers belong to, such as the PTA.
2. Contact the membership director and establish a relationship to understand their member's needs, challenges and concerns.
3. Identify non-competitive suppliers who sell to our customer to learn their challenges and look for partnering solutions.
4. Work directly with our customer and ask them what their needs are and if our business may offer a possible solution.

Our sales strategy will be targeted at obtaining both the individual and corporate clients. The individual customers will be primarily obtained through word-of-mouth referrals, but we will also advertise discount specials or introductory offers to introduce people to the different dances our studio offers. Our instructors will work with the customer on these specials to determine what it is they are looking for in Pilates, and then outline a course that satisfies the customer's needs and wants. Customers will also be given the choice between packaged private and group sessions at various program levels. The customer will then sign up for the sessions by way of a contract. The combination of the perception of higher quality and the recognition of superior value should turn referral leads into satisfied customers.

The company's sales strategy will be based on the following elements:
Advertising in the Yellow Pages - two inch by three-inch ads describing our services will be placed in the local Yellow Pages.
Placing classified advertisements in the local parenting magazines.
Word of mouth referrals - generating sales leads in the local community through customer referrals.

We also plan to hire a local independent commissioned sales rep to sell our team building services to corporations.

In addition, _____ (company name) plans to offer a Club Membership Card. There will be three different memberships offered with the following benefits:

1. The Bronze: Unlimited admission to Yoga parties as well as discounts to special events and product purchases.
2. The Gold: Limited access to group classes, unlimited admission to Yoga parties, four party guest passes, and special event discounts.
3. The Platinum: Unlimited access to group classes, unlimited admission to parties, twelve party guest passes, and discounts to special events and products.

Our basic sales strategy is to:
Develop a website for lead generation by _____ (date).
Provide exceptional customer service.
Accept payment by all major credit cards, cash, and check, and monthly installment payment plan (ACH).

Survey our customers regarding services they would like to see added.

Sponsor charitable and other community events.

Motivate employees with a pay-for-performance component to their straight salary compensation package, based on profits and customer satisfaction rates.

Build long-term customer relationships by putting the interests of customers first.

Establish mutually beneficial relationship with all vendors.

Direct Sales

The company will develop a database of customer names, addresses, email addresses, key dates and personal preferences. This information will be used for email and direct mail efforts to build customer loyalty. We will also use the services of independent commissions sales reps to approach corporations.

Indirect Sales

We will establish a referral program for customers. We will start an affiliate program for strategic business alliance partners.

6.5.1   Customer Retention Strategies

We will use the following techniques to improve customer retention and the profitability of our business:

1.   Keep the studio sparkling clean and well-organized.
2.   Use only well-trained instructors, and the highest quality equipment.
3.   Ask the customers for feedback and promptly act upon their inputs.
4.   Tell customers how much you appreciate their business.
5.   Call regular customers by their first names.
6.   Send thank you notes.
7.   Offer free new product and service samples.
8.   Change displays and sales presentations on a regular basis.
9.   Practice good phone etiquette
10.   Respond to complaints promptly.
11.   Reward referrals.
12.   Publish a monthly newsletter.
13.   Develop and publish a list of frequently asked questions.
14.   Issue Preferred Customer Membership Cards.
15.   Hold informational seminars and workshops.
16.   Run contests.
17.   Develop service contracts.
18.   Provide an emergency hotline number.
19.   Publish code of ethics.
20.   Publish our guarantees.
21.   Publish all customer reviews.
22.   Help customers to make accurate competitor comparisons.

23.   Build a stay-in-touch (drip marketing) communications calendar.
24.   Keep marketing communications focused on our competitive advantages.
25.   Offer repeat user discounts and incentives.
26.   Be supportive and encouraging, and not judgmental.
27.   Measure customer retention and look at recurring revenue and customer surveys.
28.   Issue participant progress report cards.
29.   Show no participant favoritism.
30.   Organize social events.
31.   Incorporate sports and martial arts training into Yoga sessions.

We will seek to build strong long-term relationships with our students by adhering to the following practices:
1.   Place student name on a sticker and adhere it to the corner of their mat.
2.   Ask instructors to introduce themselves to every student in the class.
3.   Express an interest what the student does for a living.
4.   Ask for the student's reason for taking the class.
5.   Create a beautiful zen space.
6.   Offer schedule of 4+ classes a day, 7 days a week.
7.   Arrange for a large diverse line-up of instructors with different points of view.
8.   Design classes so that anyone can be challenged in them.
9.   Encourage students to participate in our Referral Rewards Program.
10.   Explain to students that you have developed a comprehensive system for personal and professional growth.
11.   Teach the entire empowering full-faceted system of yoga that can serve everyone's needs.
12.   Include resources that educate and make the value of experiencing this powerful system very apparent.
13.   Get smart about part-time space-sharing with a business that targets the same target market.
14.   Keep the two-way dialogue going by developing a feedback system and a customer satisfaction survey.

We will also consider the following Customer Retention Programs:

Type of Program	Customer Rewards
Frequency Purchase Loyalty Program	Special Discounts
	Free Product or Services
'Best Customer' Program	Special Recognition/Treatment/Offers
Customer Community Programs	Special Event Participation
Auto-Knowledge Building Programs	Purchase Recommendations based On Past Transaction History
Profile Building Programs	Recommendations Based on Stated Customer Profile Information.

6.5.2   Sales Forecast

Our sales projections are based on the following:
1. Actual sales volumes of local competitors
2. Interviews with other Yoga Studio owners and managers
3. Observations of Yoga Studio sales and traffic at competitor establishments.
4. Government and industry trade statistics
5. Local population demographics and projections.
6. Discussions with suppliers.

The sales forecast outlines sales of instruction time as well as sales of products through the boutique located in the facility. Instructions will be sold in the following three ways:
1. Private lessons
2. _____ (#) week courses
3. Drop-in sessions.

The boutique will sell clothing, books, posters, books, DVDs and videos, mats, and other props for yoga. In addition, it will sell healthy pre-bottled drinks and healthy energy food. In the beginning all food will be pre-packaged, but if the facility becomes more of a destination, we will research adding a cafe.

_____ (company name) anticipates that sales will be slow for the first and second month of operation. After that point, sales will increase as membership grows.

Our sales forecast is an estimated projection of expected sales over the next three years, based on our chosen marketing strategy and assumed competitive environment. It is calculated by multiplying the forecasted number of customers we plan to acquire by the average cost of a particular lesson or product sale.

Sales are expected to be below average during the first year, until a regular customer base has been established. It has been estimated that it takes the average Yoga Studio a minimum of two years to establish a significant customer base. After the customer base is built, sales will grow at an accelerated rate from word-of-mouth referrals and continued networking efforts.

We expect sales to steadily increase as our marketing program and contact management system are executed. By using advertising, especially discounted introductory coupons, as a catalyst for this prolonged process, _____ (company name) plans to attract more customers sooner.

Our forecast assumes a 33% closing ratio for new participants who sign up for the introductory special offer and go on to purchase the Basic Package. We then assume a 50% closing ratio for existing participants, which mean 50% of the participants will move onto the next level of Yoga sessions or the Intermediate Package, and so forth. Throughout the first year, it is forecasted that sales will incrementally grow until profitability is reached toward the end of year _____ (one?). Year two reflects a conservative growth rate of _____ (15?) percent. Year three reflects a growth rate of _____ (15?) percent.

With our unique product and service offerings, along with our thorough and aggressive marketing strategies, we believe that sales forecasts are actually on the conservative side.

Table: Sales Forecast

Sales	Forecast #	x	Cost	Annual Sales 2018	2019	2020
Private Introductory Special						
Group Introductory Special						
Private Basic Package						
Group Basic Package						
Private Intermediate Package						
Group Intermediate Package						
Private Advanced Package						
Group Advanced Package						
Bronze Club Memberships						
Gold Club Memberships						
Platinum Club Memberships						
Mobile Private sessions						
Aerobic Exercise Classes						
Space Rentals						
Corporate Consulting						
Yoga Product Sales						
Snack Food/Beverage Sales						
Miscellaneous						
Total Sales Forecast						

Direct Cost of Sales:

Private Introductory Special						
Group Introductory Special						
Private Basic Package						
Group Basic Package						
Private Intermediate Package						
Group Intermediate Package						
Private Advanced Package						
Group Advanced Package						
Bronze Club Memberships						
Gold Club Memberships						
Platinum Club Memberships						
Mobile Private sessions						
Aerobic Exercise Classes						
Space Rentals						
Corporate Consulting						
Yoga Product Sales						
Snack Food/Beverage Sales						
Miscellaneous						

6.6 Merchandising Strategy

Merchandising is that part of our marketing strategy that is involved with promoting the sales of our merchandise, as by consideration of the most effective means of selecting, pricing, displaying, and advertising items for sale in our Yoga Studio.

We will develop a merchandising strategy that grabs shoppers' attention as they enter the store. The store entrance will feature a variety of bright colors and interesting merchandise displays. We will strive to carry merchandise that is not found in competitor stores and use proper and informative signage to help sell merchandise.

We plan to group similar types of merchandise together for maximum visual appeal. Product presentation will be designed to lead the customers through the entire display area.
We will monitor our sales figures and data to confirm that products in demand are well-stocked and slow-moving products are phased-out. We will improve telephone skills of employees to boost phone orders.

To illustrate our cost competitiveness on premium Yoga products, we will use shelf signs to compare our prices to those of the local discount store. This will also help to develop the client's trust in the competitive pricing of all of our products and services.

We will encourage impulse purchases with the use of descriptive adjectives in our signage. We will attach our own additional business labels to all products to promote our line of services and location.

We will adhere to the following general merchandising tips:
1. Locate specials in maximum traffic areas.
2. Group related items together.
3. Provide self-service, point-of-purchase display units.
4. Use color to create eye-catching displays.
5. Change stock and displays often to capture attention.
6. Have a trained person available to provide information and assistance at all times.
7. Create accessible displays that encourage browsing.
8. Create displays that emphasize special products or services.
9. Slide items to the front of the display to make it look full.
10. Clearly mark the price on every item.
11. Position displays near the registration counter and in the reception area.
12. Create seasonal Pilates-themed gift baskets to tie in to holiday/seasonal celebrations.
13. Update neon signage inside and outside of the store.
14. Make sure sales brochures and flyers are always available at the sales counter.

15. Encourage instructors and sales associates to utilize products in demo sessions.

6.7 Pricing Strategy

When setting prices, we will consider the following factors:
1. Direct Costs: labor, time and supplies
2. Indirect Costs: rent, utilities, taxes and expenses.
3. Demand: economic conditions, demographics, consumer behavior, etc.
4. Marketing Promotions
5. Level of Competition
6. Positioning Image
7. Goals: profit objectives, return on investment, growth objectives.

We will develop a pricing strategy that incorporates the following principles:
1. An introductory package so affordable it is impossible to pass up.
2. A package of 10 classes discounted 20 percent lower than the drop-in value.
3. Rewards for long-term membership.
4. Special offers with a 30-day expiration date.
5. Discounted automatic online payments with commitments and auto renew feature.
6. A higher drop-in rate.

Note: Some yoga classes are paid for by attendees on a donation-based payment plan. The studio suggests that those who attend classes give a donation of $ ___ (13?), but those who are able to give more often do, with those who can't afford as much giving what they can spare. Service donations are also available for those who cannot donate financially.

Source: www.mndaily.com/article/2016/10/yoga-sol-makes-yoga-available-to-all-with-its-pay-what-you-can-model

Proposed Pricing Schedule
First Class is Free for _____ (city) residents.
New Student Special: 2 Months Unlimited $80
All Classes: Buy a Package or Donate!
Everyday Yoga is committed to sharing the gift of yoga with everyone regardless of their financial means. To this end, all of our classes are Pay As You Wish / Donation classes. Suggested donation for Walk-in is $10 but offer what your financial situation allows. You can pay by cash, credit card, or use your class package. We also sell normal class packages. We do not accept checks.
No expiration date.
10 Class Pack $85 ($8.5 per class)
15 Class Pack $120 ($8 per class)
20 Class Pack $150 ($7.5 per class)

The best value for frequent visitors.
1 Month Unlimited Classes $80
3 Months Unlimited Classes $220

Locals: Try Us Out for Your First Week Unlimited for $7

Drop In Single Class	$17
5 Class Package	$70 (3 month expiration)
10 Class Package	$130 (6 month expiration)
20 Class Package	$250 (1 year expiration)
Monthly Unlimited w/Autopay	$125 (6 month minimum commitment)
One Hour Private Meditation or Yoga Class	$85-$95

Mats available to rent for $2 per class
20% Discount for Yoga Teachers, Students & Military (please provide valid ID).

Our pricing strategy will take into view factors such as our firm's overall marketing objectives, consumer demand, product/service attributes, competitors' pricing, and market and economic trends. Our pricing strategy plays a major role in whether we will be able to create and maintain participants for a profit. Our pricing statutory will be guided by the following insights:

1.   Our assessment of participant needs to develop a consistent positioning strategy.
2.   Development of a pricing strategy based on our market positioning strategy, which is _____ (mass market value leadership/exceptional premium niche value?)
3.   Our goal to differentiate our studio by providing outstanding value for tuition fees.
4.   Our pricing policy objective, which is to _____ (increase profit margins/achieve revenue maximization to increase market share/lower unit costs).
5.   We will time the price increase for the start of a new season.
6.   We will use marketplace intelligence and gain insights from competitor pricing strategy comparisons.
7.   We will consider the variable cost of producing each additional unit of service and the fixed costs that are incurred, regardless of participant volume.
8.   We will present the price increase in smaller monthly terms rather than possibly overwhelming full-year numbers.
9.   We will be prepared to justify the price, in terms of facilities improvements, quality instructor acquisitions, extra amenities and/or the results achieved for prior participants.
10.   We will solicit before and after pricing feedback from participants and parents,

using customer surveys and informal interviews.

11. We will offer the opportunity for early registration to avoid the next season planned price increase.
12. We will utilize limited time pricing incentives to penetrate niche markets, such as two for one pricing for senior couples.
13. We will conduct experiments at prices above and below the current price to determine the price elasticity of demand. (Inelastic demand or demand that does not decrease with a price increase, indicates that price increases may be feasible.)
14. We will keep our offerings and prices simple to understand and competitive, based on market intelligence.
15. We will strive to differentiate our offerings by bundling several products and/or services into a packaged deal or plan.
16. We will use focus groups or customer advisory panels of involved parents to discuss the justification for and merits of our planned price increase.
17. We will consider offering multi-class, family, participant, senior, referral and introductory discounts.
18. We will consider other Pricing Strategy Options:

Penetration Pricing	Temporary, artificially low prices to gain market share.
Economy Pricing	Everyday no frills low prices on basic offerings.
Loss Leader	Selling at or below cost to attract customers who might buy other profitable products.
Price Skimming	High prices due to temporary, but substantial competitive advantage.
Psychological Pricing	Price point perspective (Ex: $19.99)
Grand Opening Pricing	Lower tuition rate to build database faster.
Optional Product	Optional extras increase overall sale price.
Product Bundle Pricing	Combine several products and/or services into a packaged plan.
Promotional Pricing	Ex: Buy One lesson… Get One Free
Value Pricing	Bundled packages resulting from increased competition.

Determining the costs of servicing business is the most important part of covering our expenses and earning profits. We will factor in the following pricing formula: Materials + Overhead + Labor + Profit = Price

Materials are those items consumed in the delivering of the service.

Overhead costs are the variable and fixed expenses that must be covered to stay in business. Variable costs are those expenses that fluctuate including vehicle expenses, rental expenses, utility bills and supplies. Fixed costs include the purchase of equipment, service ware, marketing and advertising, and insurance. After overhead costs are determined, the total overhead costs are divided among the total number of transactions forecasted for the year.

Labor costs include the costs of performing the services. Also included are Social Security taxes (FICA), vacation time, retirement and other benefits such as health or life insurance. To determine labor costs per hour, keep a time log. When placing a value on our time, we will consider the following: 1) skill and reputation; 2) wages paid by employers for similar skills and 3) where we live. Other pricing factors include image, inflation, supply and demand, and competition.

Profit is a desired percentage added to our total costs. We will need to determine the percentage of profit added to each service. It will be important to cover all our costs to stay in business. We will investigate available computer software programs to help us price our services and keep financial data for decision-making purposes. Close contact with customers will allow our company to react quickly to changes in demand.

We will develop a pricing strategy that will reinforce the perception of value to the customer and manage profitability, especially in the face of rising inflation. To ensure our success, we will use periodic competitor and customer research to continuously evaluate our pricing strategy. We intend to review our profit margins every six months.

6.8   Differentiation Strategies

We will use differentiation strategies to develop and market unique products for different customer segments. To differentiate ourselves from the competition, we will focus on the assets, creative ideas and competencies that we have that none of our competitors has. The goal of our differentiation strategies is to be able to charge a premium price for our unique Yoga Studio products and services.

Differentiation in our yoga studio will be achieved in the following types of ways, including:

Explanation

☐ Product features   _____
☐ Complementary services   _____
☐ Technology embodied in design _____
☐ Location   _____
☐ Service innovations   _____
☐ Superior service   _____
☐ Creative advertising   _____
☐ Better supplier relationships _____
Source:
http://scholarship.sha.cornell.edu/cgi/viewcontent.cgi?article=1295&context=articles

Differentiating will mean defining who our perfect target market is and then catering to their needs, wants and interests better than everyone else. It will be about using surveys to determine what's most important to our targeted market and giving it to them consistently.   It will not be about being "everything to everybody"; but rather, "the absolute best to our chosen targeted group".

In developing our differentiation strategy will we use the following form to help define our differences:

1. Targeted customer segments _____
2. Customer characteristics _____
3. Customer demographics _____
4. Customer behavior _____
5. Geographic focus _____
6. Ways of working _____
7. Service delivery approach _____
8. Customer problems/pain points _____
9. Complexity of customers' problems _____
10. Range of services _____

We will use the following approaches to differentiate our products and services from those of our competitors to stand apart from standardised offerings:

1. Superior quality
2. Unusual or unique product features
3. More responsive customer service
4. Rapid product or service innovation
5. Advanced technological features
6. Engineering design or styling
7. Additional product features
8. An image of prestige or status

Specific Differentiators will include the following:

1. Being a Specialist in one procedure
2. Utilizing advanced/uncommon technology
3. Possessing extensive experience
4. Building an exceptional facility
5. Consistently achieving superior results
6. Having a caring and empathetic personality
7. Giving customer s WOW experience, including a professional customer welcome package.
8. Enabling convenience and 24/7 online accessibility
9. Calling customers to express interest in their challenges.
10. Keeping to the appointment schedule.
11. Remembering customer names and details like they were family.
12. Assuring customer fears.
13. Building a visible reputation and recognition around our community
14. Acquiring special credentials or professional memberships
15. Providing added value services, such as taxi service, longer hours, financing plans, and post-sale services.

Primary Differentiation Strategies:

1. We will develop a referral program to turn participants into commissioned sales agents.
2. We plan to develop alternative revenue streams as listed in the services section of this business plan.
3. We plan to publish a monthly newsletter and use classified advertising revenues

from suppliers and local merchants to partially fund the newsletter.

4. We will highlight our community involvement by preparing and conducting classes related to Yoga at our local community college.

5. We will develop an online registration form for those wanting to register for a class or event via our website.

6. We will promote our "green" practices.

7. We will customize our offerings according to the cultural influences, customs, interests and tastes of our local market to create loyalty and increase sales.

8. We will offer a consistent quality of sessions to establish our brand identity.

9. We will publish our code of ethics and service guarantees to improve our competitive advantage.

10. We will offer a broader range of Yoga products and services.

11. We will investigate new software applications that improve employee productivity and share those cost-savings with our participants.

12. We will develop training programs for our instructors and commissioned sales reps.

13. We will develop a formal participant recruiting program and encourage with incentives the participation of current and prior participants.

14. We will develop a set of participant retention strategies and make them a part of our instructor training program.

15. We will develop a Club Membership Program and clearly define the benefits of becoming a club member.

16. We will use market research surveys to open a dialogue with potential participants and ascertain what programs might be of interest to local residents.

17. We will use customer satisfaction surveys to collect feedback, solicit testimonials and referrals, and improvement suggestions.

18. We will develop a stress reduction consulting package, based on Yoga principles, for corporations, and use independent sales reps to market this service.

19. We will develop Yoga programs that are specifically focused on helping people to attain weight and stress reduction.

20. We will develop Yoga programs, with the assistance and approval of medical experts, geared to helping seniors achieve pain management.

21. We will develop a studio shuttle program to provide after-school enrichment programs and homework support for latch key kids.

22. We will develop a birthday party program, and offer these services in our studio and at the client's home, with adequate insurance protection.

23. We plan to develop a new revenue stream based on the publishing of a monthly directory/newsletter and charging businesses to place display ads in our publication.

24. We will create an 'Open Ticket' premium package that enables studio members to take any class on the schedule, for one fixed rate.

25. Our healthy snack bar will feature fruit-based smoothies and homemade oatmeal energy bars.

26. We recognize that each participant brings his/her unique needs and individual style to the mix and it is the goal of our program to embrace and build upon each individual's unique style and set of needs.

27.   Our memberships offer unlimited group reformer classes, which means a member can come to as many classes as he or she likes during the term of their membership.

6.9 Milestones

The Milestones Chart is a timeline that will guide our company in developing and growing our business. It will list chronologically the various critical actions and events that must occur to bring our business to life. We will make certain to assign real, attainable dates to each planned action or event.

_____ (company name) has identified several specific milestones which will function as goals for the company. The milestones will provide a target for achievement as well as a mechanism for tracking progress. The dates were chosen based on realistic delivery times and necessary construction times. All critical path milestones will be completed within their allotted time frames to ensure the success of contingent milestones. The following table will provide a timeframe for each milestone.

Table: Milestones

Milestones	Start Date	End Date	Budget	Responsibility
Business Plan Completion				
Secure Permits/Licenses				
Locate & Secure Retail Space				
Obtain Insurance				
Secure Additional Financing				
Get Start-up Supplies Quotes				
Establish Vendor Accounts				
Purchase Office Equipment				
Renovate Space				
Define Marketing Programs				
Install Equipment/Displays				
Technology Systems				
Set-up Accounting System				
Finalize Media Plan				
Create Facebook Business Page				
Open Twitter Account				
Conduct Blogger Outreach				
Create Demo Reel				
Develop Personnel Plan				
Hire sales associate				
Personnel Training Program				
Implement Marketing Plan				
Get Website Live				
Conduct SEO Campaign				

Form Strategic Alliances
Purchase Inventory/Supplies
Press Release Announcements
First Production Job
Advertise Grand Opening
Full Time Work Threshold
Kickoff Advertising Program
Join Community Orgs./Network
Conduct Satisfaction Surveys
Devise Growth Strategy
Monitor Social Media Networks
Respond Positively to Reviews
Measure Return on Marketing $$$
Revenues Exceed $_____
Profitability

_____

Totals:

7.0 Website Plan Summary

_____ (company name) is currently developing a website at the URL address www. (company name).com. We will primarily use the website to advertise class schedules, specials events, and to post a catalog of our Yoga products. We will use email to communicate with customers wishing to sign-up for email specials and our newsletter.

The website will be developed to offer customers a product catalog for online orders and appointment setting. The overriding design philosophy of the site will be ease of use. We want to make the process of placing an order as easy and fast as possible thereby encouraging increased sales. We will incorporate special features such as a section that is specific to each customer so the customer can easily make purchases of repeat items. Instead of going through the website every month and locating their monthly needs, the site will capture regularly ordered items for that specific customer, significantly speeding up the ordering process. This ease-of-use feature will help increase sales as customers become more and more familiar with the site and appreciate how easy it is to place an order.

We will also provide multiple incentives to sign-up for various benefits, such as our newsletters and promotional sale notices. This will help us to build an email database, which will supply our automated customer follow-up system. We will create a personalized drip marketing campaign to stay in touch with our customers and prospects.

We will develop our website to be a resource for web visitors who are seeking knowledge and information about brand comparisons, with a goal to service the knowledge needs of our customers and generate leads. Our home page will be designed to be a "welcome mat" that clearly presents our service offerings and provides links through which visitors can gain easy access to the information they seek. We will use our website to match the problems our customers face with the solutions we offer. Our website will include plenty of pictures, detailing our training programs, and describing how our instructors are relatable and personable.

We will use the free tool, Google Analytics (http://www.google.com/analytics), to generate a history and measure our return on investment. Google Analytics is a free tool that can offer insight by allowing the user to monitor traffic to a single website. We will just add the Google Analytics code to our website and Google will give our firm a dashboard providing the number of unique visitors, repeat traffic, page views, etc. This will help to stop wasting our company's money on inefficient marketing. Using an analytic program will show exactly which leads are paying off, and which ones to do without. We will find out what's bringing our site the most traffic and how to improve upon that.

To improve the readability of our website, we will organize our website content in the following ways.

1.	Headlines	2.	Bullet points
3.	Callout text	4.	Top of page summaries

To improve search engine optimization, we will maximize the utilization of the

following;

1.   Links   2.   Headers
3.   Bold text   4.   Bullets
5.   Keywords   6.   Meta tags

This website will serve the following purposes:

About Us	How We Work/
Our Studio Philosophy	
Contact Us	Customer service contact info
Frequently Asked Questions	FAQs
Yoga Glossary	
Instructors	Instructor Bios/Resumes
Newsletter Sign-up	Mailing List
Newsletter Archives	
Class Descriptions	
Yoga Class Schedule	
Prices	Tuition
Product Catalog	Online Catalog
Upcoming Events	Community Schedule
Book Introductory Session	Form
Registration Form	
About Yoga	
Testimonials	With Client Photos
Monthly Spotlight	
Photo Gallery	Studio Events
Referral Program	Details
Directions	Location directions.
Seminar Calendar	Guest Lectures
Customer Satisfaction Survey	Feedback
Hours of Operation	
Press Releases	In the News Archive
Strategic Alliance Partners	Links
Privacy Policy	
Favorite Links	Professional Associations
Our Blog	Office diary/Accept comments
Refer-a-Friend	Viral marketing
YouTube Video Clips	Seminar Presentation/Testimonials
MySpace/Facebook Link	
Code of Ethics	
Mission Statement	
Our Studio	Facility Features/Benefits/Photos
Competition Team	
Career Opportunities	
Classified Ads	

Classified Ads

By joining and incorporating a classified ad affiliate program into our website, we will create the ultimate win-win-win. We will provide our guests with a free benefit, increase our rankings with the search engines by incorporating keyword hyperlinks into our site, attract additional markets to expose to our product, create an additional income source as they upgrade their ads, and provide our prospects a reason to return to our web site again and again

Resources:

App Themes	www.appthemes.com/themes/classipress/
e-Classifieds	http://www.e-classifieds.net/
Noah's Classifieds	http://www.noahsclassifieds.org/
Joom Prod	http://www.joomprod.com/

7.1   Website Marketing Strategy

Our online marketing strategy will employ the following distinct mechanisms:

1.   Search Engine Submission
This will be most useful to people who are unfamiliar with _____ (company name), but are looking for a local Yoga Studio. There will also be searches from customers who may know about us, but who are seeking additional information.

Search Engine Optimization (SEO)
SEO is a very important digital marketing strategy because search engines are the primary method of finding information for most internet users. SEO is simply the practice of improving and promoting a website in order to increase the number of visitors a site receives from search engines. Basic SEO techniques will range from the naming of webpages to the way that other websites link to our website. We will also need to get our business listed on as many relevant online directories as possible, such as Google, Yelp, Kudzu and Yahoo Local, write a blog that solicit comments and be active on social media sites.
We will also try to incorporate local terms potential clients would use, such as "_____ (city) yoga studio." This will make it more likely that local customers will find us close to the top of their search.
Resource;
www.officerreports.com/blog/wp-content/uploads/2014/11/SEOmoz-The-
        Beginners-Guide-To-SEO-2012.pdf

2.   Website Address (URL) on Marketing Materials
Our URL will be printed on all marketing communications, business cards, letterheads, faxes, and invoices and product labels. This will encourage a visit to our website for additional information

3.   Online Directories Listings
We will list our website on relevant, free and paid online directories and manufacturer website product locators.

The good online directories possess the following features:

Free or paid listings that do not expire and do not require monthly renewal.

Ample space to get your advertising message across.

Navigation buttons that are easy for visitors to use.

Optimization for top placement in the search engines based on keywords that people typically use to find Yoga Studios.

Direct links to your website, if available.

An ongoing directory promotion campaign to maintain high traffic volumes to the directory site.

4. Strategic Business Partners

We will use a Business Partners page to cross-link to prominent _____ (city) area dance web sites as well as the city Web sites and local recreational sites. We will also cross-link with brand name suppliers.

5. YouTube Posting

We will produce a video of testimonials from several of our satisfied clients and educate viewers as to the range of our services and products. Our research indicates that the YouTube video will also serve to significantly improve our ranking with the Google Search Engine.

6. Exchange of links with strategic marketing partners.

To find suitable link partners, we will find out who is linking to our competitors. We will cross-link to non-profit businesses that accept our gift certificate donations as in-house run contest prize awards.

7. E-Newsletter

Use the newsletter sign-up as a reason to collect email addresses and limited profiles, and use embedded links in the newsletter to return readers to website. Resource: Wellworks Centre's Communique Plus www.wellworks.com

8. Create an account for your photos on flickr.com

Use the name of your site on flickr so you have the same keywords and your branded. To take full advantage of Flickr, we will use a JavaScript-enabled browser and install the latest version of the Macromedia Flash Player.

9. Geo Target Pay Per Click (PPC) Campaign

Available through Google Adwords program. Example keywords include Yoga studio, Yoga Studio, Yoga sessions, Yoga and _____ (city).

10. Post messages on Internet user groups and discussion forums.

Get involved with Yoga related discussion groups and forums and develop a descriptive signature paragraph.
Examples:
www.yoga.com/forums/forums/thread-view.asp?tid=25143

www.yogaforums.com/forums/
www.Pilates-forums.com/

11. Write up your own LinkedIn.com and Facebook.com profiles.
Highlight your background and professional interests.

12. Facebook.com Brand-Building Applications:
As a Facebook member, we will create a specific Facebook page for our business through its "Facebook Pages" application. This page will be used to promote who we are and what we do. We will use this page to post alerts when we have new articles to distribute, news to announce, etc. Facebook members can then become fans of our page and receive these updates on their newsfeed as we post them. We will create our business page by going to the "Advertising" link on the bottom of our personal Facebook page. We will choose the "Pages" tab at the top of that page, and then choose "Create a Page." We will upload our logo, enter our company profile details, and establish our settings. Once completed, we will click the "publish your site" button to go live. We will also promote our Page everywhere we can. We will add a Facebook link to our website, our email signatures, and email newsletters. We will also add Facebook to the marketing mix by deploying pay-per-click ads through their advertising application. With Facebook advertising, we will target by specifying sex, age, relationship, location, education, as well as specific keywords. Once we specify our target criteria, the tool will tell us how many members in the network meet our target needs.

13.   Blog to share our success stories and solicit comments
Blogging will be a great way for us to share information, expertise, and news, and start a conversation with our customers, the media, suppliers, and any other target audiences. Blogging will be a great online marketing strategy because it keeps our content fresh, engages our audience to leave comments on specific posts, improves search engine rankings and attracts links. In the blog we will share rehab success stories. We will also provide a link to our Facebook.com page.
Resources: www.blogger.com   www.wordpress.com

14. Other Embedded Links
We will use social networking, article directory postings and press release web sites as promotional tools and to provide good inbound link opportunities.

15. Issue Press Releases
We will create online press releases to share news about our new website.
Resources: Sites that offer free press release services include:
       www.1888pressrelease.com and www.pr.com/press-releases.

7.2 Development Requirements

A full development plan will be generated as documented in the milestones. Costs that _____ (company name) will expect to incur with development of its new website include:

Development Costs

User interface design	$_____.
Site development and testing	$_____
Site Implementation	$._____

Ongoing Costs

Website name registration	$_____ per year.
Site Hosting	$_____ or less per month.

Site design changes, updates and maintenance are considered part of Marketing.

The site will be developed by _____ (company name), a local start-up company. The user interface designer will use our existing graphic art to come up with the website logo and graphics. We have already secured hosting with a local provider, _____ (business name). Additionally, they will prepare a monthly statistical usage report to analyze and improve web usage and return on investment.

The plan is for the website to be live by __ (date). Basic website maintenance, including update and data entry will be handled by our staff. Site content, such as images and text will be maintained by _____(owner name). In the future, we may need to contract with a technical resource to build the trackable article download and newsletter capabilities.

Resources:

www.bluehost.com/

www.godaddy.com

www.yogabaronmarketing360.com/uxi-yoga-websites/?ref=yoga-baron

7.3   Sample Frequently Asked Questions

We will use the following guidelines when developing the frequently asked questions for the ecommerce section of the website:

1. Use a Table of Contents: Offer subject headers at the top of the FAQ page with a hyperlink to that related section further down on the page for quick access.
2. Group Questions in a Logical Way and group separate specific questions related to a subject together.
3. Be Precise with the Question: Don't use open-ended questions.
4. Avoid Too Many Questions: Publish only the popular questions and answers.
5. Answer the Question with a direct answer.
6. Link to Resources When Available: via hyperlinks so the customer can continue with self-service support.
7. Use Bullet Points to list step-by-step instructions.
8. Focus on Customer Support and Not Marketing.
9. Use Real and Relevant Frequently Asked Questions from actual customers.
10. Update Your FAQ Page as customers continue to communicate questions.

The following frequently asked questions will enable us to convey a lot of important information to our clients in a condensed format. We will post these questions and answers on our website and create a hardcopy version to be included on our sales presentation folder.

What are the similarities and differences between Pilates and Yoga?
Yoga is aimed to unite the mind, the body, and the spirit. Yogis view that the mind and the body are one, and that if it is given the right tools and taken to the right environment, it can find harmony and heal itself. Yoga therefore is considered therapeutic. It helps you become more aware of your body's posture, alignment and patterns of movement. It makes the body more flexible and helps you relax even in the midst of a stress stricken environment. This is one of the foremost reasons why people want to start practicing Yoga - to feel more fit, to be more energetic, be happier and peaceful.
Pilates seek to reach much the same goals, also via a series of controlled movements. The major difference is that the Pilates technique not only has a full complement of matwork, but it incorporates work on the Pilates machines. The emphasis of the exercises is to strengthen the abdominals, improve posture, stabilize and lengthen the spine, improve balance and overall strength. Pilates gives you a longer, leaner, dancer-like line. Unlike many other training programs, Pilates works the whole body, emphasizing control, precision and concentration in both the mind and the body. Movements are not performed rapidly or repeated excessively instead, the focus is on quality not quantity. The abdominal muscles, lower back and buttocks ("powerhouse") serve as the center of all movement, allowing the rest of the body to move freely. This focus on core stabilization makes one stronger from the inside out and is critical for the advancement of the client. The low impact nature of Pilates makes it ideal for injury prevention and rehabilitation. Its six principles-concentration, control, centering, breathing, flow and precision-train the body to move efficiently with minimal impact on the body. The balance between strength and flexibility creates a healthy, vigorous and symmetrical workout for all muscle groups resulting in a leaner, more balanced, and stronger body.

Why practice yoga exercises?
When it comes to achieving both physical and mental well-being, yoga exercises are by far the most effective and time-tested practices. Yoga asanas effectively strengthen and tone the body, increase flexibility, improve balance, and relieve stress. However, the most significant benefits of yoga asanas come from their profound effects on the internal systems of the body. By bending, stretching, twisting, and flexing in the various postures, you bathe your internal organs with oxygenated blood and prana, also known as "life force energy" or "chi." Yoga asanas soothe and tone the nerves and regulate the endocrine system, which is responsible for the production of hormones. They also improve digestion and elimination, strengthen the respiratory system, and tone the reproductive organs.

What Class Should I Take?
If you have never done yoga before, have injuries, or are more than 40 pounds over weight, you should start with our Easy Does It Yoga class. Over time your body will let

you know when you are able to try other classes. Your instructor will also be able to help you should you have any questions.

What to bring?

Please bring your own mat, a towel, and bottled water. If you forgot your mat or are new to Yoga and want to try it out, we have available mats for your practice inside the studio. Please leave all other belongings in the changing area at the reception and please make sure to turn off your cell phones. No phones allowed inside the class.

What to wear?

You can wear traditional comfortable exercise clothing. Avoid clothing that is too baggy as it can bunch up or slide during practice. You may want to take off any jewelry before class as it can impair movements. Please note that Yoga is practiced on bare feet for better grip and movements on your mat. Please do not use any perfume or strong lotion before and during the class. Though there are entire lines of yoga fashion, fancy gear is unnecessary.

What to expect?

Plan to get to the studio at least 10 minutes before class begins so that you can check in. If you are new to yoga, it is a good idea to let the staff know so that they can welcome you and assist with any questions or concerns you may have. Please take your shoes off before entering the class space. There is a reception area for your belongings. Classes are 60 minutes long or otherwise noted. Please notify the teacher if you need to leave before class ends, otherwise stay until the end to respect your practice and the practice of others around you. Please observe silence inside the class.

Understand that it's completely normal to feel uncomfortable during your first yoga class. However, after a couple classes you will be more comfortable with the way it works and you will feel more relaxed to enjoy your experience.

How Often Should I Practice Yoga?

We recommend practicing a minimum of 3 times per week but even if you can only fit one class in a week you will see and feel a noticeable difference.

Is Yoga Just Stretching?

Although yoga involves stretching your muscles, it is much different than the few warm-up stretches you might do at the gym. Yoga places emphasis on alignment, meaning that how you are touching your toes is more important than whether you can actually touch them or not. Most yoga poses are not stretching an isolated area, but rather involve the whole body in both stretching and strengthening.

Can I Still Do Yoga If I'm Not Flexible?

Contrary to popular belief, you do not need to be a pretzel to be able to do and benefit from yoga. Yoga is about stretching, lengthening, strengthening and relaxing–from whatever point you are at.

Should I Eat Before Class?

It is generally recommended not to eat large meals 1-2 hours before class. We do a lot of inversion poses in our classes which may not be very comfortable if you've just eaten a large meal. If you do need to eat something just before class we would recommend yogurt, fruit or some nuts.

Will Yoga Help Me Lose Weight?

Yoga can make you look and feel better, regardless of your weight. That said, Yoga can help you slim down in a couple of ways. First, the exercises will help you burn calories. In addition, they'll help tone your muscles and improve of your posture. Yoga is also about healthy living, which includes a healthy diet. That doesn't mean you have to become a vegetarian, just that you should be conscious of the foods you eat, sticking with natural, fresh fruits and vegetables, grains, etc. as much as possible while limiting your intake of junk food and foods high in fat, like red meat. Any of the basic hatha styles will help.

Can I buy a gift certificate?

Yes, we have gift certificates! They are very attractive and are individually personalized for you.

7.4 Website Performance Summary

We will use web analysis tools to monitor web traffic, such as identifying the number of site visits. We will analyze customer transactions and take actions to minimize problems, such as incomplete sales and abandoned shopping carts. We will use the following table to track the performance of our website:

Category	2018 Fcst	Act	2019 Fcst	Act	2020 Fcst	Act
No. of Customers						
New Newsletter Subscribers						
Unique Visitors						
Avg. Time on Site						
Pages per Visit						
Percent New Visits						
Bounce Rate						
No. of Products						
Product Categories						
Number of Incomplete Sales						
Conversion Rate						
Affiliate Sales						
Customer Satisfaction Score						

7.5 Website Retargeting/Remarketing

Research indicates that for most websites, only 2% of web traffic converts readers on the first visit. Retargeting will keep track of people who have visited our website and displays our ads to them as they browse online. This will bring back 98% of users who don't convert right away by keeping our brand at the top of their mind. Setting up a remarketing tracking code on our website will allow us to target past visitors who did not convert or take the desired action on our site. After people have been to our website and are familiar with our brand, we will market more aggressively to this 'warm traffic.'

Resource:
www.marketing360.com/remarketing-software-retargeting-ads/

8.0 Operations Plan

Operations include the business aspects of running our business, such as conducting quality assessment and improvement activities, auditing functions, cost-management analysis, and customer service.

Our operations plan will present an overview of the flow of the daily activities of the business and the strategies that support them. It will focus on the following critical operating factors that will make the business a success:

1. We will enjoy the following advantages in the sourcing of our inventory:
   _____

2. We will utilize the following technological innovations in the customer relationship management (CRM) process:
   _____

3. We will make use of the following advantages in our distribution process:
   _____

4. We will develop the following in-house training program to improve worker productivity: _____

5. We will utilize the following system to better control inventory carrying costs.
   _____

6. We will implement the following quality control plan:
   _____

Quality Control Plan

Our Quality Control Plan will include a review process that checks all factors involved in production of our services. The main objectives of our quality control plan will be to uncover defects, and reporting to management level to make the decisions on the improvement of the whole production process. Our review process will include the following activities:

Quality control checklist
Finished product review
Structured walkthroughs
Statistical sampling
Testing process

Operations Planning

We will use Microsoft Visio to develop visual maps, which will piece together the different activities in our organization and show how they contribute to the overall "value stream" of our business. We will rightfully treat operations as the lifeblood of our business. We will develop a combined sales and operations planning process where sales and operations managers will sit down every month to review sales, at the same time creating a forward-looking 12-month rolling plan to help guide the product development and manufacturing processes, which can become disconnected from sales. We will approach our operations planning using a three-step process that analyzes the company's current state, future state and the initiatives it will tackle next. For each initiative, such as launching a new product or service, the company will examine the related financials, talent and operational needs, as well as target customer profiles. Our management team will map out the cost of development and then calculate forecasted return on investment and revenue predictions.

We will use the Client Needs Analysis Worksheet, to precisely document participant expectations, Yoga style preferences, and time and budget constraints.

We also plan to develop a list of specific interview questions and a worksheet to evaluate, compare and pre-screen potential suppliers. We will also check vendor references and their rating with the Better Business Bureau (www.bbb.org) and Hoovers.com.

We will provide ongoing instructor training programs to assist with customer service and quality control. The training program will focus on "The Yoga System", which teaches instructors how to work the basic to advanced client through the Yoga system.

We plan to write and maintain an Operations Manual and a Personnel Policies Handbook. The Operating Manual will be a comprehensive document outlining virtually every aspect of the business. The operating manual will include management and accounting procedures, hiring and personnel policies, and daily operations procedures, such as opening and closing the store, and how to _____. The manual will cover the following topics:

- Community Relations
- Media Relations
- Vendor Relations
- Competition Relations
- Environmental Concerns
- Intra Company Procedures
- Banking and Credit Cards
- Computer Procedures
- Quality Controls
- Open/Close Procedures
- Software Documentation
- Instructor Certification
- Class Curriculum
- Referral Programs

- Customer Relations
- Employee Relations
- Government Relations
- Equipment Maintenance Checklist
- Pro Shop Sales
- Accounting and Billing
- Financing
- Instructor Scheduling
- Safety Procedures
- Security Procedures
- Studio Policies
- Independent Contractors
- Training Programs

We plan to create the following business manuals:

Manual Type	Key Elements
1. Operations Manual	Process flowcharts
2. Employee Manual	Benefits/Appraisals/Practices
3. Managers Manual	Job Descriptions
4. Customer Service Policies	Inquiry Handling Procedures

Our plan is to automate our sales process, by developing an online registration cost calculator. We plan to adapt Quickbooks to track product inventory and sales. The plan is to place special emphasis on using technology to make the transaction with customers more efficient and to accept a wide range of credit and debit card options. All systems are computer based and allow for accurate off-premises control of all aspects of our service business.

Software Options

Quickbooks	//quickbooks.intuit.com/product/accounting-software/

Online Registration Software:

Mind and Body Online	www.MindBodyOnline.com
Akada Software	www.akadasoftware.com
Studio Manager	www.triplethreatsoftware.com
Studio Director	www.thestudiodirector.com
Compete Services, Inc.	www.competeservices.com

9.0 Management Summary

The Management Plan will reveal who will be responsible for the various management functions to keep the business running efficiently. It will further demonstrate how that individual has the experience and/or training to accomplish each function. It will address who will do the planning function, the organizing function, the directing function, and the controlling function.

At the present time _____ (owner name) will run all operations for _____ (company name). _____ (His/Her) background in _____ (business management?) indicates an understanding of the importance of financial control systems. Other key personnel are the project managers. There is not expected to be any shortage of qualified staff from local labor pools in the market area.

_____ (owner name) will be the owner and operations manager of _____ (company name). His/her general duties will include the following:
1.   Oversee the daily operations
2.   Ordering inventory and supplies.
3.   Develop and implementing the marketing strategy
4.   Purchasing equipment.
5.   Arranging for the routine maintenance and upkeep of the facility.
6.   Teaching advanced participants.
7.   Hiring, training and supervision of new instructors.
8.   Scheduling and planning the Yoga group sessions and special events.
9.   Creating and pricing Yoga lesson programs and packages.
10.   Managing studio events.
12.   Managing the accounting/financial aspect of the business.
13.   Bookkeeping and payroll
14.   Contract negotiation/vendor relations.

The operations manager will take a monthly draw of $_____ month.

9.1 Owner Personal History

The owner has been working in the _____ (Pilates?) industry for over _____ (#) years, gaining personal knowledge and experience in all phases of the industry. _____ (owner name) is the founder and operations manager of _____ (company name). He/she began his/her career as a _____ .

Over the last _____ (#) years, _____ (owner name) became quite proficient in a wide range of management activities and responsibilities, becoming an operations manager for _____ (former employer name) from _____ to _____ (dates). There he/she was able to achieve _____.

_____, owner of _____ (company name), has a _____ degree in _____.
For _____ years he/she has managed a business similar to _____ (company name).
_____ (His/her) duties included _____.

Specifically, the owner brings __(#) years of experience as a ___ (Yoga instructor), as well as certification from _____.

_____ (owner name) is a certified Anusara instructor and one of the few Designated Teacher Trainers in the Anusara style of Hatha Yoga. ___(He/She) is registered with the national Yoga Alliance at the highest 500-hour level.

He/she is an experienced entrepreneur with _____ years of small business accounting, finance, marketing and management experience. Education includes college course work in business administration, banking and finance, investments, and commercial credit management.

The owner will draw an annual salary of $_____ from the business although most of this goes to repay loans to finance business start-up costs. These loans will be paid-in-full by _____ (month) of _____ (year).

9.2 Management Team Gaps

Despite the owner's and manager's experience in the _____ (gift?) industry, the company will also retain the consulting services of _____ (consultant company name). This company has over _____ (#) years of experience in the _____ industry, and has successfully opened dozens of Yoga Studio businesses across the country. The Consultants will be primarily used for market research, customer satisfaction surveys and to provide additional input in the evaluation of new business opportunities. Additionally, the business will make use of the following advisory board. A Board of Advisors will provide mentoring support on business matters. Expertise gaps in legal, tax, marketing and personnel will be covered by the Board of Advisors. The owner will actively seek free business advice from SCORE, a national non-profit organization with a local office. This is a group of retired executives and business owners who donate their time to serve as business counselors to new business owners.

Advisory Resources Available to the Business Include:

	Name	Address	Phone
Accountant			
Attorney			
Insurance Broker			
Banker			
Business Consultant			
Wholesale Suppliers			
Trade Association			
Realtor			
SCORE.org			

Other _____

Management Matrix
Note: See appendix for attached management resumes.

Name	Title	Functions	Responsibilities

Outsourcing Matrix

Company Name	Functions	Responsibilities	Cost

Note: Marketing and public relations will be handled mainly by the owner. If there is a greater need, a marketing consultant will be hired to help issue press releases and generate seminar and website content.

9.3   Personnel Plan

Employee Requirements:

1.   Skills and Abilities

Staff must have a high college education, be self-motivating, and have strong customer service skills. Previous experience as a Yoga instructor is preferred.

2.   Recruitment

Experience suggests that community and university arts programs and personal referrals are excellent sources for experienced instructors. We will also approach area Yoga Studios and attend Yoga workshops to uncover good instructor leads. We will also consider former participants who have been trained in our studio methods and post a career opportunity ad on our website.

3.   Instructor Selection

To hire the very best instructors, we will develop job descriptions and interview questions that clearly delineate expectations, roles, responsibilities, performance evaluation criteria and the structure of the position. We will also ask candidates to teach sample audition classes and evaluate their performances.

4.   Training and Supervision

Teacher training is largely accomplished through hands-on experience with supplemental instruction given on more complicated projects. Additional knowledge is gained through trade shows, and industry books, magazines, production manuals, and promotional materials. We will encourage and foster professional development by funding continuing education courses on topics such as the psychology of teaching. We will also conduct semi-annual instructor performance reviews and incorporate the survey results submitted by participants. All instructors will be cross-trained and certified as Yoga Instructors, and be capable of staffing both the retail shop and the snack bar.

Resource: www.anmolmehta.com/meditation-training-program/meditation-teacher-training.html?hop=ice610

5.   **Salaries and Benefits**

We will pay from $___ to $____ an hour depending on experience. An employee discount of ____ percent on personal sales is offered. As business warrants, we hope to put together a benefit package that includes insurance, and paid vacations. The personnel plan also assumes a 5% annual increase in salaries.

Personnel Plan

1.   We will develop a system for recruiting, screening and interviewing employees.
2.   Background checks will be performed as well as reference checks.
3.   We will develop an instructor training course.
4.   We will keep track of staff scheduling.
5.   We will develop client satisfaction surveys to provide feedback and ideas.
6.   We will develop and perform semi-annual employee evaluations.
7.   We will "coach" all of our employees to improve their abilities and range of skills.
8.   We will employ temporary employees via a local staffing agency to assist with one-time big projects.
9.   Each employee will be provided a detailed job description and list of business policies, and be asked to sign these documents as a form of employment contract.

Our Employee Handbook will include the following sections:

1.   Overview
2.   Introduction to the Company
3.   Organizational Structure
4.   Employment and Hiring Policies
5.   Performance Evaluation and Promotion Policies
6.   Compensation Policies
7.   Time Off Policies
8.   Training Programs and Reimbursement Policies
9.   General Rules and Policies
10.   Termination Policies.

9.4   Job Classifications

Job Description -- Studio Manager

The studio manager will be responsible for the complete operation of the business, which is owned by the corporation. A detailed description of his or her duties and responsibilities is as follows:

Train and supervise the ____ (#) instructors. Develop programs to motivate and compensate these employees. Coordinate advertising and sale promotion efforts to achieve sales totals as outlined in the budget. Oversee the purchasing function and inventory control procedures to insure adequate merchandise at all times at a reasonable cost. Prepare monthly and annual budgets and track actual performance against those numbers. Supervise office personnel to insure the timely preparation of records, statements, all government reports, control of receivables and payables, website updates and monthly financial statements. Perform duties as required in the areas of personnel, building leasing and maintenance, licenses and permits and public relations. Manage enrollment campaigns and referral program implementation.

Job Description --Yoga Instructor

Description

Yoga instructors train others in the Yoga methods. They may lead group classes or train clients one on one and instruct participants in a range of activities. Yoga instructors must be able to adjust routines and techniques to the individual's fitness level and ability. Through Yoga exercises, instructors help participants to meditate and reduce stress.

Duties and Responsibilities:

1. Analyze student requirement and develop yoga sessions according to same.
2. Prepare and develop music tapes for sessions and student levels.
3. Develop and assist students to develop stretching and relaxation exercises.
4. Monitor performance of all students and evaluate techniques and equipment and ensure proper use.
5. Design and demonstrate training activities to students and assist in various exercises.
6. Prepare and initiate warm up cool down exercises in program.
7. Assist students and ensure appropriate use of exercise heart beats.
8. Ensure all students come in proper shoe and dresses for exercise classes.
9. Coordinate with various students and initiate and provide feedback.
10. Assist participants and develop programs for muscle work for students.
11. Maintain and update attendance records for all students.
12. Ensure compliance to all safety procedures to operate all exercise equipment.
13. Analyze various departmental activities and recommend changes to authorities to reduce cost.
14. Analyze activities, identify risks and develop preventative measures.

Certification

In the United States, teacher-training programs that meet certain standards are registered by the Yoga Alliance, a nationally recognized organization. There are two levels of Yoga Alliance certificates- 200 Hour and 500 Hour, referring to the length of the program. Trainees first complete a 200-Hour program, which most yoga studios require as the minimum training for their teachers. Some teachers then choose to continue their studies by undertaking a 500-Hour training. Upon completion of a Yoga Alliance registered teacher-training program, teachers may use the acronym RYT (Registered Yoga Teacher) after their name.

9.5   Job Descriptions
Our job descriptions will adhere to the following format guidelines:

1.	Job Title		2.	Reports to:	
3.	Pay Rate		4.	Job Responsibilities	
5.	Travel Requirements		5.	Supervisory Responsibilities	
6.	Qualifications		7.	Work Experience	
8.	Required Skills		10.	Salary Range	
11.	Benefits		12.	Opportunities	

9.6   Staffing Plan

The following table summarizes our personnel expenditures for the first three years, with salaries increasing from $_____ in the first year to about $_____ in the third year.

Table: Personnel

	Number of Employees	Hourly Rate	Annual Salaries		
			2018	2019	2020
Director/Ops Manager					
Admin Assistant					
Membership Advisors					
Teachers/Instructors					
Assistant Instructors					
P/T Sales Rep					
P/T Bookkeeper					
Pro Shop/Snack Bar Attendant					
Receptionist					
Other					
Total People: Headcount					
Total Annual Payroll					
Payroll Burden (Fringe Benefits)		(+)			
Total Payroll Expense		(=)			

Yoga Instructor Salary Notes:

Most yoga centers hire teachers as independent contractors. If the IRS determines that a worker should have been classified as an employee, there are tremendous penalties and even criminal sanctions. However, in the yoga business, most teachers are independent contractors. Teachers hired as independent contractors are in business for themselves and are contracted by the studio owner. You should therefore have a contract with each instructor that expressly delineates the services to be rendered and the fees to be paid. Do not provide any "employee benefits," and do not allow them to represent themselves as employees of the studio company. Instructors hired as independent contractors should have their own liability insurance that names the yoga studio as co-insured, and this requirement should be included in their contract. Consult an attorney and/or CPA regarding the hiring and contracting of teachers.

In 2006 the Bureau of Labor Statistics (BLS) published information specific to the salaries of professional fitness workers to include Yoga instructors. This publication showed them earning a median annual salary of $25,910 with the middle 50% earning between $18,010 and $41,040. This same publication showed the top 10% earning as much as $56,750 yearly. Although this may be a fair representation of what Yoga instructors working in salaried positions within health clubs make, independently employed Yoga instructors are known to make considerably more than this. In 2010, the average annual income for yoga instructors in California earned an average of $42,370 per year.

Payscale.com shows a tremendous spread of between $26 and $100 per hour when looking at the wage earned by instructors in either salaried or non-salaried Yoga instructor jobs within health clubs. The factors that play most heavily into the hourly rate earned by Yoga instructors are location, experience, and professional setting. Working in an exclusive health club or Yoga Studio serving a wealthy clientele in an affluent neighborhood of a larger city will ensure a Yoga instructor salary that will be on the higher end of this spectrum. An instructor working as an employee of a health club or Yoga Studio will typically take home between 40% and 50% of the cost of the client's session with the rest going to the house.

Although Yoga teacher training program graduates can usually find work as instructors without becoming certified through the PMA or similar professional organizations, certification does have its benefits. Uncertified workers can take home $15 or $16 an hour while those with certification can expect to take home about $40 an hour.

10.0   Risk Factors

Risk management is the identification, assessment, and prioritization of risks, followed by the coordinated and economical application of resources to minimize, monitor, and control the probability and/or impact of unfortunate events or to maximize the realization of opportunities. For the most part, our risk management methods will consist of the following elements, performed, more or less, in the following order.

1.   Identify, characterize, and assess threats
2.   Assess the vulnerability of critical assets to specific threats
3.   Determine the risk (i.e. the expected consequences of specific types of attacks on specific assets)
4.   Identify ways to reduce those risks
5.   Prioritize risk reduction measures based on a strategy

Types of Risks:

_____ (company name) faces the following kinds of risks:

1.   **Financial Risks**

   Our quarterly revenues and operating results are difficult to predict and may fluctuate significantly from quarter to quarter as a result of a variety of factors. Among these factors are:

   > -Changes in our own or competitors' pricing policies.
   > - Recession pressures.
   > - Fluctuations in expected revenues from advertisers, sponsors and strategic relationships.
   > - Timing of costs related to acquisitions or payments.

2.   **Legislative / Legal Landscape.**

   Our participation in the health and wellness presents unique risks:

   > - Product and other related liability.
   > - State regulations on licensing, privacy and insurance.

3.   **Operational Risks**

   For the past __ (#) years the owner has been dealing with computers so he is comfortable with technology and understands a wide array of software applications. However, the biggest potential problem will be equipment malfunction. To minimize the potential for problems, the owner will be taking equipment repair training from the manufacturer and will deal with basic troubleshooting and minor repairs. Beyond that, we have identified a service technician who is located close-by.

   To attract and retain client to the _____ (company name) community, we must continue to provide differentiated and quality services. This confers certain risks including the failure to:

   > - Anticipate and respond to consumer preferences for partnerships and service.
   > - Attract, excite and retain a large audience of customers to our

community.
- Create and maintain successful strategic alliances with quality partners.
- Deliver high quality, customer service.
- Build our brand rapidly and cost-effectively.
- Compete effectively against better-established yoga studios.

4.   Human Resource Risks

The most serious human resource risk to our business, at least in the initial stages, would be my inability to operate the business due to illness or disability. The owner is currently in exceptional health and would eventually seek to replace himself on a day-to-day level by developing systems to support the growth of the business.

5.   Marketing Risks

Advertising is our most expensive form of promotion and there will be a period of testing headlines and offers to find the one that works the best. The risk, of course, is that we will exhaust our advertising budget before we find an ad that works. Placing greater emphases on sunk-cost marketing, such as our storefront and on existing relationships through direct selling will minimize our initial reliance on advertising to bring in a large percentage of business in the first year.

6.   Business Risks

A major risk to retail service businesses is the performance of the economy and the small business sector. Since economists are predicting this as the fastest growing sector of the economy, our risk of a downturn in the short-term is minimized. The entrance of one of the major chains into our marketplace is a risk. They offer more of the latest equipment, provide a wider array of products and services, competitive prices and 24-hour service. This situation would force us to lower our prices in the short-term until we could develop an offering of higher margin, value-added services not provided by the large chains. It does not seem likely that the relative size of our market today could support the overhead of one of those operations. Projections indicate that this will not be the case in the future and that leaves a window of opportunity for ___ (company name) to aggressively build a loyal client base. We will also not pursue big-leap, radical change misadventures, but rather strive to hit stepwise performance benchmarks, with a planned consistency over a long period of time.

The Company's start-up quarterly revenues and operating results are difficult to predict and may fluctuate from quarter to quarter as a result of a variety of factors, including changes in pricing to accommodate local market conditions, recession pressures and seasonal patterns of spending.

To combat the usual start-up risks we will do the following:
1.   Utilize our industry experience to quickly establish desired strategic relationships.
2.   Pursue business outside of our immediate market area.
3.   Diversify our range of product and service offerings.

4. Develop multiple distribution channels.
5. Monitor our competitor actions.
6. Stay in touch with our customers and suppliers.
7. Watch for trends which could potentially impact our business.
8. Continuously optimize and scrutinize all business processes.
9. Institute daily financial controls using Business Ratio Analysis.
10. Create pay-for-performance compensation and training programs to reduce employee turnover.

Further, to attract and retain customers the Company will need to continue to expand its market offerings, utilizing third party strategic relationships. This could lead to difficulties in the management of relationships, competition for specific services and products, and/or adverse market conditions affecting a particular partner.

The Company will take active steps to mitigate risks. In preparation of the Company's pricing, many factors will be considered. The Company will closely track the activities of all third parties, and will hold monthly review meetings to resolve issues and review and update the terms associated with strategic alliances.

Additionally, we will develop the following kinds of contingency plans:
Disaster Recovery Plan
Business Continuity Plan
Business Impact and Gap Analysis
Testing & Maintenance

The Company will utilize marketing and advertising campaigns to promote brand identity and will coordinate all expectations with internal and third-party resources prior to release. This strategy should maximize customer satisfaction while minimizing potential costs associated with unplanned expenditures and quality control issues.

10.1   Reduce New Business Risk Tactics

We plan to use the following tactics to reduce our new business start-up risk:
1. Implement your business plan based on go, no-go stage criteria.
2. Develop employee cross-training programs.
3. Regularly back-up all computer files/install ant-virus software.
4. Arrange adequate insurance coverage with higher deductibles.
5. Test market offerings to determine level of market demand and appropriate pricing strategy.
6. Thoroughly investigate and benchmark to competitor offerings.
7. Research similar franchised businesses for insights into successful prototype business/operations models.
8. Reduce operation risks and costs by flowcharting all structured systems & standardized manual processes.

9.   Use market surveys to listen to customer needs and priorities.
10. Purchase used equipment to reduce capital outlays.
11. Use leasing to reduce financial risk.
12. Use subcontractors to limit fixed overhead salary expenses.
13. Ask manufacturer about profit sharing arrangement.
14. Pay advertisers with a percent of revenues generated.
15. Develop contingency plans for identified risks.
16. Set-up procedures to control employee theft.
17. Do criminal background checks on potential employees.
18. Take immediate action on delinquent accounts.
19. Only extend credit to established account with D&B rating
20. Get regular competitive bids from alternative suppliers.
21. Check that operating costs as a percent of rising sales are
     lower as a result of productivity improvements.
22. Request bulk rate pricing on fast moving supplies.
23. Don't tie up cash in slow moving inventory to qualify for bigger discounts.
24. Reduce financial risk by practicing cash flow management policies.
25. Reduce hazard risk by installing safety procedures.
26. Use financial management ratios to monitor business vitals.
27. Make business decisions after brainstorming sessions.
28. Focus on the products/services with biggest return on investment.
29. Develop a network of suppliers with outsourcing capabilities.
30. Analyze and shorten every cycle time, including product development.
31. Develop multiple sources for every important input.

10.2   Reduce Customer Perceived Risk Tactics

We will utilize the following tactics to help reduce the new customer's perceived risk of starting to do business with our company.

                                                                        Status
1.   Publish a page of testimonials.   _____
2.   Secure Opinion Leader written endorsements.   _____
3.   Offer an Unconditional Satisfaction Money Back Guarantee.   _____
4.   Long-term Performance Guarantee (Financial Risk).   _____
5.   Guaranteed Buy Back (Obsolete time risk)   _____
6.   Offer free trials and samples.   _____
7.   Brand Image (consistent marketing image and performance)   _____
8.   Patents/Trademarks/Copyrights   _____
9.   Publish case studies   _____
10. Share your expertise (Articles, Seminars, etc.)   _____
11. Get recognized Certification   _____
12. Conduct responsive customer service   _____
13. Accept Installment Payments   _____
14. Display product materials composition or ingredients.   _____

15. Publish product test results. _____
16. Publish sales record milestones. _____
17. Foster word-of-mouth by offering an unexpected extra. _____
18. Distribute factual, pre-purchase info. _____
19. Reduce consumer search costs with online directories. _____
20. Reduce customer transaction costs. _____
21. Facilitate in-depth comparisons to alternative services. _____
22. Make available prior customer ratings and comments. _____
23. Provide customized info based on prior transactions. _____
24. Become a Better Business Bureau member. _____
25. Publish overall customer satisfaction survey results. _____
26. Offer plan options that match niche segment needs. _____
27. Require client sign-off before proceeding to next phase. _____
28. Document procedures for dispute resolution. _____
29. Offer the equivalent of open source code. _____
30. Stress your compatibility features (avoid lock-in fear). _____
31. Create detailed checklists & flowcharts to show processes _____
32. Publish a list of frequently asked questions/answers. _____
33. Create a community that enables clients to connect with
    each other and share common interests. _____
34. Inform customers as to your stay-in-touch methods. _____
35. Conduct and handover a detailed needs analysis worksheet. _____
36. Offer to pay all return shipping charges and/or refund all
    original shipping and handling fees. _____
37. Describe your product testing procedures prior to shipping. _____
38. Highlight your competitive advantages in all marketing materials. ____

11.0   Financial Plan

The over-all financial plan for growth allows for use of the significant cash flow generated by operations. We are basing projected sales on the market research, industry analysis and competitive environment.

_____ (company name) expects a profit margin of over ____ (60?) % starting with year one. By year two, that number should slowly increase as the law of diminishing costs take hold, and the day-to-day activities of the business become less expensive. Sales are expected to grow at ____ % per year, and level off by year _____.

The initial investment in _____ (company name) will be provided by ____ (owner name) in the amount of $ _____. The owner will also seek a ___ (#) year bank loan in the amount of $ _____ to provide the remainder of the required initial funding. The funds will be used to renovate the space and to cover initial operating expenses.

The owner financing will become a return on equity, paid in the form of dividends to the owner. We expect to finance slow and steady growth through cash flow.

Our financial plan includes:
Moderate growth rate with a steady cash flow.
Investing residual profits into company expansion.
Company expansion will be an option if sales projections are met and/or exceeded.
Marketing costs will remain below ___ (5?) % of sales.
Repayment of our loan calculated at a high A.P.R. of ___ (10?) percent and at a 10-
    year-payback on our $_____ loan.

11.1   Important Assumptions

_____ (company name) recognizes that the collection of payments for Yoga lesson packages is critical to our success, and discounts will be offered for tuition pre-payments and automated monthly payments. The Personnel Burden is low because benefits are not paid to our staff. We will continue to work on a short-term interest rate that is lower. We are also assuming the economy will continue to grow after the current recession.

The following basic assumptions need to be considered:
1.   The economy will grow at a steady slow pace, without another major recession.
2.   There will be no major changes in the industry, other than those discussed in the trends section of this document.
3.   The State will not enact 'impact' legislation on our industry.
4.   Sales are estimated at minimum to average values, while expenses are estimated at above average to maximum values.
5.   Staffing and payroll expansions will be driven by increased sales.
6.   Rent expenses will grow at a slow, predictable rate.
7.   Materials expenses will not increase dramatically over the next several years, but

8.   We assume access to equity capital and financing sufficient to maintain our financial plan as shown in the tables.
9.   The amount of the financing needed from the bank will be approximately $_____and this will be repaid over the next 10 years at $_____ per month.
10.   We assume that people in _____ (city) will be interested in learning how to Yoga and will give us the opportunity to provide such sessions.
11.   We assume that the area will continue to grow, and at present rate of _ % per year.
12.   Interest rates and tax rates are based on conservative assumptions.

will grow at a rate that matches increasing consumption.

Revenue Assumptions:

	Year	Sales/Month	Growth Rate
1.			
2.			
3.			

General Assumptions	FY2018	FY2019	FY2020
Short-term Interest Rate %	10.00%	10.00%	10.00%
Long-term Interest Rate %	10.00%	10.00%	10.00%
Payment Days Estimator	30	30	30
Collection Days Estimator	45	45	45
Tax Rate %	25.00%	25.00%	25.00%
Expenses in Cash %	10.00%	10.00%	10.00%
Sales on Credit %	15.00%	15.00%	15.00%
Personnel Burden %	15.00%	15.00%	15.00%

Resource:
www.score.org/resources/business-plans-financial-statements-template-gallery

11.2   Break-even Analysis

Break-Even Analysis will be performed to determine the point at which revenue received equals the costs associated with generating the revenue. Break-even analysis calculates what is known as a margin of safety, the amount that revenues exceed the break-even point. This is the amount that revenues can fall while still staying above the break-even point. The two main purposes of using the break-even analysis for marketing is to (1) determine the minimum number of sales that is required to avoid a loss at a designated sales price and (2) it is an exercise tool so that you can tweak the sales price to determine the minimum volume of sales you can reasonably expect to sell in order to avoid a loss.

The Break-even Analysis will give our company an idea of how many participants _____ (company name) must teach each month to cover overhead costs. Because _____ (company name) is providing a new customized service, with many participants having unique requirements, the estimates of revenue and cost are somewhat arbitrary. We also realize that we may have a slow start, until the word of mouth gets circulated about our business. Furthermore, the company experiences a high degree of seasonality in its contracts which may result in a number of unprofitable summer months.

Fixed costs are based on running costs estimated by the owner(s) of the company and include payroll for all employees. Variable costs are based on a _____% estimate of the average sales per unit. The average revenue estimate is based on the judgment of the owner(s) who have had many years of experience in the industry and on the realistic assumption of the types of contracts the company will get in the beginning and the requirements needed to complete such commitments.

Definition: Break-Even Is the Volume Where All Fixed Expenses Are Covered. Based on projections, we will need an average of __ participants each month to breakeven.

Three important definitions used in break-even analysis are:
- **Variable Costs** (Expenses) are costs that change directly in proportion to changes in activity (volume), such as raw materials, labor and packaging.
- **Fixed Costs** (Expenses) are costs that remain constant (fixed) for a given time period despite wide fluctuations in activity (volume), such as rent, loan payments, insurance, payroll and utilities.
- **Unit Contribution Margin** is the difference between your product's unit selling price and its unit variable cost.
  Unit Contribution Margin = Unit Sales Price - Unit Variable Cost

For the purposes of this breakeven analysis, the assumed fixed operating costs will be approximately $ _____ per month, as shown in the following table.

Averaged Monthly Fixed Costs:		**Variable Costs:**	
Salaries	_____	Cost of Inventory Sold	_____

Rent	_____	Inventory	_____
Insurance	_____	Direct Labor	_____
Utilities	_____	Payroll Taxes	_____
Security.	_____	Other	_____
Legal/Accounting	_____		
Advertising	_____		
Depreciation	_____		
Interest	_____		
Owner's Draw	_____		
Repairs/Maintenance	_____		
Other	_____		
Total:	_____	Total	_____

A break-even analysis table has been completed on the basis of average costs/prices. With monthly fixed costs averaging $_____ , $_____ in average sales and $_____ in average variable costs, we need approximately $_____ in sales per month to break-even.

Based on our assumed ____ % variable cost, we estimate our breakeven sales volume at around $ ____ per month. We expect to reach that sales volume by our _____ month of operations. Our break-even analysis is shown in further detail in the following table.

Breakeven Formulas:

Break Even Units = Total Fixed Costs / (Unit Selling Price - Variable Unit Cost)

_____ = _____ / (_____ - _____)

BE Dollars = (Total Fixed Costs / (Unit Price – Variable Unit Costs))/ Unit Price

_____ = (_____ / (_____ - _____)) / _____

BE Sales = Annual Fixed Costs / (1- Unit Variable costs / Unit Sales Price)

_____ = _____ / (1 - _____ / _____)

Table: Break-even Analysis

Monthly Units Break-even	_____
Monthly Revenue Break-even	$ _____
Assumptions:	
Average Per-Unit Revenue	$ _____
Average Per-Unit Variable Cost	$ _____
Estimated monthly Fixed Cost	$ _____

Ways to Improve Breakeven Point:

1. Reduce Fixed Costs via Cost Controls
2. Raise unit sales prices.
3. Lower Variable Costs by improving employee productivity or getting lower competitive bids from suppliers.
4. Broaden product/service line to generate multiple revenue streams.

11.3   Projected Profit and Loss

Pro forma income statements are an important tool for planning our future business operations. If the projections predict a downturn in profitability, we can make operational changes such as increasing prices or decreasing costs before these projections become reality.

Our monthly profit for the first year varies significantly, as we aggressively seek improvements and begin to implement our marketing plan. However, after the first ___ months, profitability should be established.

We predict advertising costs will go down in the next three years as word-of-mouth about our Yoga Studio gets out to the public and we are able to find what has worked well for us and concentrate on those advertising methods, and corporate affiliations generate sales without the need for extra advertising.

Our net profit/sales ratio will be low the first year. We expect this ratio to rise at least _____ (15?) percent the second year. Normally, a startup concern will operate with negative profits through the first two years. We will avoid that kind of operating loss on our second year by knowing our competitors and having a full understanding of our target markets.

Our projected profit and loss is indicated in the following table. From our research of the Yoga Studio industry, our annual projections are quite realistic and conservative, and we prefer this approach so that we can ensure an adequate cash flow.

Key P & L Formulas:
Gross Margin = Total Sales Revenue - Cost of Goods Sold
Gross Margin % = (Total Sales Revenue - Cost of Goods Sold) / Total Sales Revenue
This number represents the proportion of each dollar of revenue that the company retains as gross profit.
EBITDA =Revenue - Expenses (exclude interest, taxes, depreciation & amortization)
PBIT = Profit (Earnings) Before Interest and Taxes = EBIT
A profitability measure that looks at a company's profits before the company has to pay corporate income tax and interest expenses. This measure deducts all operating expenses from revenue, but it leaves out the payment of interest and tax. Also referred to as "earnings before interest and tax ".
Net Profit = Total Sales Revenues - Total Expenses

Pro Forma Profit and Loss

	Formula	2018	2019	2020

Revenue:

Private Introductory Special
Group Introductory Special
Private Basic Package
Group Basic Package
Private Intermediate Package
Group Intermediate Package
Private Advanced Package
Group Advanced Package
Bronze Club Memberships
Gold Club Memberships
Platinum Club Memberships
Mobile Private sessions
Aerobic Exercise Classes
Space Rentals
Corporate Consulting
Yoga Product Sales
Snack Food/Beverage Sales
Miscellaneous

Total Sales Revenue   **A**

Direct Cost Food & Beverage   B
Other Costs of Goods   C
Total Costs of Goods Sold   B+C=D

Gross Margin   A-D=E
Gross Margin %   E / A

Expenses

Payroll
Payroll Taxes
Delivery Labor
Temp Labor
Contracted Floral Designer
Sales & Marketing
Portfolio Materials
Conventions/Trade Shows
Depreciation
License/Permit Fees
Entertainment
Cooking Books

Dues and Subscriptions _____

Rent _____

Utilities _____

Deposits _____

Interest _____

Repairs and Maintenance _____

Janitorial Supplies _____

Uniforms Rental _____

Office Supplies _____

General Supplies _____

Leased Equipment _____

Buildout Costs _____

Insurance _____

Location Rental _____

Van Expenses _____

Gas _____

Merchant Fees _____

Bad Debts _____

Miscellaneous _____

Total Operating Expenses   **F** _____

Profit Before Int. & Taxes   **E - F = G** _____

Interest Expenses   H _____

Taxes Incurred   I _____

Net Profit   **G - H - I = J** _____

Net Profit / Sales   **J / A = K** _____

11.5 Projected Cash Flow

The Cash Flow Statement shows how the company is paying for its operations and future growth, by detailing the "flow" of cash between the company and the outside world. Positive numbers represent cash flowing in, negative numbers represent cash flowing out.

The first year's monthly cash flows are will vary significantly, but we do expect a solid cash balance from day one. We expect that the majority of our sales will be done in cash or by credit card and that will be good for our cash flow position. Additionally, we will stock only slightly more than one month's inventory at any time. Consequently, we do not anticipate any problems with cash flow, once we have obtained sufficient start-up funds. A __ year commercial loan in the amount of $_____, sought by the owner will be used to cover our working capital requirement. Our projected cash flow is summarized in the following table, and is expected to meet our needs. In the following years, excess cash will be used to finance our growth plans.

Cash Flow Management:

We will use the following practices to improve our cash flow position:
1. Become more selective when granting credit.
2. Seek deposits or multiple stage payments.
3. Reduce the amount/time of credit given to clients.
4. Reduce direct and indirect costs and overhead expenses.
5. Use the 80/20 rule to manage inventories, receivables and payables.
6. Invoice as soon as the service has been performed.
7. Generate regular reports on receivable ratios and aging.
8. Establish and adhere to sound credit practices.
9. Use more pro-active collection techniques.
10. Add late payment fees where possible.
11. Increase the credit taken from suppliers.
12. Negotiate extended credit terms from vendors.
13. Use some barter arrangements to acquire goods and service.
14. Use leasing to gain access to the use of productive assets.
15. Covert debt into equity.
16. Regularly update cash flow forecasts.
17. Defer projects which cannot achieve acceptable cash paybacks.
18. Require a 50% deposit upon the signing of the contract and the balance in full, due five days before the event.

Cash Flow Formulas:

Net Cash Flow = Incoming Cash Receipts - Outgoing Cash Payments
Equivalently, net profit plus amounts charged off for depreciation, depletion, and amortization. (also called cash flow).
Cash Balance = Opening Cash Balance + Net Cash Flow
We are positioning ourselves in the market as a medium risk concern with steady cash flows. Accounts payable is paid at the end of each month, while sales are in cash, giving our company an excellent cash structure.

Pro Forma Cash Flow

	Formula	2018	2019	2020

Cash Received
Cash from Operations

	Formula			
Cash Sales	A	_____		
Cash from Receivables	B	_____		
Subtotal Cash from Operations	A + B = C	_____		
Additional Cash Received				
Non-Operating (Other) Income		_____		
Sales Tax, VAT, HST/GST Received		_____		
New Current Borrowing		_____		
New Other Liabilities (interest fee)		_____		
New Long-term Liabilities		_____		
Sales of Other Current Assets		_____		
Sales of Long-term Assets		_____		
New Investment Received		_____		
Total Additional Cash Received	D	_____		
Subtotal Cash Received	C + D = E	_____		

Expenditures
Expenditures from Operations

	Formula			
Cash Spending	F	_____		
Payment of Accounts Payable	G	_____		
Subtotal Spent on Operations	F+G = H	_____		
Additional Cash Spent				
Non-Operating (Other) Expenses		_____		
Sales Tax, VAT, HST/GST Paid Out		_____		
Principal Repayment Current Borrowing		_____		
Other Liabilities Principal Repayment		_____		
Long-term Liabilities Principal Repayment		_____		
Purchase Other Current Assets		_____		
Dividends		_____		
Total Additional Cash Spent	I	_____		
Subtotal Cash Spent	H + I = J	_____		
Net Cash Flow	**E - J = K**	_____		
Cash Balance		_____		

11.6   Projected Balance Sheet

Pro forma Balance Sheets are used to project how the business will be managing its assets in the future. As a pure start-up business, the opening balance sheet may contain no values.

Note: The projected balance sheets must link back into the projected income statements and cash flow projections.

_____ (company name) does not project any real trouble meeting its debt obligations, provided the revenue predictions are met. We are very confident that we will meet or exceed all of our objectives in the Business Plan and produce a slow but steady increase in net worth.

All of our tables will be updated monthly to reflect past performance and future assumptions. Future assumptions will not be based on past performance but rather on economic cycle activity, regional industry strength, and future cash flow possibilities. We expect a solid growth in net worth by the year _____.

The Balance Sheet table for fiscal years 2018, 2019, and 2020 follows. It shows managed but sufficient growth of net worth, and a sufficiently healthy financial position.

Excel Resource:
www.unioncity.org/ED/Finance%20Tools/Projected%20Balance%20Sheet.xls

Key Formulas:

Paid-in Capital = Capital contributed to the corporation by investors on top of the par value of the capital stock.

Retained Earnings = The portion of net income which is retained by the corporation rather than distributed to the owners as dividends.

Earnings =   Revenues - (Cost of Sales + Operating Expenses + Taxes)

Net Worth = Total Assets - Total Liabilities
          Also known as 'Owner's Equity'.

Pro Forma Balance Sheet

	Formulas	2018	2019	2020
Assets				
Current Assets				
Cash		_____		
Accounts Receivable		_____		
Inventory		_____		
Other Current Assets		_____		
Total Current Assets	A	_____		
Long-term Assets				
Long-term Assets	B	_____		
Accumulated Depreciation	C	_____		
Total Long-term Assets	B - C = D	_____		
Total Assets	**A + D = E**	_____		

Liabilities and Capital

	Formulas	2018	2019	2020
Current Liabilities				
Accounts Payable		_____		
Current Borrowing		_____		
Other Current Liabilities		_____		
Subtotal Current Liabilities	**F**	_____		
Long-term Liabilities				
Notes Payable		_____		
Other Long-term Liabilities		_____		
Subtotal Long-term Liabilities	**G**	_____		
Total Liabilities	**F + G = H**	_____		
Capital				
Paid-in Capital	I	_____		
Retained Earnings	J	_____		
Earnings	K	_____		
Total Capital	I - J + K = L	_____		
Total Liabilities and Capital	**H + L = M**	_____		
Net Worth	**E - H = N**	_____		

11.7 Business Ratios

The following table provides significant ratios for the personal services industry. The final column, Industry Profile, shows ratios for this industry as it is determined by the Standard Industrial Classification SIC 7997(Yoga Studios)/ (NAICS) 713940, for comparison purposes.

Our comparisons to the SIC Industry profile are very favorable and we expect to maintain healthy ratios for profitability, risk and return. Use Business Ratio Formulas provided to assist in calculations.

Key Business Ratio Formulas:

EBIT = Earnings Before Interest and Taxes
EBITA = Earnings Before Interest, Taxes & Amortization. (Operating Profit Margin)

Sales Growth Rate =((Current Year Sales - Last Year Sales)/(Last Year Sales)) x 100
Ex: Percent of Sales = (Advertising Expense / Sales) x 100

Net Worth = Total Assets - Total Liabilities

Acid Test Ratio = Liquid Assets / Current Liabilities
Measures how much money business has immediately available. A ratio of 2:1 is good.

Net Profit Margin = Net Profit / Net Revenues
The higher the net profit margin is, the more effective the company is at converting revenue into actual profit.

Return on Equity (ROE) = Net Income / Shareholder's Equity
The ROE is useful for comparing the profitability of a company to that of other firms in the same industry. Also known as "return on net worth" (RONW).

Current Ratio = Current Assets / Current Liabilities
The higher the current ratio, the more capable the company is of paying its obligations. A ratio under 1 suggests that the company would be unable to pay off its obligations if they came due at that point.

Quick Ratio = Current Assets - Inventories / Current Liabilities
The quick ratio is more conservative than the current ratio, because it excludes inventory from current assets.

Pre-Tax Return on Net Worth = Pre-Tax Income / Net Worth
Indicates stockholders' earnings before taxes for each dollar of investment.

Pre-Tax Return on Assets = (EBIT / Assets) x 100
Indicates much profit the firm is generating from the use of its assets.

Accounts Receivable Turnover = Net Credit Sales / Average Accounts Receivable
A low ratio implies the company should re-assess its credit policies in order to ensure the timely collection of imparted credit that is not earning interest for the firm.

Net Working Capital = Current Assets - Current Liabilities
Positive working capital means that the company is able to pay off its short-term liabilities. Negative working capital means that a company currently is unable to meet its short-term liabilities with its current assets (cash, accounts receivable and inventory).

Interest Coverage Ratio = Earnings Before Interest & Taxes /Total Interest Expense
The lower the ratio, the more the company is burdened by debt expense. When a company's interest coverage ratio is 1.5 or lower, its ability to meet interest expenses may be questionable. An interest coverage ratio below 1 indicates the company is not generating sufficient revenues to satisfy interest expenses.

Collection Days = Accounts Receivables / (Revenues/365)
A high ratio indicates that the company is having problems getting paid for services.

Accounts Payable Turnover = Total Supplier Purchases/Average Accounts Payable
If the turnover ratio is falling from one period to another, this is a sign that the company is taking longer to pay off its suppliers than previously. The opposite is true when the turnover ratio is increasing, which means the firm is paying of suppliers at a faster rate.

Payment Days = (Accounts Payable Balance x 360) / (No. of Accounts Payable x 12)
The average number of days between receiving an invoice and paying it off.

Total Asset Turnover = Revenue / Assets
Asset turnover measures a firm's efficiency at using its assets in generating sales or revenue - the higher the number the better.

Sales / Net Worth = Total Sales / Net Worth

Dividend Payout = Dividends / Net Profit

Assets to Sales = Assets / Sales

Current Debt / Totals Assets = Current Liabilities / Total Assets

Current Liabilities to Liabilities = Current Liabilities / Total Liabilities

Business Ratio Analysis

2018   2019   2020

Sales Growth
_____

Percent of Total Assets
Accounts Receivable   _____
Inventory   _____
Other Current Assets   _____
Total Current Assets   _____
Long-term Assets   _____
Total Assets   _____

Current Liabilities   _____
Long-term Liabilities   _____
Total Liabilities   _____
Net Worth   _____

Percent of Sales
Sales   _____
Gross Margin   _____
Selling G& A Expenses   _____
Advertising Expenses   _____
Profit Before Interest & Taxes _____

Main Ratios
Current   _____
Quick   _____
Total Debt to Total Assets   _____
Pre-tax Return on Net Worth _____
Pre-tax Return on Assets   _____

Additional Ratios
Net Profit Margin   _____
Return on Equity   _____

Activity Ratios
Accounts Receivable Turnover _____
Collection Days   _____
Inventory Turnover   _____
Accounts Payable Turnover   _____
Payment Days   _____
Total Asset Turnover   _____

Debt Ratios
Debt to Net Worth   _____
Current Liabilities to Liabilities   _____

Liquidity Ratios
Net Working Capital   _____
Interest Coverage   _____

Additional Ratios
Assets to Sales   _____
Current Debt / Total Assets   _____
Acid Test   _____
Sales / Net Worth   _____
Dividend Payout   _____

Business Vitality Profile
Sales per Employee   _____
Survival Rate

12.0　Summary

_____ (company name) will be successful. This business plan has documented that the establishment of _____ (company name) is feasible. All of the critical factors, such as industry trends, marketing analysis, competitive analysis, management expertise and financial analysis support this conclusion.

Project Description: (Give a brief summary of the product, service or program.)

_____

Description of Favorable Industry and Market Conditions.
(Summarize why this business is viable.)

_____

Summary of Earnings Projections and Potential Return to Investors:

_____

Summary of Capital Requirements:

_____

Security for Investors & Loaning Institutions:

_____

Summary of expected benefits for people in the community beyond the immediate business concern:

_____

Means of Financing:
A. Loan Requirements:　　　　　$_____
B. Owner's Contribution: $　　　$_____
C. Other Sources of Income:　　 $_____
Total Funds Available:　　　　　$_____

13.0   Potential Exit Scenarios

Two potential exit strategies exist for the investor:

1. **Initial Public Offering. (IPO)**

   We seek to go public within ___ (#) years of operations. The funds used will both help create liquidity for investors as well as allow for additional capital to develop our _____ (international/national?) roll out strategy.

2. **Acquisition Merger with Private or Public Company.**

   Our most desirable option for exit is a merger or buyout by a large corporation. We believe with substantial cash flows and a loyal customer base our company will be attractive to potential corporate investors within five years. Real value has been created through the novel combination of home health care services as well as partnering with key referral groups.

3. **Sale of the Business to a third party.**

   Yoga Studios usually sell for approximately one to two times earnings given the financial strength of the business. In this event, the business would be sold by a business broker and the business loan sought in this plan would be repaid according to the covenants of the business loan agreement.

APPENDIX

Purpose: Supporting documents used to enhance your business proposal.

Tax returns of principals for the last three years, if the plan is for new business

A personal financial statement, which should include life insurance and endowment policies, if applicable

A copy of the proposed lease or purchase agreement for building space, or zoning information for in-home businesses, with layouts, maps, and blueprints

A copy of licenses and other legal documents including partnership, association, or shareholders' agreements and copyrights, trademarks, and patents applications

A copy of résumés of all principals in a consistent format, if possible

Copies of letters of intent from suppliers, contracts, orders, and miscellaneous.

In the case of a franchised business, a copy of the franchise contract and all supporting documents provided by the franchisor

Newspaper clippings that support the business or the owner, including something about you, your achievements, business idea, or region

Promotional literature for your company or your competitors

Product brochures of your company or competitors

Photographs of your product. equipment, facilities, etc.

Market research to support the marketing section of the plan

Trade and industry publications when they support your intentions

Quotations or pro-forma invoices for capital items to be purchased, including a list of fixed assets, company vehicles, and proposed renovations

References

All insurance policies in place, both business and personal

Operation Schedules

Organizational Charts

Job Descriptions

Additional Financial Projections by Month

Customer Needs Analysis Worksheet

Helpful Resources:

North American Studio Alliance   www.namasta.com

The National Exercise Trainers Association   www.ndeita.com/
Offers basic, moderate and advanced certification courses for instructors trying to help their participants.

Yoga Alliance   www.yogaalliance.org/
Cultural Arts Resources   www.carts.org
Human Kinetics   www.humankinetics.com
Cecchetti Council of America   www.cecchetti.org
Institute for Meditation and Psychotherapy   www.meditationandpsychotherapy.org
The Back Sense program for treating chronic back pain   www.backsense.org
Mindfulness-Based Stress Reduction   www.umassmed.edu/cfm
Dialectical Behavior Therapy   www.behavioraltech.com
Acceptance and Commitment Therapy www.acceptanceandcommitmenttherapy.com
Mindfullness and Acceptance Special Interest Group of the Association for the Advancement of Behavior Therapy www.listservekent.edu/archives/mindfulness/html

Equipment Suppliers:
OPTP   optp.com
Wrist Assured Gloves (WAGs)   wristassuredgloves.com
Artform   artform.it
Balanced Body   Pilates.com
Comfy Sheepskins   comfysheep.com
Fundamental Fitness Products   funfitpro.com
IMX   imxPilatesstudio.com
Power Systems   power-systems.com
Stamina Products   staminaproducts.com
Zenirgy   zenirgy.com
Floor Advice   floor advice.com

Miscellaneous:
Vista Print Free Business Cards   www.vistaprint.com
Free Business Guides   www.smbtn.com/businessplanguides/
Open Office   http://download.openoffice.org/
US Census Bureau   www.census.gov
Federal Government   www.business.gov
US Patent & Trademark Office   www.uspto.gov
US Small Business Administration   www.sba.gov
National Association for the Self-Employed www.nase.org
International Franchise Association   www.franchise.org
Center for Women's Business Research www.cfwbr.org

How to Get Started Marketing on Twitter

1. **Import Your Contacts**
   Import contacts from Gmail, Hotmail and your own address book. Start with a solid base of people who you consider friends, following you on Twitter.

2. **Make Sure that Your Profile is Complete**
   Fill in all the fields (both required and optional) and include your website URL. Personalize your Twitter page to match your company's branding.

3. **Understand the Dynamics of Twitter**
   Use Twitter as a social tool, not a classifieds site and follow these tips:
   - Don't spam others about your specials.
   - Follow other users.
   - Don't promote your company directly.
   - Tweet about an informative blog posting.

4. **Build Your Followers Base**
   - Put a link to "Follow Me on Twitter" everywhere (your email signature, forums, website, and business cards)
   - Every time you post on your blog, invite people to follow you on Twitter
   - Follow people who are smart in your business and look for people who follow them for you to follow. Get a re-follow will build our follower list with the right profile of followers. Make sure that you look for people who might be interested in what you have to offer and don't send a Tweet that is overtly asking for a sale.
   - Start by actually reading what prospective clients say in their Tweets and give a smart "tweetback" before you follow him on Twitter.

5. **Balance Your Followers/Following Ratio**
   - Strike a balance between people you follow and people that follow you.
   - Grow slowly by adding 30 friends at a time, and then wait for them to follow you back.

6. **Make it Worthwhile to Follow You**
   - Tweet only interesting stuff about your industry, and relate your tweetbacks to it and even post in some links.
   - Clients develop real interest and attention when they realize that the people who are meticulously maintaining the Twitter profile really want to help them.
   - Make sure that at least an hour is spent in maintaining the Twitter account, so that the profile is active, and remains interesting to people.

7. **Learn from the Best**
   - Find users with several hundred followers and learn their best practices.

8. **Twitter Uses**
   - Use twitter to extend the reach of an existing blogging strategy and to deepen or further ties. Ex: Carnival Cruise Lines.
   - Use to announce sales and deals. Ex: Amazon.
   - Increase the ability for frequent updates to blogs or web sites or news.
   - Build consensus or a community of supporters.
   - Build buzz for a blog. /Update breaking news at conferences or events.

Advertising Plan Worksheet

Ad Campaign Title: _____

Ad Campaign Start Date: _____ End Date: _____

What are the features (what product has) and hidden benefits (what product does for consumer) of my products/services?

Who is the targeted audience?

What problems are faced by this targeted audience?

What solutions do you offer?

Who is the competition and how do they advertise?

What is your differentiation strategy?

What are your bullet point competitive advantages?

What are the objectives of this advertising campaign?

What are your general assumptions?

What positioning image do you want to project?
__ Exclusiveness	___ Low Cost	___ High Quality
__ Speedy Service	___ Convenient	___ Innovative

What is the ad headline?

What is the advertising budget for this advertising campaign?

What advertising methods will be used?
__ Radio	___ TV/Cable	__ Yellow Pages
__ Coupons	___ Telemarketing	___ Flyers
__ Direct Mail	___ Magazines	___ Newspapers
__ Press Release	___ Brochures	___ Billboards
__ Other		

When will each advertising method start and what will it cost?

Method	Start Date	Frequency	Cost

Indicate how you will measure the cost-effectiveness of the advertising plan?
Formula: Return on Investment (ROI) = Generated Sales / Ad Costs.

Marketing Action Plan

Month: _____

Target Market: _____

Responsibilities: _____

Allocated Budget: _____

Objectives _____

Strategies _____

Implementation _____

Tactics _____

Results
Evaluation _____
_____

_____
_____
_____
_____
_____
_____
_____
_____
_____
_____
_____
_____
_____
_____
_____

sessions Learned:

_____
_____
_____

Viral Marketing

Definition: Also known as word-of-mouth advertising.
Objective: To prompt your customers to deliver your sales message to others.
Strategy: Encourage and enable communication recipients to pass the offer or message along to others.
Benefit: Provides an excellent advertising return on investment and builds the trust factor.

Methodologies:
1. Encourage blog comments and two-way dialogue.
2. Use surveys to solicit feedback.
3. Use refer-a-friend forms or scripts.
4. Provide discount coupon or logo imprinted giveaway rewards for telling a friend.
5. Utilize pre-existing social networks.
6. Participate in message boards or forums.
7. Add a signature line with a refer-a-friend tagline to all posts and emails.
8. Enable unrestricted access.
9. Facilitate website content sharing.
10. Write articles and e-books, and encourage free reprints with byline mention.
11. Submit articles with 'about the author' box to article directories, such as www.articlecity.com.
12. Develop attention-grabbing product line extensions to stay connected.
13. Do the unexpected by offering a surprise benefit.
14. Deliver a remarkable offering that exceeds customer expectations.
15. Provoke a strong emotional response by getting involved with a cause that is important to your customers.
16. Provide referral incentives.
17. Get free samples into the hands of respected opinion leaders.
18. Educate customers, as to your product benefits and competitive advantages, to act as spokespersons for your company.

Explain Your Viral Marketing Program

_____

_____

_____

_____

_____

Integrate Marketing into Daily Operations

Objective: To seamlessly integrate marketing processes into daily, routine operations.

Strategies:
1. Develop form to ask for referrals upon new customer registration and annual renewal.
2. Present a sales presentation folder upon registration or contract sign-up with needs analysis worksheets, testimonials, new product introduction flyers, innovative application ideas, etc.
3. Develop a second sales presentation folder version for presentation upon job completion or sale, with referral program details, warranty service contract blank, and accessory suggestions.
4. Include business cards and coupons with all product deliverables.
5. Install company yard signs during job set-up.
6. Include a thank you note/comment card with all deliverables.
7. Include flyers and helpful articles in all customer correspondence, especially mailed invoices and statements.
8. Attach logo and contact info to all finished products.
9. Conduct customer satisfaction surveys while clients are waiting to be served.
10. Develop enclosed warranty card to build customer database and feed drip marketing program.
11. Provide competitor product/service comparisons that highlight your strengths.
12. Incorporate feedback cards into merchandise displays.
13. Train all employees to also be sales and customer service agents.
14. Print your Mission Statement or slogan on all forms and correspondence.
15. _____
16. _____

Indicate how you will incorporate marketing into daily operations.

Sales Stage	Business Processes	Opportunities to Incorporate Marketing Techniques
Pre-sale		_____
		_____
		_____
Transaction		_____
		_____
		_____
Post Sale		_____
		_____
		_____

Monthly Marketing Calendar

Instruction: Use to plan your monthly marketing events or activities and
evaluate individual event results and marketing sessions learned
for the month.

Month/Year: _____

Event/ Activity	Responsibility	Cost	Comments	Date	Results Evaluation

Monthly Evaluation of sessions Learned:

_____

_____

_____

Form Strategic Marketing Alliances

Definition: A collaborative relationship between two or more non-competing firms with the intent of accomplishing mutually compatible and beneficial goals that would be difficult for each to accomplish alone. Also referred to as 'Collaboration Marketing'.

Note: Usually, potential alliance partners sell distinct or complementary products and/or services to the same target market audience.

Advantages: Improve marketing efficiency by achieving synergy in resource allocation with strategic partners.
Improve marketing effectiveness by creating a one-stop or wraparound shopping experience.
A way to inexpensively test the market for growth potential.

Types of Co-Ventures:
1. Informal Strategic Alliances
2. Contractual Relationships (Attorney review recommended)
3. New Business Entity (Set-up by attorney)

Informal Strategic Alliances
1. Most involve consultations regarding:
   a. Mutual Referrals
   b. Research for product improvements
   c. Promotion of products or services (affiliate programs).
   d. Creative product bundling arrangements.
2. May or may not require a written agreement.
3. May or may not require compensation.

Topics to be Covered:
1. The specific strategic goals and objectives of the alliance.
2. The performance expectations of the parties..
3. The scope of the alliance.
4. The period of performance.
5. Termination and renewal procedures.
6. Strategic marketing plan to promote the alliance.
7. Dispute resolution procedures.
8. Performance tracking methods.
9. Periodic evaluation of reciprocal benefits realized.
10. Website pages/links to promote alliance partners.

Example: The mutual referral relationship between a sports bar and a fitness club or physical fitness trainer.

Referral Program Tips

Objective: To formalize your referral program so that it can be easily
and consistently integrated into your operating processes.

1. Define the stages in the sales process when you will ask for a referral. Ex: Registration, Renewals, Annual Drive, etc.)

2. Document your referral asking script (include objection handling responses).

3. Include a request for referrals in your customer satisfaction survey and your registration forms.

4. Stress the dependence of your business on referrals in all your marketing communications.

5. Set-up a follow-up procedure and tracking form to convert referral leads into actual customers.

6. Publish your referral incentives, awards criteria and timetable for settlement.

7. Customize your referral program to the motivational needs of a select number of potential 'Bird Dogs' or 'Big Hitters'.

8. Educate potential referral agents as to the characteristics of your ideal prospect. (Develop Ideal Prospect Profile)

9. Set-up special, mutual referral arrangements with strategic business alliance partners and track the reciprocity of efforts.

10.   Join or start a local lead group.

11.   Set-up 'thank-you note' templates to facilitate your expression of gratitude.

12.   Use logo imprinted giveaways, such as T-sheets, as referral thank you expressions.

Seminar Outline Worksheet

Objective: To establish your expertise on the subject matter, and produce future possible networking contacts by offering a newsletter sign-up and/or business card exchange.

Warning: Make seminar information rich and not a sales presentation.

1. Start with Attention-Grabbing Headline
   Ex: Hard-hitting Quotation, Thought Provoking Question, Startling Fact

   _____

2. Introduce Yourself and Establish Your Credentials

   _____

3. Present Seminar Overview

   _____

4. Discuss Attendee Participation Guidelines

   _____

5. Solicit a sampling of attendee interests, backgrounds and concerns.

   _____

6. Establish Learning Objectives

   _____

7. Preview the Bulleted Topics To be Covered

   _____

   _____

8. Share a Relevant Success Story (Case Study).

   _____

9. Use analogies and comparisons to create reference points.

   _____

10. Use statistics to support your position.

    _____

    _____

11. Conclusion: - Summarize Benefits for Attendees / Appeal to Action

    _____

    _____

    _____

12. Hold Question and Answer Session

13. Final Thoughts
    - Appreciation for Help Received
    - Indicate after-seminar availability

14. Handout A Remembrance
    - Business Cards
    - Seminar Outline
    - Glossary of Terms
    - Feedback Survey

YouTube Marketing Tips

Definition: An online video destination to watch and share original video clips.
(World-wide approx. 55 million unique users/month)

1. Focus on something that is funny or humorous, so that people will feel compelled to share it with friends and family.
2. Make the video begin and end with a black screen and include the URL of your originating website to bring traffic to your site.
3. Put your URL at the bottom of the entire video.
4. Clearly demonstrate how your product works.
5. Create how-to videos to share your expertise and develop a following.
6. Build contests and events around special holidays and occasions.
7. Run a search on similar content by keyword, and use the info to choose the right category and tags for your video.
8. Make sure the video is real, with no gimmicks or tricks.
9. Add as many keywords as you can.
10. Make sure that your running time is five minutes or less.
11. Break longer videos into several clips, each with a clear title, so that they can be selectively viewed.
12. Encourage viewer participation and support.
13. Take advantage of YouTube tags, use adjectives to target people searching based on interests, and match your title and description to the tags.
14. Use the flexibility provided by the medium to experiment.
15. Use the 'Guru Account' sign-up designation to highlight info videos and how-to guides.
16. Create 'Playlists' to gather individual clips into niche-targeted context so viewers can easily find related content.
17. Use 'Bulletins' to broadcast short messages to the world via Your YouTube Channel.
18. Email 'The Robin Good YouTube Channel' to promote a new video release.
19. Join a 'YouTube Group' to post videos or comments to the group discussion area and build your network of contacts.
20. Use 'YouTube Streams' to join or create a room where videos are shared and discussed in real-time.
21. Use 'Active Sharing' to broadcast the videos that you are currently watching, and drive traffic to your profile.
22. Use the 'Share Video' link found under each video you submit and then check the box 'Friends' to send your video to all your friends.
23. Create your own YouTube Channel when you sign-up for a new YouTube account.

Basic Monthly Marketing Plan Checklist

1. Send birthday greetings to existing clients. _____
2. Contact referral sources and express appreciation for their referrals. _____
3. Implement program to develop new referral sources. _____
4. Research new ways to solve more problems of your target clients. _____
5. Research possible new target audience needs. _____
6. Make your friends/family/associates/social contacts aware of your expanding capabilities. _____
7. Train all employees to assist in marketing efforts. _____
8. Conduct selected client interviews to assess performance, changing needs and suggestions. _____
9. Forward copies of articles of interest to contacts. _____
10. Take contact to breakfast, lunch or dinner. _____
11. Invite contact to sporting or cultural event. _____
12. Distribute articles that demonstrate your expertise. _____
13. Invite contacts to an informative seminar. _____
14. Send personal notes of congratulation. _____
15. Join organizations important to your contacts. _____
16. Update your mailing list. _____
17. Issue a press release on a firm accomplishment or planned marketing event. _____
18. Update your firm's list of competitive advantages. _____
19. Attend a networking event. _____
20. Update the helpful content on your website. _____
21. Arrange to speak on your area of expertise. _____
22. Become actively involved in the community. _____
23. Track your ad results to determine resource focus. _____
24. Develop alliances with complementary businesses. _____
25. Conduct customer satisfaction surveys. _____
26. Implement client needs analysis checklist. _____
27. Distribute newsletter featuring clients. _____
28. _____ _____
29. _____ _____
30. _____ _____

Networking Insights

Definition: A reciprocal process in which you share ideas, leads, information, and advice to build mutually beneficial relationships.

Networking Tips:

1. Start your own local referral group with other business owners.
2. Understand your long-term networking goals.
3. Become a helpful resource to networking members.
4. Research people and companies to know their goals and interests.
5. Offer referrals, resources and recommendations to receive same in return.
6. Consistently try to meet new people and make new friends.
7. Develop good listening skills.
8. Frequently express your gratitude for assistance.
9. Know what interests, strengths and availability you bring to the table.
10. Stay in touch with a newsletter, blog, postcards or email messages.
11. Keep asking questions to get others to tell you more about themselves.
12. Show warmth, display confidence, smile and shake hands firmly.
13. Explore organizations that offer accreditation and directory listings.

Entrepreneur Networking Possibilities

1. Meet Up — www.meetup.com
2. FaceBook, Friendster, Myspace — www.facebook.com
3. LinkedIn — www.linkedIn.com
4. Ryze — www.ryze.com
5. Int'l Virtual Women's Chamber of Commerce — www.ivwcc.org
6. Business Network International — www.BNI.com
7. Club E Network — www.clubENetwork.com
8. Local Chamber of Commerce
9. Rotary Club — www.rotary.org
10. Lion's Club — www.lionsclubs.org
11. Jaycees
12. Toastmasters — www.toastmasters.com
13. Woman Owned Network — wwwwomanowned.com
14. Alumni Associations
15. Parent Teacher Associations (PTA)
16. Trade Shows — www.tsnn.com
17. Trade Associations — www.associationscentral.com
18. EONetwork — www.eonetwork.org
19. Prof. Organizations, Economic Clubs, Charities, Churches, Museums, etc.

Perfect Your Elevator Pitch

A brief, focused message aimed at a particular person or niche segment that summarizes why they should be interested in your products and/or services.

**I am a/we are _____(profession) and we help _____
(target market description) to_____(primary problem solved).**

Press Release Cover Letter Worksheet

Instructions: Use this form to build a ready-to-use cover letter.

Your Letterhead.

Date

Dear _____,

As a company located in your coverage area, we thought the attached Press Release would be of special concern to your readers/viewers, as it touches upon something that we all have in common, an interest in

_____.

Brief overview purpose of the press release.

_____

I have also enclosed a media kit to give you background information on _____ Company and myself. I hope to follow-up with you shortly.

I also possess expertise in the following related areas:

- _____
- _____
- _____

Should you wish to speak to me or require additional information, I can be reached at _____ or via email at _____.
Additional assistance with company supplied photos can be requested at the same number. This Press Release can also be downloaded from my company website at www. _____.

Thank you for your time and attention,

Contact Name
Company Title
Phone Number
Email Address

New Release Template

News Release

For Immediate Release
(Or Hold for Release Until …(date)….)

Contact:
Contact Person   _____
Contact Title   _____
Company Name   _____
Phone Number   _____
Fax Number   _____
Email Address   _____
Website Address   _____

Date: _____
Attention: _____ (Target Type of Editor)

Headline: Summarize Your Key Message:
                       _____

Sub-Headline: Optional: _____

Location of the Firm and Date.

_____

Lead Paragraph: A summary of the newsworthy content.
                       _____

                       Answers the questions:
                       Who: _____
                       What: _____
                       Where:_____
                       When: _____

Second Paragraph:
Expand upon the first paragraph and elaborate on the purpose of the Press Release.

_____
_____

Third Paragraph:
Further details with additional quotes from staff, industry experts or satisfied clients.

_____
_____

For Additional Information Contact:

_____

_____

About Your Expertise:
Presentation of your expert credentials

_____

_____

About Your Business:
Background company history on the firm and central offerings.

_____

_____

Enclosures: Photographs, charts, brochures, etc.

Special Event Release Format   Notes

1.   Type of Event   _____
2.   Sponsoring Organization   _____
3.   Contact Person Before the Event   _____
4.   Contact Person at the Event   _____
5.   Date and Time of the Event   _____
6.   Location of the Event   _____
7.   Length of Presentation Remarks   _____
8.   Presentation Topic   _____
9.   Question Session (Y/N)   _____
10. Speaker or Panel   _____
11. Event Background   _____
12. Noteworthy Expected Attendees   _____
13. Estimated Number of Attendees   _____
14. Why readers s/b interested in event.   _____
15. Specifics of the Event.   _____
16. Biographies   _____

Track Ad Return on Investment (ROI)

Objective: To invest in those marketing activities that generate the greatest return on invested funds.

Medium	Cost	Calls Received	Cost/Call	No. Act. New Clients	Cost/New Client
Formula:	A	B	A/B=C	D	A/D=E
Newspaper					
Classified Ads					
Yellow Pages					
Billboards					
Cable TV					
Magazine					
Flyers					
Posters					
Coupons					
Direct Mail					
Brochures					
Business Cards					
Seminars					
Demonstrations					
Sponsored Events					
Sign					
Radio					
Trade Shows					
Specialties					
Cold Calling					
Door Hangers					
T-shirts					
Coupon Books					
Transit Ads					
Press Releases					
Word-of-Mouth					
Totals:					

Internet Article Writing Template

1.   Article Title

Maximum 100 characters (including spaces) - about 12 words.
Write it to catch the attention of readers and publishers. Start with your primary search engine keyword phrase. In printed media titles starting "How to…" or "10 top tips for…" are very popular, but they are not very helpful for search engines. The article title will go into the title of a web page.

2.   Abstract

Maximum 500 characters - about 90 words but 50 or 60 is better.
Make it enticing to hook the publisher and make them want to read the full article. The abstract is primarily targeted at the publisher and will be displayed just below the title on the search pages in the directory, but is secondary to the title in getting attention. Some publishers may also use it.

3.   Description – Meta Tag

Maximum 200 characters but preferably 150 – two lines of text.
This should be a shorter version of the abstract, which must contain your primary keywords. The Mega Tag is needed if you publish on your own website.

4.   Keywords – Meta Tag

Maximum 100 characters - about 12 words comma separated
Start with your primary keyword of phrase then add the other relevant keywords that are used in the article.

5.   Article Text

Length depends on your topic, market and writing style. Research suggests about 500 to 800 words, but some publishers want more of an in-depth analysis. Research your specific market and be flexible, with a prepared mix of lengths, including long and short versions of the same article. Write the basic article with no formatting. If you are using word, disable all the auto-formatting like smart quotes, automatic hypertext links and paragraph spacing because they will all cause problems later.

Include the 'Primary Keyword Phrase' into the first sentence. Include the liberal usage of keywords throughout the article, but don't overdo it. The article still has to be a good read. Remember that even though you are writing for several audiences, content must still be king. Do not promote your own products and services or your article will not be published. Also, do not include self-serving links to your web site or affiliate sites in the body of the article, but rather save them for the 'Resource or Byline Box'. If you have links to resources show them as text, as many sites do not allow live html links in the body of the article.
Introduction
1.   Brief outline of what will be covered in the article.
2.   The motivating factor behind why this particular topic was selected and why you

are qualified to address the subject.

3. A brief statement on your credentials, experience and exposure.
4. What you have achieved from your experience to convince readers that you know the subject very well.

Core Subject Matter
1. Define the problem or address the subject areas that will define the gap between the uninformed and the knowledgeable.
2. Provide the benefits the reader will realize from reading the article.
3. Start with simple and general background knowledge, and gradually intensify the technicality of the subject matter.
4. State the expected challenges to be faced in tackling the problem.
5. Discuss the pros and cons of your proposed solution to create the link between the norm and the desired state.

Expand Upon Subject Matter
1. Add technical information to convince readers of the merits of your solution.
2. State a range of requirements needed to implement your solution and their options.
3. Compare players in the market and promote good practice.
4. Place emphasis on desired actions, taking a chronological approach to each stage.
5. Attempt to indirectly answer any questions you think your readers may have.
6. Give supporting points to gain confidence in the approach you recommend.
7. Suggest other options based on price and availability.

Conclusion
1. Summarize problem solution recommendations.
2. Refer readers to other helpful resources.

6. Copyright

Copyright, date, name, country. Few directories ask for this but it makes sense to put it at the bottom of the article or in the field requested.

7. Resource Box

Maximum 500 characters, "including spaces and html code."
This is your opportunity to promote yourself but limit content to 1 or 2 self-serving links. Refer to the links in the "Third Person." The directory publisher has to function with this link on their site or ezine so make it acceptable to them. Offer an incentive or reward for people to visit your web site, but make sure that live links show the web address not just keywords. If the publisher doesn't use live links, you still want to present your website address for later referral.

Classified Ad Worksheet

Ad Budget: _____

Ad Objective: ___ Go to Website ___ Request More Info ___ Mail a Check
___ Introduce a new product/service ___ Announce a Sale
___ Increase awareness of product
___ Other _____

Target Market: _____

Target Market:
Demographics:
- Age _____
- Gender _____
- Income _____
- Education _____
- Location _____

Reading Interests:
- Daily Newspapers _____
- Weekly Magazines _____
- Magazines _____
- Trade Journals _____

Product. Knowledge Level _____

Purchase Motivators _____

Best Category Heading _____

Select Type of Message
- Strong Offer with Best Value for Money _____
- Point of Difference from Competitors _____
- Listing the Benefits _____

Product Price: $_____

Ad Cost: $_____

Number of Responses: _____
Cost/Response: _____
Number of Sales: _____
Cost/Sales: _____

Yellow Pages Ad Design Checklist

Check

1.   Include the following key information:
      Phone Number, Website Address, Logo, Slogan or Motto.

      _____

2.   Use red ink to make the ad standout.   _____
3.   Surround the ad with a decorative border.   _____
4.   Offer something for 'Free' to capture attention.   _____
      Ex: Pamphlet, checklist, consultation, schedule.
5.   Make your headline scream a key client benefit or
      competitive advantage.   _____
      Ex: Physical Fitness and Social Development Skills
             For the Whole Family.
6.   Include your primary service guarantee.   _____
      Ex: Your Complete Satisfaction is Guaranteed.
7.   Make your telephone number standout.   _____
8.   Do not make your company name the headline.   _____
9.   List some of your solutions to common client problems.   _____
             - The Perfect Cure for the Feeling of Isolation.
             - Yoga Your Way to Physical Fitness
             - One Stop for All Yoga Styles
10.   Include your professional credentials and associations.   _____
11.   Use a consistent company logo in all your ads.   _____
12.   Avoid the use of cute symbols, abbreviations and excessive
      punctuation.   _____
13.   Indicate your acceptance of specific credit cards.   _____
14.   Include a Call to Action!   _____
             Ex: Call Now to Make an Appointment
                  for a Free Introductory Lesson!
15.   Indicate if you "Se Hablo Espanol".   _____
16.   Choose an ad size comparable to that of your competitors.   _____
17.   Indicate length of time in business.   _____
19.   Indicate use of any well-branded products.   _____
20.   Use a dedicated phone line to track ad return on investment.   _____

Marketing Plan

Month: _____

Planned Accomplishments for month:
_____

Describe target audience:
_____
_____

Success Measures:

Number of New Prospects   _____

Number of New Contacts to Referral Network

Sales Revenues of _____ by _____

Other measure: _____

Referral Network Action Plan:

We will attend the following events:

      Event   Date   Objective
_____
_____

We will contact the following people in my network:

      Name   Date   Reason
_____
_____

We will meet the following people in person:

      Name   Date   Reason
_____
_____

We will keep in touch with the following people by sending them information, including articles and newspaper clippings:

      Name   Date   Information Type
_____
_____

Past Client Action Plan:

We will contact the following past clients:

Method Options: In-person, Mail, email, phone.

      Name   Date   Reason   Method
_____
_____

Prospecting Action Plan:

Distribution Methods: Publications, Website, Organizations, Email, etc.

Method	Date	Subject	Distribution Method
Article			
Speech			
Newsletter			
Press Release			

Other Activities:

Activity Type	Date	Target

Sample Flyer Template

Company Name
Address
City, State, Zip code
Website
Main Phone:
Email Address

Service Area:

What We Do:

Products:

Services:

Specialties:

Associations:

Awards / Certifications:

Open Hours

Special Offer:

Additional Info:

Coupon:

$_____ Off Any _____ Service
Name: _____
Address: _____
Phone: _____
Problem: _____
Expiration Date: _____
Offer valid for 90 days from _____ (date) . Limit one (1) coupon per contract. Cannot be combined with any other offer. Not redeemable on minimum service charge. Coupon must be presented at time of visit.

Made in the USA
San Bernardino, CA
30 August 2018